The Beginning of Terror

Literature and Psychoanalysis
General Editor: Jeffrey Berman

1. The Beginning of Terror: A Psychological Study of
Rainer Maria Rilke's Life and Work
DAVID KLEINBARD

The Beginning of Terror

A Psychological Study of
Rainer Maria Rilke's Life and Work

David Kleinbard

NEW YORK UNIVERSITY PRESS
NEW YORK AND LONDON

NEW YORK UNIVERSITY
New York and London

Library of Congress Cataloging-in-Publication Data
Kleinbard, David
    The beginning of terror : psychological study of Rainer Maria
Rilke's life and work / David Kleinbard.
        p.   cm. — (Literature and psychoanalysis : 1)
    Includes bibliographical references and index.
    ISBN 0-8147-4626-8 (alk. paper)
    1. Rilke, Rainer Maria, 1875-1926—Biography—Psychology.
2. Authors, German—20th century—Biography.   I. Title.
II. Series.
PT2635.I65Z753   1993
831'.912—dc20   92-32630
[B]   CIP

Manufactured in the United States of America

c 10 9 8 7 6 5 4 3 2 1

This book is dedicated to
Maureen Waters, my wife,
and Joseph Kleinbard, my father,
with much love.

For beauty is nothing
but the beginning of terror, which we are just able to bear,
and we wonder at it so because it calmly disdains
to destroy us.

Contents

Foreword

As New York University Press inaugurates a new series of books on literature and psychoanalysis, it seems appropriate to pause and reflect briefly upon the history of psychoanalytic literary criticism. For a century now it has struggled to define its relationship to its two contentious progenitors and to come of age. After glancing at its origins, we may be in a better position to speculate on its future.

Psychoanalytic literary criticism was conceived at the precise moment in which Freud, reflecting upon his self-analysis, made a connection to two plays and thus gave us a radically new approach to reading literature. Writing to his friend Wilhelm Fliess in 1897, Freud breathlessly advanced the idea that "love of the mother and jealousy of the father" are universal phenomena of early childhood (*Origins*, 223–24). He referred immediately to the gripping power of *Oedipus Rex* and *Hamlet* for confirmation of, and perhaps inspiration for, his compelling perception of family drama, naming his theory the "Oedipus complex" after Sophocles' legendary fictional hero.

Freud acknowledged repeatedly his indebtedness to literature, mythology, and philosophy. There is no doubt that he was a great humanist, steeped in world literature, able to read several languages and range across disciplinary boundaries. He regarded creative writers as allies, investigating the same psychic terrain and intuiting similar human truths. "[P]sycho-analytic observation must concede priority of imaginative writers," he declared in 1901 in *The Psychopathology of Everyday Life* (*SE* 6:213), a concession he was generally happy to make. The only exceptions were writers like Schopenhauer, Nietzsche, and Schnitzler, whom he avoided reading because of the anxiety of influence. He quoted effortlessly from Sophocles, Shakespeare, Goethe, and Dostoevsky, and was himself a master prose stylist, the recipient of the coveted Goethe Prize in 1930. When he was considered for the Nobel Prize, it was not for medicine but for literature. Upon being greeted as the discoverer of the unconscious, he disclaimed the title and instead paid generous tribute to the poets and philosophers who preceded him.

And yet Freud's forays into literary criticism have not been welcomed uniformly by creative writers, largely because of his allegiance to science rather than art. Despite his admiration for art, he viewed the artist as an introvert, not far removed from neurosis. The artist, he wrote in a well-known passage in the *Introductory Lectures on Psycho-Analysis* (1916–17), "is oppressed by excessively powerful instinctual needs. He desires to win honour, power, wealth, fame and the love of women; but he lacks the means for achieving these satisfactions" (*SE* 16:376). Consequently, Freud argued, artists retreat from reality into the world of fantasy, where they attempt to make their dreams come true. While conceding that true artists manage to shape their daydreams in such a way as to find a path back to reality, thus fulfilling their wishes, Freud nevertheless theorized art as a substitute gratification. Little wonder, then, that few artists have been pleased with Freud's pronouncements.

Nor have many artists been sympathetic to Freud's preoccupation with sexuality and aggression; his deterministic vision of human life; his combative, polemical temperament; his self-fulfilling belief that psycho-analysis brings out the worst in people; and his imperialistic claim that psychoanalysis, which he regarded as his personal creation, would explore and conquer vast new territories. He chose as the epigraph for *The Interpretation of Dreams* (1900) a quotation from *The Aeneid:* "Flectere si nequeo superos, Acheronta movebo" ("If I cannot bend the Higher Powers, I will move the Infernal Regions"). Although he denied that there was anything Promethean about his work, he regarded himself as one of the disturbers of the world's sleep. The man who asserted that "psycho-analysis is in a position to speak the decisive word in all questions that touch upon the imaginative life of man" (SE 19:208) could hardly expect to win many converts among creative writers, who were no less familiar with the imaginative life of humankind and who resented his intrusion into their domain.

Freud viewed psychoanalysts as scientists, committed to the reality principle and to heroic self-renunciation. He perceived artists, by contrast—and women—as neurotic and highly narcissistic, devoted to the pleasure principle, intuiting mysterious truths which they could not rationally understand. "Kindly nature has given the artist the ability to express his most secret mental impulses, which are hidden even from himself," he stated in *Leonardo da Vinci and a Memory of His Childhood* in 1910 (*SE* 11:107). The artist, in Freud's judgment, creates beauty, but the psychoanalyst analyzes its meaning and "penetrates" it, with all the phallic implications thereof. As much as he admired artists, Freud did not want to give them credit for knowing what they are doing. Moreover, although he always referred to artists as male, he assumed that art itself was essentially female; and he was drawn to the "seductive" nature of art even as he resisted its embrace, lest he lose his masculine analytical power. He wanted to be called a scientist, not an artist.

From the beginning of his career, then, the marriage Freud envisioned between the artist and the analyst was distinctly unequal and patriarchal. For their part, most creative writers have remained wary of psychoanalysis. Franz Kafka, James Joyce, and D. H. Lawrence were fascinated by psychoanalytic theory and appropriated it, in varying degrees, in their stories, but they all remained skeptical of Freud's therapeutic claims and declined to be analyzed.

Most artists do not want to be "cured," fearing that their creativity will be imperiled, and they certainly do not want psychoanalysts to probe their work; they agree with Wordsworth that to dissect is to murder. Vladimir Nabokov's sardonic reference to Freud as the "Viennese witch doctor" and his contemptuous dismissal of psychoanalysis as black magic are extreme examples of creative writer's mistrust of psychoanalytic interpretations of literature. "[A]ll my books should be stamped Freudians Keep Out," Nabokov writes in *Bend Sinister* (xii). Humbert Humbert speaks for his creator when he observes in *Lolita* that the difference between the rapist and therapist is but a matter of spacing (147).

Freud never lost faith that psychoanalysis could cast light upon a wide variety of academic subjects. In the short essay "On the Teaching of Psycho-Analysis in Universities" (1919), he maintained that his new science has a role not only in medical schools but also in the "solutions of problems" in art, philosophy, religion, literature, mythology, and history. "The fertilizing effects of psycho-analytic thought on these other disciplines," Freud wrote enthusiastically, "would certainly, contribute greatly towards forging a closer link, in the sense of a *universitas literarum,* between medical science and the branches of learning which lie within the sphere of philosophy and the arts" (*SE* 17:173). Regrettably, he did not envision in the same essay a cross-fertilization, a desire, that is, for other disciplines to pollinate psychoanalysis.

Elsewhere, though, Freud was willing to acknowledge a more reciprocal relationship between the analyst and the creative writer. He opened his first published essay on literary criticism, "Delusions and Dreams in Jensen's *Gradiva*" (1907), with the egalitarian statement that "creative writers are valued allies and their evidence is to be highly prized, for they are apt to know a whole host of things between heaven and earth of which our philosophy has not yet let us dream" (*SE* 9:8), an allusion to his beloved Hamlet's affirmation of the mystery of all things. Conceding that literary artists have been, from time immemorial, precursors to scientist, Freud concluded that the "creative writer cannot evade the psychiatrist nor the psychiatrist the creative writer, and the poetic treatment of a psychiatric theme can turn out to be correct without any sacrifice of its beauty" (*SE* 9:44).

It is in the spirit of this equal partnership between literature and psychoanalysis that New York University Press launches the present series. We intend to publish books that are genuinely interdisciplinary, theoretically sophisticated, and clinically informed. The literary critic's insights into psychoanalysis are no less valuable than the psychoanalyst's insights into literature. Gone are the days when psychoanalytic critics assumed that Freud had a master key to unlock the secrets of literature. Instead of reading literature to confirm psychoanalytic theory, many critics are now reading Freud to discover how his understanding of literature shaped the evolution of his theory. In short, the master-slave relationship traditionally implicit in the marriage between the literary critic and the psychoanalyst has given way to a healthier dialogic relationship, in which each learns from and contributes to the other's discipline.

Indeed, the prevailing ideas of the late twentieth century are strikingly different from those of the late nineteenth century, when literature and psychoanalysis were first allied. In contrast to Freud, who assumed he was discovering absolute truth, we now believe that knowledge, particularly in the humanities and social sciences, is relative and dependent upon cultural contexts. Freud's classical drive theory, with its mechanistic implications of cathectic energy, has given way to newer relational models, such as object relations, self psychology, and interpersonal psychoanalysis, affirming the importance of human interaction. Many early psychoanalytic ideas, such as the death instinct and the phylogenetic transmission of memories, have fallen by the wayside, and Freud's theorizing on female psychology has been recognized as a reflection of his cultural bias.

Significant developments have also taken place in psychoanalytic literary theory. An extraordinary variety and synthesis of competing approaches have emerged, including post-Freudian, Jungian, Lacanian, Horneyan, feminist, deconstructive, psycholinguistic, and reader response. Interest in psychoanalytic literary criticism is at an all-time high, not just in the handful of journals devoted to psychological criticism, but in dozens of mainstream journals that have traditionally avoided psychological approaches to literature. Scholars are working on identity theory, narcissism, gender theory, mourning and loss, and creativity. Additionally, they are investigating new areas, such as composition theory and pedagogy, and exploring the roles of resistance, transference, and countertransference in the classroom.

"In the end we depend/On the creatures we made," Freud observed at the close of his life (*Letters*, 425), quoting from Goethe's *Faust;* and in the end psychoanalytic literary criticism depends on the scholars who continue to shape it. All serious scholarship is an act of love and devotion, and for many of the authors in this series, including myself, psychoanalytic literary criticism has become a consuming passion, in some cases a lifelong one. Like other passions, there is an element of idealization here. For despite our criticisms of Freud, we stand in awe of his achievements; and even as we recognize the limitations of any single approach to literature, we find that psychoanalysis has profoundly illuminated the human condition and inspired countless artists. In the words of the fictional "Freud" in D. M. Thomas's extraordinary novel *The White Hotel* (1981), "Long may poetry and psychoanalysis continue to highlight, from their different perspectives, the human face in all its nobility and sorrow" (143n.).

JEFFREY BERMAN
Professor of English
State University of New York at Albany

Works Cited

Freud, Sigmund. *The Letters of Sigmund Freud*. Ed. Ernst Freud. Trans. Tania and James Stern. New York: Basic Books, 1975.

————. *The Origins of Psychoanalysis*. Ed. Marie Bonaparte, Anna Freud, and Ernst Kris. Trans. Eric Mosbacher and James Strachey. New York: Basic Books, 1954; rpt. 1977.

————. *The Standard Edition of the Complete Psychological Works of Sigmund Freud*. Ed. James Strachey. 24 vols. London: Hogarth Press, 1953–74.

Nabokov, Vladimir. Introduction, *Bend Sinister*. New York: McGraw-Hill, 1974.

————. *Lolita*. London: Weidenfeld and Nicolson, 1959.

Thomas, D. M. *The White Hotel*. New York: Viking, 1981.

Preface

I am deeply grateful to Maureen Waters, my wife, and Fred Kaplan for all their useful criticisms and suggestions for the revision of *The Beginning of Terror.* I take this opportunity to thank the members of the History of Psychiatry Seminar at Cornell Medical Center, who were very helpful in their responses to my paper on the relationship between Rilke and Rodin, and especially Barbara Leavy, whose support and encouragement will stay with me as a model of generous friendship. I have benefited as an interpreter of literature from the discussions of the Columbia University Literature and Psychology Seminar. The warm and thoughtful responses of Jason Renker, my editor at New York University Press, Jeffrey Berman, the editor of the Literature and Psychoanalysis Series, and New York University Press's final anonymous reader have played a creative role in revisions of my book.

For thirty-five years I have been studying Rilke's work and translating it for my own pleasure, along with the works of other German writers. During this time I have been interested in translations of Rilke by others and am, no doubt, indebted to them in my own interpretations and translations of his poems.

Acknowledgments

I would like to thank the following: Random House, Inc., for permission to quote from *The Selected Poetry of Rainer Maria Rilke,* by Rainer Maria Rilke, edited and translated by Stephen Mitchell. Copyright © 1982 by Stephen Mitchell; North Point Press for permission to quote portions of the poetry of Rainer Maria Rilke from *New Poems (1907),* by Rainer Maria Rilke, translated by Edward Snow. Translation and copyright © 1984 by Edward Snow; Random House, Inc., for permission to quote from *The Notebooks of Malte Laurids Brigge,* by Rainer Maria Rilke, translated by Stephen Mitchell. Copyright © 1982, 1983 by Stephen Mitchell; W. W. Norton & Company, Inc., for permission to quote from *Letters of Rainer Maria Rilke, 1892–1926* (two volumes), translated by Jane Bannard Greene and M. D. Herter Norton. Copyright © 1945, 1947, and 1948, W. W. Norton & Company.

Abbreviations

The following abbreviations are used in parenthetical citations through-out *The Beginning of Terror*. Full information concerning these texts is given in the Notes and the Selected Bibliography.

ET	*Ewald Tragy*
Letters 1	*Letters of Rainer Maria Rilke: 1892–1910*
Letters 2	*Letters of Rainer Maria Rilke: 1910–1926*
LYP	*Letters to a Young Poet*
R&B: IC	*Rilke and Benvenuta: An Intimate Correspondence*
SO	*The Sonnets to Orpheus* (trans. Stephen Mitchell)
SP	*The Selected Poetry of Rainer Maria Rilke*
WDB	*Werke in drei Bänden*
WSR	*Where Silence Reigns*

The Beginning of Terror

CHAPTER 1

Introduction

I

This is a psychological study of Rainer Maria Rilke's life and writings.
Beginning with his novel, *The Notebooks of Malte Laurids Brigge,* published in 1910, I explore the relationship between illness and genius in
the poet and his work, a subject to which he returned time and again.
His letters describing his experiences when he first came to Paris in 1902
reveal that the anxieties which bring Malte, the main character of the
novel, close to psychosis, plagued Rilke himself. The letters and *The
Notebooks* show that Rilke felt that he was losing his sanity. In the summer of 1903 he wrote to Lou Andreas-Salomé, his old friend, lover, and
acknowledged surrogate mother, imploring her to help him, declaring
that she alone knew who he was and could tell him what he need and
need not fear. Salomé had cut off all communication when he decided to
marry in February 1901, but she had also promised that she would help
him if he should be in dire need at some time in the future. Answering
his appeal, she expressed surprise at the maturity of the gifts and skills
revealed by his descriptions of his frightening experiences in Paris. She
assured him he was mistaken in believing that he would be destroyed by
mental illness. The mastery, artistic cunning, and understanding which
his letters disclosed clearly distinguished him from the helpless victims
of illness with whom he was identifying himself. In the first few months
of the following year, encouraged by her praise, Rilke began *The Notebooks,* drawing upon the experiences he had described in his letters to

her. Some passages of this memorable novel differ but little from those anguished letters.

The Notebooks expresses the belief that it might be necessary for "every meaning" to "dissolve like a cloud and fall down like rain," necessary, that is, to endure something like mental disintegration or dying to be able to "see everything differently." A poet might have to risk undergoing a process of fragmentation closely resembling the onset of psychosis (we would say "schizophrenia," but the term was not introduced until 1911, the year after Rilke completed his novel)[1] before his hand would "write words that are not mine," "that other interpretation."[2] Such experiences gave rise to "agony" and "disconsolations"; they were also sources of "most painful insights" and "a negative mold" from which the poet hoped to cast "real still things," works of art, "that it is serenity and freedom to create and from which, when they exist, reassurance emanates. . . . "[3]

Obviously these ideas raise questions for anyone writing a study of Rilke and his work, or interested in the psychology of his genius. With such questions in mind and with help from a number of psychologists and psychoanalysts, I attempt to define the nature of the emotional illness which often preoccupied the poet, its complex relation to his genius, its origins in his childhood, and its development.

Studies of creativity have made me wary of the old myth that has "great wits . . . to madness near allied" and poets "mad as the mist and snow."[4] Artists often reveal exceptionally strong capacities for organization and control which are absent or weak in insanity. But psychological analyses of the creative process also suggest that there are significant affinities between certain kinds of mental illness and talent or genius in art and science. In subsequent chapters I refer to a number of these findings, for example, Anton Ehrenzweig's argument in *The Hidden Order of Art* concerning the striking similarities and essential differences between Picasso's painting and Joyce's writing and schizophrenic art and language. His comparative analysis applies, as well, to *The Notebooks,* with its fragmentary form, its dreamlike scenes and images, and its portrayal of a breakdown in mental integration and in the ability to differentiate self from world and fantasy from reality.[5]

Writing to Lou in the summer of 1903, Rilke expressed the fear that he "would belong irretrievably to the lost if some passer-by merely looked at me and half unconsciously counted me with them" (*Letters*

1:111). He felt that a stranger's unspoken judgment could change him into an outcast, a dehumanized, broken thing, empty of mind and feeling, living on dust. Imagining that he was in danger of becoming one of "those who no longer hear their wills going in the noise" of the city, he thought he understood the fear that seemed to have "grown" "over" Parisians who were "beginning to read things differently from the way they were meant" (*Letters* 1:110–11). As his sense of self, distinctive identity, and autonomy became painfully uncertain and the "noise" of the city threatened to engulf him, he began to doubt his ability to distinguish fantasy from objective reality.

Writing the novel for which these experiences provided raw material helped the poet to master them and thus to defend himself against the illness that was threatening to destroy his sanity. In retrospect he believed the book was "something like an underpinning" for all the work that followed. It had opened up "a whole octave" of poetry in him. As a result of his writing *The Notebooks,* "everything reaches farther up" and "almost all songs are possible" (*Letters* 1:361).

Having received a commission to write a monograph on Auguste Rodin, Rilke came to Paris late in August 1902 to meet the sculptor. His two essays on the Frenchman (published in 1903 and 1907 as parts 1 and 2 of a book entitled *Rodin*) study Rodin's decompositions and reconstructions of the physical world and illuminate his fascination with Rodin's art at the time he was having the fantasies of disintegration described in the letters and in *The Notebooks.* In this sculpture he discovered that the "artist has the right to make one thing out of many and a world out of the smallest part of a thing."[6] This model licensed, inspired, and shaped his fictional evocations of the fantasies which had been so frightening to him. Thus, a sculptor became his "master" during the years in which his writing matured and established his place among leading modern writers with the completion of the *New Poems* (1907 and 1908) and *The Notebooks* (1910), though Rodin's personal hold on Rilke began to decline after a temporary rupture in the relationship in May 1906. This part of the story is told in chapter 8.

Rodin's example may have helped Rilke to discover, or at least to accept, the fragmentary form of his novel, the fractured personality of his central character, and the apparent incoherence of a life presented "as if one found disordered papers in a drawer" (*Letters* 1:362). A similar influence on *The Notebooks* was Paul Cézanne, whose painting also provided inspiration and guidance for some of the *New Poems*. In 1924 Rilke wrote that "from 1906 on" Cézanne's painting was his "most forceful model" (*Letters* 2:334). The precise nature of this influence is delineated in a number of letters, including the eloquent ones written to the poet's wife, Clara, in October 1907 when Rilke saw the Cézannes on exhibition in the Salon d'Automne. Picasso painted *Les Demoiselles d'Avignon* in 1907, and Braque was doing cubist landscapes in 1908. But I have not seen any evidence that Rilke was aware of their work that early. He may have known about some of the new ideas in science and psychology which were inspiring a revolution in painting and sculpture as they radically changed conceptions of nature and the mind—relativity theory, quantum physics, non-Euclidean geometry, and the psychology of the unconscious. All made it necessary to "learn to see" (Malte's phrase) the world and self as they had never been seen or dreamt of in earlier times. These new ideas dismembered nature, converted solid matter into volatile, moving energy, demolished the old Newtonian assumption that the behavior of individual entities was as predictable as clockwork, formulated new relationships between space and time and between the spectator and what he or she sees, and proposed that a large part of the mind was a mass of seemingly chaotic unconscious energies, emotions, and ideas, shaping conscious thought and precariously restrained by fragile defenses from engulfing it. A number of passages in *The Notebooks* raise the possibility that Rilke had a vague awareness of some of the new theories in physics, mathematics, and psychology when he wrote his novel. But I know of no compelling evidence from his letters, from biographies, or from recollections of friends and acquaintances which shows that at this time he had any precise knowledge of the revolutionary ideas in these disciplines.[7]

It would be absurd to classify Rilke as a schizophrenic, but the anxieties and fantasies we find in his writings about his first year in Paris closely resemble some of those characteristic of this disease. According to Harold Searles, a widely respected authority on this form of mental illness, the schizophrenic "feels that his body is not his." [8] Parts of it separate themselves and act autonomously. Alien personalities and objects invade him and are experienced as "foreign bodies within his personality," which threaten to devour or to annihilate him.[9] He may be sucked in, enveloped, or obliterated by the personality, mind, or will of another person, or by some animated part of his environment. (In a similar experience, as a boy, looking at himself in a mirror, Malte feels engulfed by a suffocating, inescapable mask and costume.) Relationships with other people threaten to obliterate all traces of his own face and to replace it with one responsive to their needs, closely resembling theirs. In this fantasy the face is felt to be synonymous with the sense of self. In *The Nonhuman Environment,* Searles analyzes the motives for the desire to turn oneself into a dehumanized object and the inclination to turn other people into such objects, tendencies which appear frequently in *The Notebooks.*

Studies of closely related forms of narcissistic and borderline illness by Heinz Kohut, R. D. Laing, and D. W. Winnicott have enlarged my understanding of what Rilke was going through when he first came to Paris. Like the poet at this time, like Malte, their patients felt so ill-defined and uncertain of their differentiation from the world and from other people that mere contact with others often threatened to transform them into helpless responses or imitations. Sustained relationships could be engulfing. The contours of the body, the basis gradually discovered in infancy for one's sense of one's separate self, failed to hold against an impinging, invading, or "imploding" world. One defense against engulfment or invasion is "schizoid," splitting into a "true" inner core of the self and a false, compliant, imitative outer self or selves, which shield the inner self against the dangers of alteration or annihilation by others or by an impinging environment.

In Rilke such defenses were crippling, but they also became creative. In subsequent chapters I discuss the self-protective, self-concealing personas which Rilke developed and consider their origins in his childhood. In this part of my commentary I refer to Winnicott's and Laing's concepts of the false self in schizoid illness and Winnicott's argument that this has a healthy counterpart, the socially compliant facades which protect the inner core of the self in the experience of most mentally healthy people. Rilke's conceptions of face and mask seem to have evolved out of intervals of illness. But Rilke, like Nietzsche, was convinced that masking protects the gifted artist's cultivation and nurturing of his or her depth, power, and art from intrusion, distraction, and adulteration. The poet's writings, like Nietzsche's and Kierkegaard's, may be seen as masks which conceal as much as they reveal. They fulfilled "the urgent need to communicate and the still more urgent need not to be found" which Winnicott observed in artists.[10]

Rilke's illness also became creative in another way. As the hard reality of things around him invades his body and drives him out of it, Malte tries to defend himself by passing his fingers over his face in an effort to reestablish his sense of his boundaries. Malte is overwhelmed particularly by the multitude of unbearable phenomena that seem to press in on him. External realities invade, overflow, drown, and suffocate him. Driven out of himself, he is squashed like "a beetle" underfoot (*The Notebooks*, 74). But Rilke's bouts of boundary loss evolved into an ability to release himself from the trap of separateness and opposition between subject and object in which most of us find ourselves caught by rigid defensiveness. In 1913 he went through an experience in which the boundaries between "inner" and "outer" dissolved as he felt "within him the gentle presence of the stars" ("An Experience," *WSR*, 36). On this occasion Rilke closed his eyes to keep out of mind the contours of his body, a response which seems to be the opposite of Malte's reaction to the threat of invasion. At other times he experienced the "inviolable presentness and simultaneity" of everything which in ordinary consciousness comes to us as "mere 'sequence' " (*Letters* 2:342). Distinctions between past, present, and future faded. So did the common sense opposition between the living and the dead, for the dead continue to exist for us and "we are incessantly flowing over and over to those who preceded us, to our origins" (*Letters* 2:373). Such experiences of what Rilke called "das Offne" ("the open") seem to have grown out of the kinds of fragmentation and boundary loss described in his letters and fiction. Yet they make "normal" ideas and perceptions of time, space, self, and world seem fragmentary in comparison. They must have occurred during intervals of ego strength and health (wholeness, integration) between stretches of barrenness, emotional illness, and depression.

They prepared for and shaped the thinking and imagery of the *Duino Elegies*, and *The Sonnets to Orpheus*. They seemed to the poet to bring an interchange of being between him and the surrounding world, in which metamorphosing world and self were continually re-created, as he tells us, quietly rejoicing, in the first and last sonnets of the second cycle.

Fantasies of engulfment, impingement, and depersonalization, which we find in Rilke's letters and *The Notebooks*, often lead to defensive isolation. *The Notebooks* demonstrates the dangers of isolation such as Malte's, which feeds the demons of disease it is meant to defend against. Malte's solitude is extreme. He has no relationships in the present time of the novel. This was not true of Rilke. But the poet was almost obsessively devoted to an ideal of solitude, as his letters, fiction, and poetry show. If psychological infirmities were an acknowledged source of his need to be alone, nineteenth-century thinkers, such as Nietzsche and Kierkegaard, strongly supported his belief that solitude was a necessary condition for creative work. His contemporary and fellow native of Prague, Franz Kafka, equally influenced by these philosophers, emphasized the same theme in his diaries and letters.

Rilke was often with other people. He complained that being with them did him little good and much harm, shutting off the sources of his poetry. Beginning with the "boundlessly frightful pains of childhood," solitude had given him "all that was greatest" (*Letters* 2:106–7). Yet the severe anxieties which isolation fostered often led him to seek company and to lose the poet in himself among friends and acquaintances. His relationships with Lou Andreas-Salomé and Auguste Rodin, which I interpret in chapters 5 and 8, reveal the psychodynamics of his dependence on others in its most extreme forms.

The insights of Harold Searles, Heinz Kohut, R. D. Laing, D. W. Winnicott, and Arnold Modell have helped me to elucidate Rilke's dependence on Salomé and Rodin and his extravagant idealization of these two surrogate parents.[11] If we can trust his memory, his extreme neediness in both relationships was due largely to his mother's and father's failings, which are amply described in his letters, fiction, and poetry. He feared that he had inherited his mother's disconnectedness and unreality. He complained bitterly about Phia Rilke's dishonesty with herself, narcissistic self-absorption, blindness to his real qualities, and inability to love him for what he was. His father's failure to fulfill his aspirations to a career as an army officer weighed heavily on René during his childhood. The poet was haunted by Josef's emotional constriction, his expectation that his son would vicariously fulfill his own frustrated ambitions, his disappointment at René's leaving military school and rejecting a military career, and his anxiety about the poet's unwillingness to find a job which would protect him, his wife, and daughter from shameful poverty and give them a respectable place in society. But Rilke was able to see or imagine generosity and an inclination to love in his father, struggling against such narrow-minded anxiety and rigidity.

Psychoanalysts who have studied narcissistic illness theorize that the kinds of failures in mothering and fathering which Rilke attributed to his parents often leave the psyche severely impaired. As an adult a child of such parents may look for surrogates who will provide the empathetically responsive maternal "mirroring" required to strengthen a sense of self which remains weak because the individual did not receive adequate "mirroring" in early childhood. He may also seek a surrogate who can be invested with the fantastical omnipotence ascribed to parents by small children, because of their need, in their sense of their own helplessness and fragility, to participate, through identification, in such power. Having failed as a child to internalize idealized parents who calm anxiety, foster the tolerance of unsatisfied cravings, provide models and guidance, distinguish reality from fantasy, make possible accommodations with environmental realities, and offer love and admiration, an adult suffering from narcissistic illness may seek such parents in other people, idealizing them so that they can supply these needs, which persist with an infantile intensity. My chapters on Salomé and Rodin show how they fulfilled such needs in Rilke.

Analysts have also written about the ways in which the impairments and injuries characteristic of narcissistic illness can be repaired and healed. This is an important part of my subject. My chapters on Salomé, Clara Rilke, the poet's father, and Rodin show how, through his relationships with them and through his work, which he called "nothing but a self-treatment of the same sort" as analysis, he mastered the severest forms of his anxieties and developed a remarkable ability to move, sometimes swiftly, sometimes gradually, from fear, despair, and near mental paralysis to the writing of his greatest poems (*Letters* 2:42).

Writing to his wife in April 1903, Rilke defended the distance between them with the argument that his work was the center of his life, which he must find again if he was to be able to make progress toward the realization of his gifts. To do this he said, he must be alone, unwatched, unselfconscious. He must be solitary long enough to enable his loneliness to become "firm and secure again like an untrodden wood that is not afraid of footsteps." The worst thing that could happen to him was "to become unaccustomed to loneliness" (*Letters* 1:105–6). Though the poet did rediscover the center of his life in his work recurrently (the long period of sustained creativity between 1906 and 1910, when he wrote many of the *New Poems* and completed *The Notebooks,* was especially gratifying), the problem that he defined in this letter remained very much alive for him until the completion of the *Elegies* and the writing of the *Sonnets* at Muzot in February 1922.

D. W. Winnicott's observations about "the capacity to be alone" seem especially relevant to Rilke. Winnicott sees this capacity as "one of the most important signs of maturity in emotional development." He argues that from "this position everything is creative."[12] In chapter 9 I take a close look at Winnicott's ideas on this subject as I discuss Rilke's attainment of his long-sought home in isolation during the winter of 1921–22.

Winnicott suggests that we achieve "the ability to be truly alone" by internalizing an "ego-supportive mother." Such a mother, empathetically responsive to her infant's needs, creates a sense of a "protective environment."[13] The introjection of this maternal figure may enable one to maintain a strong, if unconscious, sense of such an environment throughout one's life. This is essential to the artist especially because he needs to be able to lapse into the strange and often frightening unintegrated, undifferentiated state of mind in which he is open to normally repressed ideas and feelings and to alien structures of thought. Rilke's letters make it clear that he needed to be alone in order to fall into such a condition, to exist solitary in an imagined cocoon so that he could come apart before coming together again. In this raw, naked, fragmentary state of mind he felt both too vulnerable and too repulsive to be near anyone, except a servant. His attempts to live with mothering women—above all, Lou Andreas-Salomé—usually resulted in painful failure.

Chapter 9 brings to a conclusion my study of the ways in which Rilke attempted, in his fiction, his poetry, and a number of his relationships, to create the benevolent, supportive, protective, mirroring mother he felt Phia had not been for him. From the time that he wrote *The Book of Hours* (1899, 1901, and 1903, revised in 1905), with its prayer that he might be granted a hermaphroditic nature as a mothering male, his works and letters reveal a fascination with the idea that *he* might be both man and woman, mother and son, brother and sister, lover and beloved. The painful memories of his mother's games during the first five years of his life, in which she had converted him into a little girl, a substitute for his sister, who had died before he was born, were put to good use in his fiction and poetry. In chapter 9 I consider the poems which, beginning with "Turning" (June 1914), show the evolution of an inner beloved woman or female presence. This process culminates in his transformation of Vera Knoop, a young dancer, artist, and musician, the daughter of friends, who had recently died at nineteen, into the inner woman, "almost a girl" ("fast ein Mädchen"), who inspired *The Sonnets to Orpheus*, as the poems, themselves, their dedication, and his letters about them tell us. In the second sonnet he imagines that she has made her bed within his ear and slept there and that her sleep within his "auditory imagination" included the world and brought it within him, allowing him at last to hear the Orphic lyre resounding in his ordinarily "unheard center." (The "auditory imagination" is T. S. Eliot's concept. "Unheard center" ["unerhörte mitte"] comes from the twenty-eighth sonnet of the second cycle, which is clearly about Vera, though she is not named, and which is dedicated to her.) With this figure in the *Sonnets*, with the silent, invisible female friend of the Seventh Duino Elegy, and with the beloved Earth in the Ninth Elegy, whom he imagines yearning to become invisible within him, Rilke brought to perfection his efforts to give vivid, compelling life and form to the loving, "mirroring" maternal figure, present in *The Notebooks* and in so many of his poems. In the young woman, "almost a girl," of the *Sonnets* this mental presence found a disguise which concealed its real, felt meaning from the poet as well as his readers.

By giving such evocative, if disguised, forms of existence to the beloved maternal figure within him he was able to convert narcissistic illness into creative narcissism and to find in his isolation at Muzot the wholeness and fertile, potent self-sufficiency that made it possible for him to complete the *Elegies* and to write the *Sonnets*. The writing of the *Sonnets* and the final Elegies brought the psychological processes which I have described to completion.

Although a number of biographies have been published, only one earlier book has answered the need for a psychological study of this great poet—Erich Simenauer's *Rainer Maria Rilke: Legende und Mythos*, published in 1953 and never translated into English. I am indebted to Simenauer for his perceptive readings of Rilke's works and his letters. But his book is limited by its narrow reliance on early Freudian concepts. His "classical" analysis focuses on the consequences of a "fixation" in the "oedipal stage" with its murderous hatred of the father and incestuous longings for the mother. He is concerned with the largely unconscious roles which "id," "ego," and "superego" play in the poet's "oedipus complex," including the ego's responses to the superego and its defenses against the id, such as "repression" and "reaction formation" (unconscious exaggeration of a feeling or wish in consciousness in order to reinforce repression of its opposite). For the most part, Simenauer classifies aspects of the poet's psychology according to the taxonomy of primitive Freudian orthodoxy.

I draw upon the same set of concepts, but, as this introduction makes clear, I also move beyond them to psychological theory and knowledge concerned with the child's pre-oedipal experience and its long-term effects. Discussions of narcissistic, borderline, schizoid, and schizophrenic forms of mental illness and their origins in this earlier period of childhood have been helpful in my study of Rilke's life and writings. My interpretations reflect an interest in works concerned with the formation and development of ego and identity; the evolution of the sense of self, its separation and integration; the experience of "the non-human environment" ("Things" for Rilke) in mental health and illness; the fear of death and the variety of ways in which it may be mastered; the psychology of the creative process; comparisons and contrasts of language and thought in literature and schizophrenic speech and writing; and new conceptions of "identification," "introjection," and "incorporation" which have helped me to elucidate Rilke's conception of relationships between the living and the dead, his notion of the woman within himself, and the ideas about internalization and transformation which form the central "argument" of the seventh and ninth Duino Elegies.

Much of the psychological theory and knowledge which I have found helpful postdates the publication of Simenauer's study. I have also benefited from recent biographies of Rilke by Wolfgang Leppmann, Donald Prater, and J. F. Hendry, as well as a wealth of scholarship and commentary written since 1953.[14]

How would the poet, himself, have responded to the news that someone had written a psychoanalytic study of his life and work? His conflicting feelings about psychoanalysis are clearly expressed in his letters. Rejecting his wife's advice that he go into analysis, on January 14, 1912, when the first Duino Elegy had just come to him, he wrote to the Freudian therapist, Emil Baron von Gebsattel, a friend of Lou Andreas-Salomé, expressing the fear that such a system of classification would disturb the "much higher order" of his imagination (*Letters* 2:43). Ten days later he wrote to Salomé and again to Gebsattel, saying that, with the exorcism of his devils, his angels too might leave. A January 20 letter to Salomé acknowledges that the idea of undergoing psychoanalysis occurred to him from time to time. If he found Freud's writings "uncongenial," nonetheless, he could "conceive of Gebsattel's using it [psychoanalysis] with discretion and influence" (*Letters* 2:44). In this letter he gives a detailed account of his imprisoning, hypochondriacal misery. But his fear that analysis might result in "a disinfected soul," "a monstrosity," a mind like a student notebook page covered with corrections—a fantasy which he acknowledged was "silly" and "false"—kept him from entering treatment (*Letters* 2:44, 43). Repelled and fascinated by the new ideas and therapies of the depth psychologists, suffering often from uncontrollable anxieties and an inability to sustain a loving relationship, a recurrent inability to work, cruel depression, and a sense of his unreality, he sought explanations and therapeutic advice from Salomé, whose growing knowledge of Freudian theory and eccentric devotion to it after 1911 influenced her interpretations of his illness and his writings in her letters to him, their conversations, and her own books, including her study of Rilke (1928), *The Freud Journal of Lou-Andreas Salomé*, which she kept in 1912 and 1913 (*Aus der Schule bei Freud*), and her memoir, *A Look Back at Life* (*Lebensrückblick*).[15]

II

In a recent essay on Rilke, "Paris/Childhood: The Fragmented Body in Rilke's *Notebooks of Malte Laurids Brigge*," published in *Modernity and the Text: Revisions of German Modernism* (1989), Andreas Huyssen observes that "the insights of psychoanalysis have by and large been shunned by Rilke scholars as irrelevant for the literary and aesthetic assessment of the novel."[1] Most of my book was complete before I discovered Huyssen's essay, but we draw upon some of the same psychological concepts and share a sense of the ways in which psychoanalytic approaches to literary criticism have changed substantially since the days when all too many reductive, simplistic psychological exegeses of poetry, fiction, and drama provided ample justification for the antagonism of literary scholars and critics. Huyssen also discusses Rilke's por-

trayal of Malte's reactions to Paris from a sociological perspective, in
relation to Walter Benjamin's and Georg Simmel's accounts of the big
city's effects on the individual and on modern literature (in Simmel's
essay "The Metropolis and Mental Life" and Benjamin's, "Some Motifs
in Baudelaire"). This part of Huyssen's analysis indicates a direction in
which interpretations of Rilke's fiction should be developing. At the end
of my review of recent Rilke criticism I shall say more about this approach, in my reflections on Brigitte Bradley's study of *The Notebooks.*

A number of recent commentators on Rilke's work continue to divorce the poetry from the poet's life, as if any attempt to read the *Duino
Elegies, The Sonnets to Orpheus,* and other great poems by Rilke with
understanding enhanced by consideration of his life and by psychoanalytic insights demeans the poetry and deprives it of proper aesthetic
appreciation. Some critics, Huyssen argues, see Rilke as representing "a
modernism of disembodied subjectivity, metaphysical negativity, and
textual closure, the classicism of the twentieth century."[2] Such criticism
may develop perceptive readings of individual poems and passages, but
it often suppresses much of the emotional and intellectual complexity,
vitality, richness, and subtlety of Rilke's work.

One of the strongest statements of antipathy to psychoanalytic and
biographical criticism among Rilke scholars is to be found in the foreword to Jacob Steiner's book *Rilkes Duineser Elegien* (1962 and 1969).
Steiner goes to the extreme of insisting that the more boldly the biographical "I" of the poet stands out in the "i" of the work, so much the
worse is the poetry ("Aber es lässt sich vermuten, dass das biographische
Ich des Dichters umso stärker durch das *ich* des Werks hervortritt, je
schlechter die Dichtung ist").[3] Attacking Simenauer's analysis, Steiner
says he forgets that "the private person Rilke is not yet the poet in his
productive hours and that ... from the productive poet to his product
there is a distance to be overcome whose breadth, unfathomable depth,
and complexity have not been measured up to the present time" ("Aber
er vergisst dabei, dass die private Person Rilke noch nicht der Dichter in
seinen produktiven Stunden ist und dass auch vom producktiven Dichter zu seinen Produkt ein Abstand zu überwinden ist, dessen Weite,
Abgründigkeit und Komplexität bisher nicht ermessen worden sind").[4]

This doctrine foreshadows more sophisticated and carefully argued
attempts to define and justify the critical concept of "das lyrische Ich"
(the lyric I) in each poem, such as Käte Hamburger's in *Die Logik der*

Dichtung (1968) and Anthony Stephens's in *Rainer Maria Rilke's "Gedichte an die Nacht"* (1972), which are reminiscent of earlier endeavors by the English and American New Critics to analyze the narrative persona in a poem or a work of fiction without reference to the life and personality of the poet or the novelist. Steiner's desire to separate and distance "the productive poet" from the person and his purist Aestheticism in arguing that the reflection in the "I" of the poem of the "private person" in his nonproductive hours makes for a bad poem seem wildly defensive and curiously naive. In her very perceptive study *Transcending Angels: Rainer Maria Rilke's Duino Elegies* (1987), Kathleen Komar finds even Steiner guilty of digressing into the personal and the biographical, when he remarks that a passage in Elegy IV reflects Rilke's relationship with his father (though he immediately qualifies this observation, saying that the relationship between father and son is so fully generalized in these lines of the Elegy that reference to a biography would make no further contribution to an understanding of the poem). Noting that, "as Steiner points out, the passage concerning the father may well have biographical overtones concerning his bureaucratic-military father's questioning of Rilke's poetic vocation," Komar remarks, "the more general implications for the male and female factors of human life provide a more fruitful focus for our discussion of the *Elegies.*"[5] The clumsy vagueness of this comment suggests an evasive, skittish response to the personal and psychological dimensions of Rilke's poetry, a response which flaws and limits an otherwise excellent book.

Komar brackets off the poet's life in a three page "Biographical Sketch" that appears as an appendix at the end of her study. Her decision to exclude the life from the rest of her book imposes substantial limitations upon her valuable, detailed analyses of content and form. And the more's the pity. For, her elucidations of verbal nuances, multiple meanings, and the connections among passages and poems which contribute to the integrity of each Elegy and to the coherence and development of the cycle are the work of an exceptionally gifted and knowledgeable interpreter.

Richard Exner and Ingrid Stipa argue that psychoanalytic interpretation is largely irrelevant in reading Rilke's later poetry, in another valuable recent contribution to Rilke criticism: "Das Phänomen der Androgynie des Schaffenprozesses im späten Rilke: Das Beispiel. 'Solang du Selbstgeworfnes fängst . . . ,' " (The Phenomenon of the Androgyny of the Creative Process in Late Rilke: Example, "As long as you catch what you yourself have thrown . . . "), published in *Rainer Maria Rilke*, as part of the "Wege der Forschung" series (1987). Referring to Simenauer's contrast between the archaic, analyzable, comparatively unformed perceptions of Rilke's earlier work and the form-giving harmonies of the later poetry, Exner and Stipa conclude that the creative processes responsible for the latter were grounded, to a large extent, in "bewussten Denkvorgänge" ("conscious thought processes"), which these critics see as providing "logische Ausdrucksformen zur Kommunikation" ("logical forms of expression for communication").[6] One can find support in Rilke's work for their hypothesis that poetry should not be read primarily as an expression of the complex and largely unknown psychic life of the poet, for example, in *Sonnet to Orpheus* I.3, which tells us, "Gesang ist Dasein," "Ein Hauch um nichts" ("Song is existence," "A breath without purpose or object"). But their choice of a focal example, "As long as you catch what you yourself have thrown . . . ," is unintentionally ironic. This poem suggests that the writing of great poetry is a profoundly mysterious process and experience, in which suddenly the poet becomes the one who catches the ball thrown to him, to his center, by an eternal female partner. In this experience all conscious courage and power, all conscious calculation, are gone, and the poem seems to come from him of its own accord, like a meteor leaving his hands and raging into its own spaces. This is only a partial paraphrase, but it suffices to show that the creative processes the poem envisions are very largely unconscious, unknown, mysterious.[7]

Exner and Stipa maintain that in "Solang du Selbstgeworfnes fängst . . . " Rilke conceives of poetry as arising out of its own logic and language, as if it were largely or entirely disconnected from the poet's unconscious thought processes. They use the word "poetologische" ("poetological") to label this purely self-sufficient logic and process. Though their critical methods and concepts are very different from Jacob Steiner's, their affirmation of rarefied aestheticism, like his, seems strangely naive and psychologically defensive. Like so many other Rilke scholars, they are defending the purity of poems which we all value as great treasures. But the poems do not become less extraordinary if we see them in relation to the poet's life and with the help of psychoanalytic insights. Exner's and Stipa's method of defining the "poetological" processes and results is to identify "lexische Fäden" ("lexical strings" or "threads"), "lexische Gewebe" ("lexical webs" or "wefts" or "textures"), and "Wortfelder" ("word fields") in a poem or a series of selected poems. This mode of operations enables them to trace the development of connected themes and closely related words and images through quite a number of poems written in different stages of Rilke's creative life. And although at times their terminology seems a pseudoscientific jargon, their careful tracings of "lexical strings" or "threads" and "word fields" do accumulate a large, persuasive picture of the developing relationship between Rilke's evolving sense of himself, his feelings and thoughts about androgyny, and his conception of the poet's (especially his own) creative processes.[8]

One cannot help being drawn to the argument that this very great poet must have become increasingly self-aware in his shaping of his own work, as he became ever more skillful and knowledgeable. But, if you postulate, as Exner and Stipa do, that the earlier work is shaped by Rilke's unconscious, as Simenauer and Lou Andreas-Salomé describe it, you will have a hard time making the case that the later work somehow floats completely free of the poet's psychic depths, as if it had no connection with its antecedents. And if, at times, as in the line from Sonnet I.3, quoted above ("Gesang ist Dasein" ["Song is existence"]), Rilke seems to resemble other purists of modernist Aestheticism, such as Mallarmé, much of his prose and poetry, including the *Duino Elegies,* shows affinities with works of nineteenth- and early twentieth-century literature, philosophy, and psychology which weigh heavily against such a position. Among the writers and thinkers most important to Rilke were Kleist, Jens Jacobsen, Kierkegaard, Dostoevsky, Flaubert, Baudelaire, Nietzsche, Freud, and Lou Andreas-Salomé.

I have mentioned Anthony Stephens's study, *Rainer Maria Rilke's "Gedichte an die Nacht"* (1972), a nonpsychoanalytic commentary which shows an intelligent openness to a variety of approaches to Rilke's extraordinarily complex, problematic, and elusive writings. Stephens finds that the "intellectual structures" of the "Gedichte an die Nacht" [Poems to the Night], written in 1913–14, "have their roots determined largely by emotion." Quoting Rilke's early definition of his aim in writing poetry—"Bilder zu finden für meine Verwandlungen" ("to find images for my transformations")—Stephens proposes that "in his later work intellectual structures [of human experience] may function precisely as *im-*

ages." (Among the structures which seem most important to him in Rilke's poems is "Gegenständlichkeit," the radically alien quality and opacity of external objects for the person who feels unrelated to them and feels that he is not at all at home in a world in which he is like a tenant constantly in danger of eviction. Opposed to "Gegenständlichkeit" in Rilke's thinking and writing is "Weltinnenraum," a term which Stephens and other critics read as a means of conceptualizing "a feeling of participation and emotional identification with the objects of experience." In other words, "The concept of 'Weltinnenraum' is based on a feeling of the homogeneity of inner and outer worlds and on the absence of any barriers to emotional identification."[9] The argument that such concepts function in Rilke's poetry as images rather than as rational abstractions in logical relationship to one another leads Stephens to the following conclusion: "What determined the succession of Rilke's 'Verwandlungen' ("transformations") is a psychological question and hence unanswerable within the framework of this book."[10] That is to say, one should not study the transformations of "Gegenständlichkeit" into "Weltinnenraum" in exclusively logical, metaphysical, or epistemological terms if one wants to give a clear and full analysis of the works which represent and realize them. Such transformations in Rilke's poetry involve complexities of feeling and thought which need help from psychological insights if we are to understand them.

But I do not want to give the impression that Stephens is an avid supporter of psychoanalytic criticism. He faults both Ulrich Fülleborn and the "Freudian" critics for approaches to Rilke which try to fit poetry to "a priori" assumptions, absolute preconceptions; if "these conditions do not appear to pertain, then the 'Synthesis a priori' supplies them in terms of what *ought* to be there if the presuppositions are correct." Stephens shows that this is the case with Fülleborn, but does not mention any "Freudian" critics specifically, as examples of this failing.[11]

My interpretations of Rilke's work in *The Beginning of Terror* resemble Stephens's questioning approach to the work, his emphasis on the problematic nature of the poetry, his sense of its great complexity, subtlety, and richness, as well as its difficulty and elusiveness, and his belief that, possessed of these qualities, it invites a variety of critical perspectives. *The Beginning of Terror* shuns the kind of prescriptive "a priori" narrowness found in some primitive, reductive psychoanalytic criticism.

For the most perceptive literary critics and psychoanalysts share a sense of the fertile overdetermination of meaning in the metaphors, images, and formal patterns of great poems and other works of art.

In his concluding chapter, "An Approach to Rilke," Stephens discusses "two opposing tendencies, or attitudes, or techniques" in Rilke's work, focusing on "the poem as a closed system and the poem as a reaching out beyond the limits of given experience."[12] Stephens is interested in the interaction between these two tendencies and opposing views of poetry in Rilke's work, and in the poet's oscillating emphases, now on the one, now on the other. The former view may be associated with the poet's inclination, in his studies of Rodin and his letters about Rodin's sculpture, to magnify art into something that has an absolute value, something, like a god, unapproachable, magical, untouchable, and in its essence incomprehensible. As Stephens points out, Rilke inherited this idealization of the work of art and the artist from the Romantics. In *The Beginning of Terror* I explore this tendency in Rilke's thought and work at length, especially in my discussion of the poet's relationship with Rodin (see chapter 8). Describing the opposing tendency, Stephens focuses on Rilke's lecture, *Moderne Lyrik* (1898), where the poet says that the "specifically modern impulse is . . . to penetrate to the furthest regions of the self and express the result in poetry." An excerpt from that lecture makes the same point in the poet's words:

Sehen Sie: seit den ersten Versuchen des Einzelnen, unter der Flut flüchtiger Ereignisse *sich selbst zu finden,* seit dem ersten Bestreben, mitten im Gelärm des Tages hineinzuhorchen bis in die tiefsten Einsamkeiten des eigenen Wesens,— giebt es eine *Moderne Lyrik.*[13]

Look: since the first attempts of the individual, amid the flood of fleeting events, *to find himself,* since the first endeavors, amid the noise of the day, to listen within down to the deepest solitudes of his own being—there [has been] a *Modern Poetry.*

Stephens argues persuasively that this early association of modern poetry with "an exploration of the self and its relation to the world" is an enduring and central concern of Rilke's writings. In my chapters on *The Notebooks of Malte Laurids Brigge* and my studies of Rilke's later poems, including the *Duino Elegies* and *The Sonnets to Orpheus,* with questions and suggestions arising from the insights of a number of analysts and from Rilke's own writings, I examine this aspect of his work.

Chapters 2, 3, and 4 of this book are largely concerned with *The Notebooks*. One of the most valuable recent studies of the novel, Brigitte L. Bradley's "*Die Aufzeichnungen des Malte Laurids Brigge*: Thematisierte Krise des literarischen Selbstvertändnisses" (*The Notebooks of Malte Laurids Brigge*: Thematicized Crisis of Literary Self-Understanding) (1980), reveals close affinities with Andreas Huyssen's attempt to integrate psychological and sociological perspectives on Rilke's work. Bradley argues that Malte's responses to Paris reflect the conflict in Rilke between his early interest in the oppressiveness of the modern urban, technological, industrialized environment, with its crowded living conditions, and his belief that a writer corrupts and degrades his work if he allows it to be shaped by an ideology or by political, sociological, and economic ends.

Bradley argues that a number of passages in *The Notebooks* reflect Rilke's sense of the ways in which the old ideal of individuality, according to which a person could hope to become master of his or her circumstances, rather than be mastered by them, had been undermined by modern methods of mass production and the pervasion of human existence by technology, commercialization, and huge bureaucracies. Bradley points out that in a number of episodes, such as the ones in which Malte encounters the blind seller of cauliflowers and the blind newspaper vendor, Rilke focuses on human figures who may be seen as examples of social problems, "as representative of alienation conditioned by the economic system of production in relation to the sphere of work" ("als repräsentativ für die vom ökonomischen Produktionssystem bedingte Entfremdung dem Arbeitsbereich gegenüber").[14]

Bradley analyzes the complex relationship between Malte's responses to these aspects of modern urban life and his efforts to rediscover himself as a writer in his new environment. Malte has broken away from his past life, work, and sense of himself so completely, it seems to him, as he sits in his room, that he is "nothing." "And yet this nothing begins to think and thinks, five flights up, on a gray Paris afternoon, these thoughts" (*The Notebooks*, 22). In his letters Rilke defines Malte's ultimate failure as a writer in terms of his inability to achieve, except in one or two sections of *The Notebooks*, what the poet calls "anonymous work" and "objective expression," exemplified by Flaubert's fiction, Baudelaire's poems, and Cézanne's paintings (*Letters* 1:311 and 314–16).

As I have indicated, Bradley discusses Malte's failure and Rilke's abandonment of attempts to write prose fiction as reactions to an unsolvable conflict between two opposing sets of aesthetic values. She points to Rilke's 1898 lecture, *Moderne Lyrik,* mentioned above in my discussion of Stephens's book, as one means of understanding this conflict. What interests Bradley in that lecture is the poet's argument that writing or painting which finds its justification in usefulness and which clings to topics and phenomena of current interest or places itself "in the service of 'political or social factional interests' " ("in den Dienst 'politischer oder sozialer Parteiinteressen' ") is not art, but journalism.[15] Opposed in Rilke's mind to such corrupted forms of writing, painting, or sculpture are "autonomous art" and the self-sufficient work. Bradley links these concepts to *Jugendstil* art and the French symbolists, and says that Rilke came into closer contact with the aesthetic ideas of the latter through Rodin, during 1902 and 1903.[16]

Bradley finds that Malte's attempts to describe the blind newspaper vendor reveal the underlying causes of his ultimate failure to achieve a new, clear understanding of himself and his task as a writer. Malte's accounts of the vendor create a double perspective on that blind man. Reading these passages in *The Notebooks,* one can see him as an exemplary consequence of dehumanizing social and economic conditions, but he can also be seen as a man, "full of resignation" ("ergebungsvoll"), who bears his condition "as a misfortune ordained by fate" ("als ein vom Schicksal verhängtes Unglück").[17] When, after painful failure, Malte at last feels his portrait of the newspaper vendor successfully portrays the man, he takes this as proof of God's existence, which places him under "a huge obligation." And he imagines the Creator takes pleasure from his (Malte's) belief that his experience in struggling to portray the vendor has taught him "That we should learn to endure everything and never to judge" (*The Notebooks,* 211). Bradley observes that Malte's conclusions curiously alienate his work (the portrait) from himself. In this respect he reveals a latent affinity with his subject, the vendor, who is obviously alienated from his task, selling newspapers which he cannot read.

Bradley also sees a connection between an earlier episode, in which Malte's father forces himself to endure the terrifying visit of a ghost without questioning, and Malte's belief that his success in doing the portrait of the vendor at last has taught him to endure everything without ever judging or questioning, as the vendor, too, suffers his fate. Retreating from "the position of social and ideological criticism into which he has ventured," Malte seems frightened by this "function of the writer" into which he has been drawn (" ... Malte vor der gesellschafts- und ideologiekritischen Position, in die er sich begeben hat, zurückschreckt bzw. dass er sich mit einer sogearteten Funktion des Schriftstellers nicht identifizieren kann").[18] Incapable of developing such critical perceptions in his work, he seems unable to realize the power which comes, as he has understood, from "no longer being anybody's son" (*The Notebooks*, 189). If we accept Bradley's connections, we can follow her argument that he is unable to free himself from attitudes and behavior obviously learned from his father. Here, as elsewhere, her essay reflects an attempt to integrate sociological and psychological insights.

Bradley sees Rilke abandoning prose fiction for poetry because in the latter he could resolve the conflict between opposing sets of values which ultimately keeps Malte from redefining and re-creating himself as a writer. Freed from the "goal-directed semantics of everyday or commonplace idiom" in an "economically-minded society," Rilke could make his poetry "an affirmation" of his concept of "autonomous art" ("von der zweckgerichteten Semantik des Alltagsidioms. . . . eine Bejahung der autonomen Kunst").[19]

Some of Rilke's later poems do show an interest in social, political, and economic matters, but these are usually of secondary importance, at best. A salient example is Sonnet II.19, which implicitly attacks bourgeois, capitalist society for its obsession with money and its neglect of the poor. But even in that poem, the poet is not primarily interested in the blind beggar because of the social, economic, and political failures which he represents. He sees the beggar as "the silent one" ("der Schweigende"), standing in the breathing pauses of pampered money, his hand held out by fate. And the poet wishes that someone seeing this "luminous, miserable, endlessly destructible" hand ("hell, elend, unendlich zerstörbar") might, in wonder, praise its endurance in song which only a god could hear.[20]

Although Bradley's analysis of *The Notebooks* offers a very partial and limited reading of Malte's efforts to achieve a clear understanding of his task as a writer as he responds to his new environment, I have given it this lengthy summary in my review of recent criticism because I believe that it serves as a valuable theoretical complement to my own exploration of the novel's psychodynamics. It also points the way toward the kind of complex, sophisticated discussion of Rilke's work, in literary criticism with historical and sociological dimensions, which still needs to be done. And it provides an encouraging counterbalance to Egon Schwarz's heavy-handed attempt, in *Das verschluckte Schluchzen: Poesie und Politik bei Rainer Maria Rilke* (The Swallowed Sobbing: Poetry and Politics in Rainer Maria Rilke's Writings) (1972),[21] to interpret Rilke's work and thought in terms of the admiration for Mussolini which the poet expressed in correspondence with the Duchess Aurelia Gallarati-Scotti, and other expressions of the poet's ideas and attitudes which Schwarz sees as repellently right-wing.

CHAPTER 2

Learning to See

Integration and Distintegration in *The Notebooks of
    Malte Laurids Brigge* and Other Writings
Illness and Creativity

I

Rilke came to Paris late in August 1902 to talk with Auguste Rodin and
to study his sculpture in order to write a monograph on him. This monograph had been commissioned by Richard Muther, professor of art history at Breslau. The poet was twenty-six. He had published several
volumes of poetry and short stories, mainly juvenilia, among them *Leben
und Lieder* (Life and Songs) (1894), *Larenopfer* (Offerings to the Lares)
(1896), *Traumgekrönt* (Dream-Crowned) (1897), *Advent* (1898), *Zwei
Prager Geschichten* (Two Prague Stories) (1899), *Mir zur Feier* (In Celebration of Myself) (1899), *Die weisse Fürstin* (The White Princess)
(1899), and *Die Letzten* (The Last Ones) (1901). *Vom lieben Gott und
Anderes* (Of the Dear God And Other Things) (1900), a book of tales,
and *Das Buch der Bilder* (The Book of Images) (1902), a volume of
poems, show that his extraordinary gifts and skills were beginning to
mature; these works foreshadow the distinctive qualities of those, soon
to come, which would establish him as a major poet and novelist. He
had already written early versions of "The Book of the Monastic Life"
and "The Book of Pilgrimage," two sections of *Das Stunden-Buch* (The
Book of Hours), which many readers have considered his first work of
enduring genius, although these poems do not move decisively beyond

the excessive subjectivity, facile rhymes, and callow thinking of his early volumes.

Rilke's move to Paris definitively ended his attempt, for little more than a year, to live as husband and father with his wife and daughter in their small house at Westerwede, near Bremen. In Paris he looked forward to long periods of solitude and the opportunity to give uninterrupted devotion to his writing. Clara would come as soon as she could, but they would live in separate quarters, and he intended that they should see each other only on weekends. Ruth, at nine months of age, would be left in the care of her mother's parents.

My chapter on Rilke's relationship with Clara offers a detailed examination of his motives for marrying her and the reasons for his decision to give up their home in Westerwede, where he had hoped that they would guard each other's solitude and foster each other's writing and sculpture, while raising a child. Here I shall give a brief, selective account of Rilke's life at the time in order to provide a biographical context for my analysis of the novel begun in January 1904, which draws on his experiences during his first year in Paris.

In the summer of 1902 Rilke's cousins cut off the allowance which his Uncle Jaroslav had provided for his university studies. Forewarned by his cousins in January, Rilke had begun looking for other means of support, but he was determined never to take the kind of full-time job his father had long been urging on him. The many letters he sent to potential patrons brought little in return. He was commissioned to do a study of the artists whom he had known in the Worpswede colony (in which he had met Clara and her friend, the painter, Paula Becker, while living there during September 1900)—Fritz Mackensen, Otto Modersohn (Paula's husband), Hans am Ende, Fritz Overbeck, and Heinrich Vogeler, the gifted *Jugendstil* designer and illustrator, whose work and cloistered style of living he admired. At the time he did not foresee that Paula Becker, who had fascinated him no less than Clara in those heady days of September 1900 at Worpswede, would someday be recognized as the only major artist to have come out of that group. He does not mention her in his monograph on the Worpswede artists. A grant from the Concordia Society of Prague also helped support the couple in Westerwede during the spring of 1902, as did the fees for his book reviewing. But there was nowhere near enough to keep the family of three going.

Rilke had other reasons for breaking up his family. His letters tell us that the little household in Westerwede did not give him the emotional support, nurture, and fulfillment he had hoped for in marrying. On the contrary, his home there had remained painfully foreign to him. For some time his wife and child had seemed unwelcome intruders. Having his own home and family had done nothing to remedy his sense of his unreality. They had only intensified it. He felt that his existence as husband and father, under pressure to find an adequate income, in the village so close to Clara's parents, was "destroying" him.[1] His state of mind in Paris during 1902 and 1903 was influenced by the failure of his expectations that his marriage with Clara would give him the strength he needed to overcome his fears and that a house and family of his own would provide a refuge from the menacing chaos of the world around him without endangering his solitude.[2]

The focus of Rilke's working life during his first few months in Paris was Rodin. In chapter 1 I offered some indications of the ways in which Rilke's study of the sculptor's methods and his work may have influenced the writing and structuring of *The Notebooks of Malte Laurids Brigge*. My chapter on the poet's relationship with the sculptor provides a detailed analysis of Rodin's effect upon Rilke and his writing. When Rilke first arrived in Paris, the great artist seemed a center of strength in the frightening disorder of the city. At the beginning of August 1902 he had written to Rodin, addressing him as "My Master," revealing the extent to which he had idealized the sculptor before meeting him and the nature of his expectations. He expressed the wish that the books which he had published might be in Rodin's possession. Unfortunately, the sculptor could not read German, and Rilke's works had not yet been translated. He confessed, "All my life has changed since I know that you exist, my Master," and he contrasted his own good fortune with that of young aspiring artists who feel forsaken because they cannot find a master who will provide them with "an example, a fervent heart, hands that make greatness" (*Letters* 1:77).

Warmly welcomed by the sculptor, he was not disappointed. His adulation grew. One can find it in letter after letter during the next few years. Writing to Otto Modersohn on December 31, 1902, after four months in Paris, he described the "cruelty," "confusion," and "monstrosity" of the city in which the dying, the physically and mentally ill, the grotesque forms of dehumanization, the people who had lost their way in the city's noise and chaos and could not find purpose or direction or any sense of self among the anonymous masses, all threatened to overwhelm his sanity. "To all that," he wrote to Modersohn, "Rodin is a great, quiet, powerful contradiction" (*Letters* 1:93–94). Possibly, the sculptor's "example" fostered the artistic mastery, the control and skill which Salomé found, the following summer, in his vivid descriptions of his borderline experiences, the accounts of his own troubled life which he used with slight revisions in creating the Paris existence of Malte Laurids Brigge. (Malte is twenty-eight—Rilke's age when he began the novel—and lives on the rue Toullier near the Luxembourg Gardens, where Rilke himself had lived during September 1902; even the month is the same.) But for many months even the powerful presence of the "Master" could not effectively contradict the deeply disturbing effects of the city and the multitude of fears which it aroused in the young poet.

"Oh a thousand hands have been building at my fear," he wrote to Lou in July 1903. The people he saw were "fragments of caryatids on whom the whole pain still lay. . . . twitching like bits of a big chopped-up fish that is already rotting but still alive. They were living on nothing, on dust, on soot, and on the filth on their surfaces" (*Letters* 1:108–9). His letters and *The Notebooks of Malte Laurids Brigge* make it clear that he was projecting his sense of himself onto these people.

Malte's thoughts about radical alterations of mind, self, and world teeter on a thin ledge of uncertainty between the fear that he is mentally disintegrating and the hope that he is going through a frightening process which will bring the poet in him to birth. In the following passage he is responding to the dying of a stranger in a crémerie: "Yes, he knew that he was now withdrawing from everything in the world, not merely from human beings. One more moment, and everything would lose its meaning, and this table and the cup and the chair he was clinging to would become unintelligible, alien and heavy." Malte realizes that something very similar is taking place in him. He understands the experience of someone dying who cannot find anything familiar in the world around him. Filled with fear, he wishes that he could console himself with "the thought that it's not impossible to see everything differently and still remain alive" (51–52).

Malte wonders if these disturbing changes in him may be a necessary preparation for truly original perception and thought. Near the beginning of *The Notebooks* he expresses the belief that he is "learning to see" (5, 6). He has discovered that each person has several faces. Some wear the same face for thirty years and keep the others "in storage" (6). These faces will be worn by their children and, sometimes, by their dogs. If we follow Malte thus far, interpretation seems relatively easy. Roughly speaking, a face in this passage seems to mean a personality or an identity. He has discovered that a child may take on a face which has remained hidden in his parent. Often children unconsciously assume the latent personalities of their parents by identifying with them.

Malte does not say all this. But it is implicit in what he does say. And it is consonant with Rilke's belief, repeatedly expressed throughout the novel and in his poems and letters, that so much of what goes on in the mind and between persons is unconscious. Thinking of mind or psyche as space, Rilke imagines "an interior" inaccessible to consciousness, into which all our thoughts and perceptions sink. We do not know what is going on in the "interior." But images which come up out of those depths reveal the ways in which earlier perceptions have been trans- formed there. Malte's conception of "learning to see" has obvious affin- ities with Freud's ideas about unconscious mental processes, though there is no clear evidence that Rilke was influenced by Freud's theory while he was writing the early parts of *The Notebooks:* "I don't know why it is, but everything enters me more deeply and doesn't stop where it once used to. I have an interior that I never knew of. Everything passes into it now. I don't know what happens there" (5).

Malte notes that we "wear" our faces "like gloves." Everyone knows that a face can become a mask. But, reading further, you can see that this is not what Malte means when he turns from people whose personalities are fairly consistent throughout much of their lives to those who "change faces incredibly fast," until at an early age, maybe forty, "their last one is worn through ... has holes in it, is in many places thin as paper." Through the widening holes, "little by little," we begin to see "the non- face" ("das Nichtgesicht"), "and they walk around with that on" (6–7). Is he thinking about people who burn themselves out too quickly? Cer- tainly not just that. The notion of a person going through a rapid suc- cession of personalities suggests instability, an absence of psychic continuity and integrity, an inability to develop a strong, lasting sense of identity. The image of a face "thin as paper" suggests that the sense of self is tenuous and fragile.

But what is the "Nichtgesicht," the "nonface"? Does this refer to someone who continues to function without any strong sense of self or

inner coherence, a person whose existence is unthinking, uncomprehending, guided by momentary impulses and feelings, external pressures
and influences? That might be a description of many people lost in the
confusion of modern urban life. A number of Rilke's poems about faces
warn us not to settle for this simple conclusion. In *Rilke, Valéry and
Yeats: The Domain of the Self,* Priscilla Shaw connects the "nonface" in
The Notebooks with a poem about faces which Rilke wrote in December
1906.[3] Here "das Nicht-Gesicht" does not refer to the facelessness of
those who have lost self and soul in the chaos of the great cities. The
poet asks if we do not implore whoever or whatever allots us our portion
"for the non-face/ which belongs to our darkness":

> flehen wir zu dem Bescheidenden
> nächtens nicht um das Nicht-Gesicht,
> das zu unserem Dunkel gehört?[4]

He asks his face how it can be the face for such an inner life, in which
continually the beginning of something is rolled together with its dissolving:

> Gesicht, mein Gesicht:
> . . . .
> Wie kannst du Gesicht sein für so ein Innen,
> drin sich immerfort das Beginnen
> mit dem Zerfliessen zu etwas ballt.

The poet thinks of forest, mountain, sky, and sea, heaving themselves
out of their depths. They have no face like ours. Those great masses
provide him with images of the serene perfection and harmony of something completely at one with itself, utterly lacking in self-consciousness
and any sense of the division between world and self. Rilke reflects that
even animals sometimes find their faces too heavy and ask that they be
taken from them. These lines recall the dogs in *The Notebooks* that wear
their masters' faces. The thought that animals have faces which they find
oppressive implies that they do not lack self-consciousness and a sense
of the separation and opposition of self and world, self and other, however vague such awareness may be in them.

The poet's longing for the "non-face" "which belongs to our darkness" seems to be a desire to lapse without fear into the internal flux,

which is chaotic, unfathomable, and incomprehensible. This would involve a complete release from the strain of self-consciousness, which awareness of one's own face intensifies. Rilke imagines the inner darkness as a vortex and as depths ("Wirbel" and "Tiefen"), as a wilderness ("Wildnis") in which paths are lost in the dread of the abyss ("sich verlieren ins Abgrundsgraun") almost as soon as one is lucky enough to find them (WDB 2:11).

What the poet seeks in his longing for the "non-face" which belongs to his darkness, what he thinks he may find by waiting patiently in unfathomable inner flux, is the radiant unity and intensity of being which he hears in a bird's call. Its call makes its tiny heart "so large" and "at one/ with the heart of the air, with the heart of the grove":

> wenn ein Vogellaut, vieltausendmal,
> geschrien und wieder geschrien,
> ein winziges Herz so weit macht und eins
> mit dem Herzen der Luft, mit dem Herzen des Hains. ...
> (WDB 2:13)

This passage brings to mind the prose fragment "An Experience" (1913), Rilke's description of his sense of fusion with the cosmos, concentrated in his feeling that a bird's call was vibrating just as intensely within him as in outer space, that he and the universe were completely absorbed into that single resonant sound. This experience in a garden on Capri made the space within and around him "one region of the purest, deepest consciousness." With eyes shut so that he might forget his body's separateness from the environment, he felt "the gentle presence of the stars" within him.[5]

In the poem quoted above the bird's luminous cry is heard by someone who, time and again, as often as it dawns, soars like "steepest stone," implicitly like a mountain or a colossus. This seems to be the god invoked at the beginning of the poem, "in whom I alone ascend and fall and lose my way" ("in dem ich allein/steige und falle und irre" [WDB 2:11]). The poet discovers this god in himself in the whirling, unfathomable darkness, when suddenly, without warning, he becomes capable of song which has the luminous unity and intensity of the bird's cry, expressing his affinity with air, sky, forest, mountain, sea, and grove. The poem implies that the poet must give up his face or faces, allow the non-face to come through, and wait in the unfathomable inner darkness, if he is to find and to become that deeper unity, power, and radiance of being which is his genius, the god who towers above his ordinary self (*WDB* 2:13).

Malte's reflections upon faces and the "non-face" culminate in a passage which differs in substance and mood from this poem, as he recalls a frightening experience of radically original perception when he startled a woman holding her face in her hands on a Paris street corner:

The woman sat up, frightened, she pulled out of herself, too quickly, too violently, so that her face was left in her two hands. I could see it lying there: its hollow form. It cost me an indescribable effort to stay with those two hands, not to look at what had been torn out of them. I shuddered to see a face from the inside, but I was much more afraid of that bare flayed head waiting there, faceless. (7)

A face comes off. A head is flayed. Perhaps no other image of mutilation is so threatening, not even the cutting off of breasts or genitals. Nothing can be more horrifying than the photo of a face blasted away in war, or eaten away by fire, acid, or animals. Obviously, this is because we associate or identify the face with the person.

Underlying the passage quoted above is a fantasy of psychic disintegration. The language seems to imply that the woman is unselfed, left without self or soul. Like so many other figures in the novel, she is an image of what Malte fears may happen to him. Implicit also is fear of sudden exposure of the selfless, amorphous, helpless mass of psychic plasma underlying the coherent, self-aware person and public personality.

The imagery of faces thin as paper, wearing through, riddled with holes, expresses the fear that one's private thoughts and feelings will show, despite one's efforts to hide them. And there is the related fear, implied in the description of the woman, that we shall be seen as selfless, amorphous, and dehumanized, like the dead, the living dead whom Malte describes as husks, and the insane.

Malte sees the woman's face lying in her hands. Does this suggest that in the moment of violent fear the woman's hands have become as expressive as a face? Rodin taught Rilke that hands could express the inner life as well as faces do. But it is the hollow form of the face which Malte sees in the woman's hands. I take this to mean that the sight of the woman's hands gives him the idea that her face has come off. He has seen her fall forward into her hands and then pull herself up out of them "too quickly, too violently." The sight of them, emptied, frightened, open, thin as they are, flashes upon his mind, by way of association, the image of the face peeled away, and then the image of her naked, helpless facelessness in this moment of shock and fear.

I have said that, in this *Notebooks* entry, faces seem to represent personalities or identities. In the description of the woman the face seems to mean something deeper, more inclusive, a sense of self, a sense of oneself as a person, for whom the inner life has or seems to have the unity given it by a viewpoint, by the feeling that there is some*one* experiencing, desiring, fearing, choosing, not just a flux of experiences, desires, fears, choices. In *Beyond Good and Evil*, Nietzsche, like Hume before him, argues that this is an illusion, a fiction. But many psychoanalysts, beginning with Freud, have observed that such a sense of self does have a basis in the unifying organization of an "ego" and in the unity and separateness of the body. The *sense* of self has a number of sources. The privacy of the mind suggests its separateness and autonomy. Action following upon choice suggests that there is an agent who makes decisions and acts upon them. Consistent patterns of feeling and thought and consistency in the way things are viewed suggest that someone is there (where?) who experiences these feelings and has this viewpoint. The description of the woman whose face comes off in her hands reflects the fear that this someone, this person or self who Malte feels he is, may be lost.

A number of clinician-observers and theorists have discussed the origins of the association of face with self and person. One of the most highly respected observers of early infant behavior, R. A. Spitz, tells us, "The inception of the reality principle is evident at the three-months level, when the hungry infant becomes able to suspend the urge for the immediate gratification of his oral need. He does so for the time necessary to perceive the mother's face and to react to it. This is the developmental step in which the 'I' is differentiated from the 'non-I.' "[6] D. W. Winnicott and other analytic theorists have concluded that an infant experiences a responsive mother's face as a reflection and thus a confirmation of his own existence. Watching an empathetic mother's face, an infant also gets to know a great deal about what he is like. Her face is a mirror in which her baby finds himself.[7]

Phyllis Greenacre points out that we never see our own face in the flesh, only in a pane of glass or water or some other mirroring surface, only as a reflected image or as an image in a photograph or a painting, which is felt to be unreal and disconnected, not the living thing itself. (This truth brings to mind Plato's cave and the myth of Narcissus, who cannot find adequate confirmation of his existence and reality in his mirror image. His death can be read as a metaphor for the dissolution of the isolated or solipsistic self. Narcissus fascinated Rilke, who valued solitude. In Malte he portrays the ways in which isolation strengthens the imagination but also fosters narcissistic illness.) As the reflected image in a pane of glass or in water is felt to be unreal, Greenacre argues, a child needs someone else, whose face responsively mirrors his, to support his sense of the living reality of his own distinctive self.[8] In *Collected Papers on Schizophrenia and Related Subjects,* Harold Searles observes that for the patient whose sense of self is weak the analyst's face often performs the maternal function of mirroring.[9] I shall return to this subject in subsequent chapters when I focus upon Rilke's relationships with his mother and other women.

This preliminary discussion of mirrors and mirroring will make some readers think of Jacques Lacan's well-known essay "The mirror stage as formative of the function of the I as revealed in the psychoanalytic experience." Lacan calls "the mirror stage," lasting from six to eighteen months of age, "a drama . . . which manufactures for the subject . . . the succession of phantasies that extends from a fragmented body image to a form of its totality that I shall call orthopaedic—and, lastly, to the assumption of the armour of an alienating identity."[10] For Lacan the child's experience of his mirror reflection at approximately six months results in his assumption of an image. This early "identification," however, is at odds with the infant's experience of its own body at that time as fragmented and uncoordinated and with the closely related lack of any developed sense of psychic coherence and integration. The image offered the child in the mirror foreshadows the gradual development of an integrated sense of self and ego. But it also helps to lay the foundation for enduring, if often unconscious, alienation from oneself and others. The mirror image is, obviously, external, inverted, reflected, and its physical unity is sharply out of sync with the infant's other experiences of psyche-and-body. The child's identification of himself (herself) with the image in the mirror, a misperception, anticipates the mediation of his (her) relationships with self and others by such images and, hence, that underlying, often unconscious sense of alienation. Eventually, Lacan argues, language and other kinds of symbols, too, will mediate these relationships and play a large part in the creation of the sense of a unified self. I have interpreted mirrors and mirroring in Rilke's life and work with the help of other psychoanalytic theorists (among them, Searles, Spitz, Winnicott, R. D. Laing, and Heinz Kohut) rather than Lacan, because I have found their insights and the matrices of clinical experience which support and substantiate them more illuminating than his writings.

II

The image of the woman's face coming off in her hands, frightening, horrifying as it is, obliquely suggests Malte's dread of mental disintegration, which a number of passages in *The Notebooks* reveal. If Malte were a real person giving us a report of an experience, we might say that he has unconsciously projected the psychic disintegration which he fears in himself onto the woman, embodying it in a fantasy of a face coming off. Is this a hallucination? Is it imaginative perception? Perhaps, Rilke would have wanted us to retain our negative capability in reading this *Notebooks* entry, and to refrain from forcing it into one category, excluding the other.

Malte's fantasies of physical and mental fragmentation and of the dissolution of boundaries between himself and his world originate in his childhood. In a subsequent entry he recalls an episode, from that time in his life, which clearly represents a lapse in the integrity of body, mind, and will. While drawing, he lets a crayon fall under the table. Kneeling on an armchair has made his legs so numb that "I didn't know what belonged to me and what was the chair's." Boundaries between the self and the external world have dissolved. In the child's mind differentiation and integration break down at the same time. Under the table Malte sees his own hand as a separate creature with a mind and will of its own:

[A]bove all I recognized my own outspread hand moving down there all alone, like some strange crab, exploring the ground. I watched it ... almost with curiosity; it seemed to know things I had never taught it, as it groped down there so completely on its own, with movements I had never noticed before ... it interested me. I was ready for all kinds of adventures. (94)

Then the boy sees another hand come "out of the wall." The two hands grope blindly toward each other. The boy is horrified. "I felt that one of the hands belonged to me and that it was about to enter into something it could never return from. With all the authority that I had over it, I stopped it, held it flat, and slowly pulled it back to me without taking my eyes off the other one, which kept on groping. I realized that it wouldn't stop, and I don't know how I got up again" (94).

This delusion expresses the child's sense that the integrity of body and self has broken down. What he has long thought was a part of himself is threatening to cross the boundaries which separate him from everything and everyone else and to become a part of the world of resistant objects and opposing wills. There is an implicit danger that, if this can happen, perhaps any part of body or psyche can separate itself from the child and cross that line into the alien, threatening other. For a little while Malte does not think he has the power to stop his hand from joining that strange other hand and thus entering "into something it could never return from" (94).

In *The Ego and the Id* (1923), Freud observed that the sense of a separate, unified ego develops with the gradual discovery that the body is a separate entity. Psychiatrists and psychologists working with schizophrenics often find that the disintegration of the self is reflected in the decomposition of the body image. Harold Searles describes the fantasy of a schizophrenic patient "that the building in which she was housed consisted, in actuality, of the disjointed fragments of a human female body." The same patient expressed her belief that Searles was "anatomically unintegrated." Searles says that these fantasies "had to do with her coming closer to an awareness of the full depth of ego fragmentation . . . which had long prevailed in herself."[1]

He also cites two 1961 studies of disturbances in body image during experiments in sensory deprivation, comparing the disturbances reported in these studies with those of his schizophrenic patients. According to one of these reports, in the minds of several subjects "the arms seemed to be dissociated from the body." In another experiment one of the subjects "feared that his body parts would disappear and disintegrate."

In *The Nonhuman Environment*, Searles cites a 1955 study of "Variations in ego feeling induced by d-lysergic acid diethylamide (LSD-25)," which reports that persons taking LSD-25 felt that their skin and their hands and feet no longer belonged to their bodies. "The individual feels that his body is not his, that it functions automatically." His hands seem to move autonomously. Searles observes that some schizophrenics go through this kind of experience for long periods of time.[2] Ultimately, as this study suggests, the loss of integration involves a withdrawal of "ego feeling" not only from parts of the body and then the body as a whole, but also from mental phenomena, from emotions and thoughts, so that they too seem separate, independent, and alien.

In *Autobiography of a Schizophrenic Girl*, not a body but a face disintegrates into separate, independent parts, like a cubist painting, in the mind of the schizophrenic girl, who suspects that the "independence of each part" is the source of her fear and that it keeps her from recognizing the face, though she knows it belongs to her analyst, whom she calls "Mama."[3] Unconsciously she projects the psychic disintegration which she fears in herself onto "Mama." Her unconscious confusion of Mama with herself reflects the pervasive weakness of her ability to differentiate between herself and others.

Of course, we can also read Malte's story about the hand as an account of the supernatural, something concocted out of Rilke's fascination with ghosts and kindred phenomena, which was encouraged by his visit to Scandinavia in 1904. And one can see in this story, as in the passage about faces, the influence of Rodin. In the first part of his book on the sculptor, written in 1902, Rilke argues that the unity of an artistic object, a painting or a sculpture, does not have to coincide with the unity of some other object in the world. The artist discovers new unities, drawing upon a number of things to make one of his own, creating "a world out of the smallest part of a thing." Rilke's chief examples are the hands sculpted by Rodin. Though they stand alone, separate, they are no less alive. A number of them seem as expressive as faces of emotions, states of mind, and personality types—anger, irritation, sleep, waking up, weariness, loss of desire, criminal tendencies, for example. "Hands have a history of their own, they have, indeed, their own civilization" (*WSR*, 104–5).

Rodin's sculpture fostered Rilke's development of ideas originating in fantasies and fantastical experiences remembered from the poet's childhood, many of which returned in Paris, brought back by the illness portrayed in Malte. Conversely, accounts of psychic disintegration or fragmentation in *The Notebooks,* insofar as the novel is autobiographical, reveal at least part of the motivation for Rilke's absorption in Rodin's disintegrative and reintegrating sculpture.

In the second half of *The Notebooks,* Malte's account of Charles the Bold, duke of Burgundy, obliquely echoes the story of the hand in Malte's childhood. The duke's hands seem to have a life and a will of their own. Malte compares them to "the heads of madmen, raging with fantasies." But it is the duke's blood which becomes the focus of Malte's implicit belief that the essential weakness which defeated and destroyed this bold lord was a lack of integration. Malte imagines that the duke was "locked in" with his "foreign" blood, that it terrified him in the expectation "that it would attack him as he slept, and tear him to pieces." In Malte's fantasy this powerful noble, remembered as Charles the Bold, was completely subject to this alien, half-Portuguese blood, which he could not comprehend. He could not "persuade" it that he was emperor or that it should fear him. As Malte imagines Burgundy, eventually his blood, realizing that he was "a lost man," "wanted to escape." And, of course, it had its way when the duke died (192–93).

Rilke wrote to his Polish translator, Witold von Hulewicz, that the historical figures in *The Notebooks* should be seen as the "*vocabula* of [Malte's] distress," and that the "evocations and images" of these accounts of historical figures "are equated" with "his period of distress" (*Letters* 2:371). But the portrait of Charles the Bold shows Malte distancing himself, to some extent, from the fear of fragmentation, as his artistic mastery enables him to externalize and objectify his anxiety in this interpretation of the duke's life.

In earlier sections of *The Notebooks,* Malte's attempts to retrieve his childhood threaten to shatter whatever psychic wholeness he has been able to develop. The episode of the hands seems too distant to be dangerous, "an event that now lies far back in my childhood" (91). Not long before this, however, thirty pages earlier, Malte notes that, with the return of his childhood in memory, at the age of twenty-eight he is no less vulnerable and susceptible to his old anxieties.

Describing the recurrence of a childhood illness, Malte writes that it brings up out of the unconscious whole "lives" which he has never known about. Yet these strange "lives" have greater strength and a more powerful hold on his mind than familiar memories of what he once was and did. Amid the "tangle of confused memories" arises the terrifying childhood delusion of "the Big Thing." As much as anything else in *The Notebooks,* this delusion, which comes back with all its original power, epitomizes Malte's continuing lack of integration. He compares the Big Thing to a cancer, an alien hostile life in the body over which a person often has little or no control and which is likely to destroy him from within. His blood flowed through it. Like a dead limb it was a part of him but did not belong to him, which is to say, it did not respond to his will. He compares it to a second head. In its ambiguity it resembled an alien personality which emerges from the unconscious to engulf the individual. It swelled and grew over his face, "like a warm bluish boil," covering his mouth, and then his eyes were "hidden by its shadow" (61–62).

The Big Thing calls to mind accounts of advanced schizoid and schizophrenic illness, in which an individual becomes increasingly anxious that he will be absorbed, ingested, and annihilated by the introjects ("distorted representations of people"), which are, as Searles explains, experienced "as foreign bodies in his personality." These "infringe upon and diminish the area of what might be thought of as his own self" and often threaten to obliterate the self.[4] The fantasy that the Big Thing covers Malte's face, his mouth and eyes, suggests that it threatens to prevent him from eating, speaking, breathing, and seeing, as well as from being seen.

This account of the return of a childhood delusion follows descriptions of patients in a hospital. Among these are several images of partial or complete effacement. Bandages cover a head, except for one eye "that no longer belonged to anyone" (56). On his right is a large, unintelligible mass, which, Malte then realizes, has a face and a hand, but the face is empty of memories, of character, of will. The clothes look as if undertakers had put them on, and the hair as if it had been combed by members of that indispensable profession. All around him in the hospital Malte sees faces, heads, and bodies in which a person has been lost, obliterated. His fascination with these sights reflects his fear of being depersonalized or dehumanized. He imagines that the chair in which he is sitting must be the one he has been "destined for" and that he has come to "the place in my life where I would remain forever" (59–60).

Another closely related episode is one in which Malte, as a child, puts on a costume, then confronts himself masked in a mirror. The reflection of the masked figure destroys the child's sense of self. Worse still, he feels that a "stranger" invades his body and takes it over. This experience, like the delusion of the Big Thing and the episode of the hands, reveals the weakness of differentiation in Malte. His sense of boundaries between himself and other people and objects is tenuous. He is apt to merge with them. Ambiguously, he is engulfed by the mirror ("I was the mirror") and by the "monstrous reality" of the "stranger" in it. His account of his earlier vulnerability to annihilation and engulfment also suggests a flimsy, fragile sense of identity in the adult who feels that he has changed very little since that time in his childhood.

The terrifying experience of engulfment is triggered by the boy's feeling that he is trapped in a mask and costume. Fearing that he will be caught inside the close-fitting mask, with his hearing muffled and his vision obstructed, feeling that he is being strangled by the strings of the cloak and that the turban and the mask are pressing down on him, he rushes to the mirror. His hands, moving frantically, seem disconnected from the invisible boy and the mask in the mirror. In this disturbed state of mind he imagines that the mirror has come to life, that it is stronger than he is, that it has the power to invade, obliterate, and completely replace him. It forces upon him

an image, no, a reality, a strange, incomprehensible, monstrous reality that permeated me against my will. . . . I lost all sense of myself, I simply ceased to exist. For one second, I felt an indescribable, piercing, futile longing for myself, then only *he* remained: there was nothing except him. (107)

III

The fantasy of "the Big Thing" expresses, among other feelings, the fear of death. It is connected with an earlier passage in which Malte wonders if the "almost nourishing smile" on the faces of pregnant women doesn't come from their sense of having "*two* fruits" growing in them, "a child and a death" (16). In this passage Rilke has converted the fantasy of death developing within one like another organism, not subject to one's will or control, from a source of fear into an idea which gives comfort and even pleasure and is, for this reason, an aid against the dread of death which is the central and most pervasive fear in the novel. The fantasy of the Big Thing and the notion that death is like a fetus within us reflect the same kind of anxiety, the same sense of separate lives or even autonomous beings, within us that are part of us and yet independent of us. They are both rooted in an experience of body and psyche which can develop into paranoid schizophrenia.[1] But the conception of death as fetus and fruit growing within also reflects the strengths of ego and imagination that enabled Rilke to defend himself against the threat of mental disintegration by transforming the worst of all internal dangers, the developing potential sources and causes of death in body and mind, into images which suggest natural, healthy growth and creativity.

The idea that a person's death grows in him like a fruit, evolving out of his genetic inheritance and his experience, conscious and unconscious, gives meaningful coherence to Malte's account of the end of his paternal grandfather, Christoph Detlev Brigge. In this narrative, which Rilke considered Malte's most fully achieved piece of writing, the chamberlain is transformed into the regal, frightening personality and thunderous voice of the death which has been developing within him throughout his lifetime: "This voice didn't belong to Christoph Detlev, but to Christoph Detlev's death. Christoph Detlev's death was alive now, had already been living at Ulsgaard for many, many days, talked with everyone, made demands. . . . Demanded and screamed" (13). Malte imagines that this swollen, shouting figure was nurtured by every "excess of pride, will, and authority that [Christoph Detlev] had not been able to use up during his peaceful days" (15). One can see how this notebook entry might come from the mind that produced the delusion of the Big Thing. Here the fantasy of an autonomous, latent inner being which emerges from within and engulfs the self, giving rise to terrifying delirious behavior, becomes creative, shaping the conception of death which unfolds in this compelling narrative. With this entry, Rilke thought, Malte achieved the "inexorability" of "objective expression" which he (the poet) had discovered in Baudelaire's "Une Charogne" and Cézanne's paintings (*Letters* 1:314).

Here dying brings disintegration of the ego, with all its structure and defenses. Malte's recollection that the chamberlain was no longer there, that he could no longer see what was going on around him, that his face was unrecognizable, that the shouting voice seemed to belong to someone or something else—these remembered details call to mind the delirium which often overwhelms the dying. Defenses are down; control is gone. Much of what the dying have not expressed in life, much that was repressed, comes out.

The Notebooks reveals Rilke's unusual access to large areas of experience ordinarily denied and repressed. This access was often involuntary, and it made life perilous and sanity precarious. Rilke was willing to endure frightening experiences of partial disintegration because he felt that they were the price he had to pay for sustaining his contact with the sources of feeling, fantasy, and insight which were the reservoirs of the extraordinary wholeness essential to his genius.

IV

Concerning the "monsters" and "dragons" which he had discovered in the "horrible dungeons" of his own psyche, Rilke wrote in 1904, "We have no reason to mistrust our world, for it is not against us. Has it terrors, they are *our* terrors; has it abysses, those abysses belong to us; are dangers at hand, we must try to love them."[1] A letter to "Merline" (Baladine Klossowska), written sixteen years later, develops and clarifies this point, arguing that "the monsters" within us "hold the surplus strength" which makes it possible for men and women of genius to transcend their ordinary human frailties and limitations.[2]

The third Duino Elegy, begun in January 1912 and completed late in the fall of 1913, reflects these ideas in language and imagery which suggest Rilke's growing interest in psychoanalysis at the time. Lou Andreas-Salomé introduced the poet to Freud late in the summer of 1913. The following year, recalling this meeting with Freud and the Swedish analyst Poul Bjerre, he wrote, "These men were important and significant for me, their whole orientation and method certainly represents one of the most essential movements of medical science."[3] In the Third Elegy the poet imagines himself as a child going down into a beloved inner wilderness, a primeval forest within him. As he descends with love into the gorges of his own interior, into more ancient blood, what he encounters is fearful, still satiated with devoured fathers. Every terrible thing he meets recognizes him, winking with mutual understanding. What is hideous and shocking smiles. The poet wonders how the child, going down into his own depths, can help loving these monstrosities which are parts of himself and smile at him with narcissistic tenderness seldom equaled even by maternal love.

> ... Liebend
> stieg er hinab in das ältere Blut, in die Schluchten,
> wo das Furchtbare lag, noch satt von den Vätern. Und jedes
> Schreckliche kannte ihn, blinzelte, war wie verständigt.
> Ja, das Entsetzliche lächelte ... Selten
> hast du so zärtlich gelächelt, Mutter. Wie sollte
> er es nicht lieben, da es ihm lächelte. ...
> (WDB 1:451)

If, as the first Duino Elegy tells us, the realization of beauty depends upon our capacity for enduring terror, how does an artist come to trust, take possession of, and even love the objects of his fear and the fear itself? Psychoanalysis can sometimes help patients to achieve mastery over their anxieties or, at least, make it possible to feel more at ease with them. Rilke, who had been "on the verge of undergoing analysis," decided not to because he thought that it would tame the lions and monsters in him and thus kill the energy he needed to surpass himself. Exposing his *"most secret powers,"* it would undermine "an existence that owed its strongest impulses precisely to the fact *that it did not know itself"* (R&B:IC, 109).

One alternative to undergoing psychoanalytic therapy was to find guidance for mastering his fears and using them creatively and models with whom he could identify in some of the artists whom he most admired, especially several in his father's generation—Tolstoy, Cézanne, and Van Gogh.

Death was among the most fearful monsters living in the psychic depths. It was also among the greatest potential sources of creative energy. In 1915, reacting to the slaughter going on around him, Rilke wrote a letter in which he conceived of God and death as parts, "never before broached, of the human mind" (Letters 2:148). (His ideas on this subject have obvious affinities with the theory of a death "drive" which Freud formulated in Beyond the Pleasure Principle [1920]. But the poet's intuitions are free from the pretentions to scientific validity which have aroused criticism of Freud's speculations.) Death, he thought, was something we feel alive at the center of our being. In our fear of it we repress this sense of it and project death into the world around us, where it seems to threaten us from a multitude of sources. We find external means to defend ourselves against it: science, in particular, medical science, with its increasing capacity for controlling nature; religion, which Rilke attacks for glossing over death with its notion of an afterlife (*Letters* 2:316), and the distractions and narcotics of modern urban life, which Rilke describes in the tenth Duino Elegy, including a bitter beer named "Deathless" ("Todlos"). As we all know, these stratagems produce emptiness and numbness.

Rilke found an alternative to such defensiveness in Tolstoy, whom he met twice during his travels in Russia with Salomé (April 1899 and May 1900). Both Salomé and Rilke have left accounts of those two visits. When they met Tolstoy in Moscow in the spring of 1899, the travelers were full of excitement about the religious fervor of the crowds celebrating Easter in the city's chapels and churches. The old man expressed his indignation against Russian Orthodoxy, urging them not to be taken in by "the superstitions of the people."[4] A year later, visiting Tolstoy at Yasnaya Polyana, they found him in a dreadful mood, arguing loudly with his wife, who was equally inhospitable. After encountering him briefly, they were kept waiting for hours, until at last he offered them a choice between having lunch with his family and walking with him on his estate. They accompanied him while he talked about the landscape, Russia, God, and death, picking flowers, savoring their fragrance, then tossing them away. Rilke's accounts of this walk differ. According to one, the poet understood everything their host was saying, except, occasionally, when the wind interfered. Elsewhere he recalls that much of what Tolstoy said was inaudible in the windy meadows, among the birches.[5]

Rilke's reactions to the author of *War and Peace* were complex and varied. Among the most fertile was his image of Tolstoy as an artist exceptionally gifted with "a feeling for life," a responsiveness which did not deny or repress the multifarious forms of death that pervade it, "contained everywhere in it as an odd spice in the strong flavor of life" (*Letters* 2:150). He had opened himself to the full intensity of his fear of death; yet, at the same time, because of "his natural composure," he was a perceptive observer of even his most emotional states of mind. Rilke's conception of such a division in consciousness resembles the psychoanalytic notion of splitting the ego. "One thinks, feels, and acts subjectively, but at the same time observes such behavior in a quasi-objective manner."[6] Tolstoy's openness to his own fear of death and his gift of self-observation enabled him to infuse that terror with "grandeur" in his works, to transform it into "a gigantic structure ... with corridors and flights of stairs and railless projections and sheer edges on all sides" (*Letters* 2:150–51). His freedom from ordinary defensiveness against the dread of death and his ability to create and sustain the combination of the feeling man and the introspective observer helped to make it possible for him to write his strongest works, including "The Death of Ivan Ilych." This story, like his great novels, reveals the force with which he felt his fear as well as his ability to transform it into "unapproachable reality" (*Letters* 2:151).

For Rilke, the creative process leading to the achievement of great work places the artist "in danger" because he must be open to his "personal madness" and must go all the way through an experience which that "madness" makes increasingly "private," "personal," "singular," and lonely. The unsupported isolation of his striving is necessary because discussing one's "personal madness" with someone else would deflate its energy and force. Rilke's letters reveal that this sense of the creative process originated in his own experience. Describing his work on *The Notebooks,* he says, "[I]n it I seemed to be clutching all my tasks together and running them into me, like that single man who in hand-to-hand fighting takes on all the lances opposed to him" (*Letters* 2:25). He was also clearly aware of the motives that led him to place himself in such danger. The work of art, he wrote, brings "enormous aid" to the artist, because it provides evidence of his integrity and authenticity. If he seems close to insanity at times, the completed work reveals the internal "law[s]" which have remained invisible in his disordered thoughts, like the form of an organism contained in genetic codes in the first fetal stages, affording the artist ample "justification" of his deviations from accepted norms.[7]

To the great poet his poems can reveal what for the ordinary person it might take years of analysis to disclose—the unconscious ("invisible") laws which govern one's experience, are at least partly responsible for one's misery and happiness, and, once known, are open to change. In June 1907, when Rilke explored these ideas, such revelations, coming from his own art, did not seem to threaten the efficacy of the "secret [inner] powers" which in 1912 and 1913 the temptations of psychoanalytic therapy made him anxious to protect against exposure by some disciple of Freud.

Writing to his wife on June 7, 1907, Rilke named another motive for subjecting himself to the inner "violence" which makes great art possible (*Letters* 2:17, 41, and 19). Because he felt such a need for solitude, his communion with his poems, fiction, and nonfiction prose was often far more satisfying and fulfilling than his contacts with other people (see *Letters* 1:121). He also observed that the artist's accomplished works make possible a deeply satisfying kind of communication in which people show one another what they have become through their work and in this way offer mutual help and support (*Letters on Cézanne*, 5). Aspiring to an extraordinary degree of self-sufficiency which would sustain the long periods of solitude he required to do his work, he nonetheless understood that he needed other people's responses to confirm the sense of his own reality, of his "unity and genuineness," and the self-esteem which his poems and fiction nurtured.

Rilke indicates another way in which his work was a form of "self-treatment" (*Letters* 2:42). In one of his *Letters to a Young Poet* he supposes that emotional illness "is the means by which an organism frees itself of foreign matter," and he urges the young poet not to try to suppress his neurosis, but to encourage it, to "have [the] whole sickness and break out with it" (*LYP*, 70). Perhaps, in *The Notebooks*, more than in any of his other works, Rilke felt that his writing could help him free himself from alien thoughts and feelings brought to consciousness by his fears. When his anxieties had flourished to the point of threatening to destroy his sanity, he projected them into the mind and life of his fictional surrogate. The process of exorcising "foreign matter" would be complete only when Malte could be detached from himself and given a separate existence. On finishing the novel, he felt he had managed to do this (see *Letters* 1:362).

Earlier interpreters of *The Notebooks* have argued that Malte served as a kind of psychological scapegoat for his author, taking upon himself the illness that plagued Rilke, carrying it away.[8] This line of thought recalls Freud's observations about Dostoevsky's characters in his essay "Dostoevsky and Parricide." Freud argues that some of the characters in Dostoevsky's works enact the crimes which the author and his readers unconsciously would like to commit, and thus bring fulfillment of forbidden desires through the author's and the reader's unconscious identification with them. Then they satisfy the demands of the author's and the reader's superegos by going through punishment for these crimes.[9] Rilke himself encourages the "scapegoat" interpretation in a letter to Salomé in which he asks whether Malte, "who is of course in part made out of my dangers, goes under in it, in a sense to spare me the going under" (*Letters* 2:32).

By externalizing and objectifying his sickness in a novel, a writer may be able to distance and detach himself from it. Seeing it more clearly in the images and language of his novel, he may gain a better understanding of the illness and thus achieve a larger degree of control over it. The imposition of literary form and style on the raw material of the novel deriving from his illness may help to give him the confidence that he can master it.

But Rilke's letters also express the belief that the writing of *The Notebooks* may have exacerbated his sickness. He feared that his attempt at self-exorcism had been a disastrous failure, that instead of enabling him to externalize his illness and detach himself from it, his long involvement with Malte had exhausted and gutted him. And he wondered if, having written *The Notebooks* and created Malte, he was sinking into irremediable, unchanging "aridity" (*Letters* 2:33).

Rilke's frightening experiences in Paris and the fantasies which he embodied in Malte, the young Dane's fears of death and mental disintegration and his belief that he must go through something like death and disintegration in order to arrive at the degree of originality in seeing and saying which permits work of genius, bring to mind Anton Ehrenzweig's theory in *The Hidden Order of Art* that the first stage of the creative process may involve an artist in unconscious projections which are experienced as fragmented, accidental, and alien, and often as persecutory. The artist must be psychologically strong enough to get through this schizoid stage of fragmentation without being overwhelmed by the anxieties arising from it. Reading Ehrenzweig's description of schizophrenic self-destructiveness, one can see how close Malte is to this illness and Rilke too during those early days in Paris: "The schizophrenic. . . . attacks his own ego functions almost physically, and projects the splintered parts of his fragmented self into the outside world, which in turn be-

comes fragmented and persecutory."[10] This shredding and projection of
the self accompanies the schizophrenic's attack on "his own language
function and capacity for image making." In this respect artists and writers, especially the "modernists" and "post-modernists," may resemble
the schizophrenic as he "twists and contorts words in the same weird
way in which he draws and paints images." One may think of Picasso
as a model of physical and mental health and toughness. But Ehrenzweig
points out that his savage attacks on his imagery, his dismemberment of
it, his scattering of the bits and pieces in the picture, have obvious affinities with the schizophrenic's ripping up of his own ego and the world.
The essential difference between Picasso's cubist painting and schizophrenic painting lies "in the coherence of [the master's] tough pictorial
space." Unconsciously the shredded and scattered images have been integrated. The violently shattered world of a cubist masterpiece is held
together and "animated by a dynamic pulse. It draws the fragments together into a loose yet tough cocoon that draws the spectator into itself."
The "linkages" which do this ordinarily remain unconscious in painter
and spectator, author and reader.

In Joyce, according to Ehrenzweig, under the surface of the "language
splinters," "dreamlike phantasies . . . link the word clusters into an un-
ending hypnotic stream."[11] Despite the irritating vagueness of this explanation, if I think of Picasso's cubism, Joyce's *Finnegans Wake,* and
Rilke's fragmentary *Notebooks* in their apparent disconnectedness and
underlying coherence, I can see the pertinence of Ehrenzweig's attempt
to define the similarities and differences between schizophrenic art and
the works of such modern masters.

Ehrenzweig suggests that the motif of the dying god in literature and
other arts reflects the artist's sense of his own "heroic self-surrender" in
the process of creation. The artist has to face death without anticipating
rebirth. When the schizophrenic loses his grasp on reality, his images of
world and self break up into "chaos," and he feels that he is undergoing
"final destruction."[12] The dying god motif in some works of art hints at
the fact that the artist has endured a similar experience of the void opening when world and self are torn to pieces, but with a different outcome.
An artist with a sufficiently strong ego can confront the frightening
"void" within himself and live with his fear. Even when "loss of ego
control" brings the feeling that mind and self are disintegrating, he can
"absorb" this experience "into the rhythm of creativity" before emerging

from it newly integrated and coherent, possibly with an enriched mental and emotional life and a strengthened sense of self.[13]

Rilke does not introduce the dying-god motif into *The Notebooks*, but Malte's response to the dying man in the crémerie prepares him for a new understanding of the artist's development. And this sequence of experience and realization in the novel does bring to mind the implicit sense of the creative process which Ehrenzweig finds in typical versions of the motif. Twenty pages after his account of the death in the crémerie Malte once more takes stock of his sense of his separation from others and of the radical changes in his perception of the world. Now the developments in his recent life, which have made dying or mental disintegration seem to resemble his own condition all too closely, have become, on the contrary, reasons for hoping that he is developing imaginative, creative intelligence and perception: "I have had certain experiences that separate me from other people. . . . A different world. A new world filled with new meanings. For the moment I am finding it a bit difficult, because everything is too new" (72).

On the same page Malte thinks of "Une Charogne," Baudelaire's "incredible poem," as an example of radically new and different perception, which seems unmistakably valid. This is genius, not madness. Malte now welcomes the painful and often frightening emergence of a strange world. He has gladly given up the fulfillment of all his earlier expectations in the belief that what he has discovered is "real, even when that is awful" (73).

CHAPTER 3

A Mask of Him Roams in His Place

Differentiation between Self and Others in *The Notebooks* and Rilke's Letters

I

During his first year in Paris, 1902–3, Rilke's ability to differentiate himself from other people was often impaired. A letter to Salomé describes an experience in which the sense of mental and bodily separateness from others which underlies most adult relationships and contacts gave way to a frightening fantasy of being pulled into close identification, involving a partial merging of bodies and minds. This was his encounter with a man suffering from St. Vitus' dance: "I was close behind him, will-less, drawn along by his fear, that was no longer distinguishable from mine." Imagining that this stranger's "fear had been nourished out of me, and had exhausted me," he felt "used up" (*Letters* 1:115). As they became increasingly connected and the stranger seemed to feed on him, he felt that "everything" within him was being consumed. This experience was the source of an entry in *The Notebooks*.

Malte is drawn to an "emaciated" figure who becomes the focus of attention on the block, an object of laughter. Following the man despite an urge to cross the street to get away from him, he notices that he hops on one leg. When this hopping travels from his legs to his neck and hands, Malte feels "bound to him" (68). As the spasms increase, his anxiety grows with the stranger's. With pounding heart he gathers his "little strength together" and begs the struggling St. Vitus dancer to take it.

When the fellow finally loses control and the nervous spasms take over his body, exploding into "a horrible dance," Malte is left feeling like "a blank piece of paper" (65–71).

What does the encounter mean to him? Why is he drawn into such close identification with this stranger?

The spectacle of St. Vitus' dance speaks to his fear of going insane, of losing himself to uncontrollable forces which often seem on the verge of overwhelming him. The scene around the St. Vitus dancer awakens in Malte a dread of becoming an object of derision and revulsion. His desire to help the stranger is motivated by compassion, but also by his sense of affinity. If this fellow can overcome the convulsive compulsion of his nerves, his victory might answer Brigge's need to believe that strength of will can win the struggle against his own fears and tensions. But Malte is also curious to see what happens if and when the fellow gives in, because he anticipates that he may soon go through a mental disintegration not unlike the cataclysm against which the other man is struggling. At the end of the episode the victim of St. Vitus' dance is invisible, engulfed by his involuntary spasms and by the crowd that surrounds him.

In a highly illuminating essay, "The Devolution of the Self in *The Notebooks of Malte Laurids Brigge*," Walter H. Sokel argues that when the St. Vitus dancer "gives in and his will collapses, something incomparably mightier, and truer leaps forth from him." Professor Sokel supports his interpretation with the argument that the "expansive gesture," "the spreading out of his arms, with which the dancer lets go of his cane indicates relief and liberation." Sokel notes that an "elemental force" seems to take over this sick man. The imagery of the scene, according to his essay, suggests the destruction of the conforming bourgeois, the conventional personality, the constricting will, the little ego which Malte both wishes and fears to transcend.[1]

As Sokel's detailed analysis makes clear, the language and imagery of this scene evoke an ambivalent response. But the emphasis at this point in *The Notebooks* is upon fearful devastation by illness. When Malte remembers that the St. Vitus dancer's "gaze wobbled over sky, houses, and water, without grasping a thing," the scene recalls the dying man in the crémerie. As the convulsive spasms overwhelm the victim of St. Vitus' dance, he stretches "out his arms as if he were trying to fly." But he does not succeed in flying. And if he does a "dance," it is the "horrible dance" of a man dragged and bowed and flung like a puppet by his spasms. The end of the scene leaves one in little doubt about its meaning. The crowd swallows the sufferer, and Malte feels annihilated, as his own ego boundaries have almost evaporated and he has been sucked, half helplessly, half willingly, into mergence with this embodiment of devastation and dehumanization.

At the time he was writing *The Notebooks* Rilke believed that the little ego must be shattered by the exploding titanic forces of the unconscious in order that the aspiring poet may gain access to essential energies. But in the St. Vitus' dance victim Rilke encountered an image of the annihilation that might come from courting and encouraging such a Dionysian shattering of the ego. He did not underestimate the dangers of mental illness. Suffering often in severe neurotic and borderline states of mind, he sometimes felt he was close to complete breakdown.

Malte fears that the world around him or objects in it will invade his body, drive out his insecurely established and feebly defended self, and replace it. In *The Divided Self,* the English analyst, R. D. Laing, describes a closely related fantasy of "implosion": "This is the strongest word I can find for the extreme form of what Winnicott terms the *impingement* of reality. Impingement does not convey, however, the full terror of the experience of the world as liable at any moment to crash in and obliterate all identity."[2] In his fear of impingement or invasion Malte reconfirms the contours of his body, the physical boundaries between himself and the world. He draws the outline of his face, and the renewed sense of his differentiation reassures him that most of what is out there in the vast world cannot get into his very limited interior space. But he quickly realizes that he could be wrong. He imagines external reality flooding over the frail border barriers of body and mind, filling him up, through the last branching of his capillaries, pushing out breath, life, and self, increasing until it spatters his insides outside, and nothing is left of the conscious individual within (see 74). In this terrifying fantasy of invasion, the boundaries of body and self are easily breached, the "surface hardness and adaptability" on which he has relied to protect him are no more dependable than the Maginot Line.

Impairment of the ability to differentiate between self and other obviously goes along with a weak sense of identity. These defects may give rise to fantasies of engulfment in which something or someone else incorporates or swallows a person, takes over his will, smothers him with possessive, pressuring love, fixes him in formulas which he feels he cannot escape, blots out his sense of a separate self, draws him into an identification so complete that there is little or nothing left of him apart from this mergence with the other person. Rilke makes the threat of engulfment a focus of interest in the final section of *The Notebooks,* Malte's reinterpretation of the Prodigal Son story as "the legend of a man who didn't want to be loved" (251).

This version of the parable of the Prodigal Son is a vehicle for Rilke's fear that intimacy opens one to the danger of being effaced and changed through and through into the person or nonperson other people need one to be:

Once you walked into [the] full smell [of the house], most matters were already decided . . . on the whole you were . . . the person they thought you were; the person for whom they had long ago fashioned a life, out of his small past and their own desires; the creature belonging to them all, who stood day and night under the influence of their love, between their hope and their mistrust, before their approval or their blame. . . .

Can he stay and conform to this lying life of approximations which they have assigned to him, and come to resemble them all in every feature of his face? (253–54).

The final sections of the novel emphasize the fear of being loved. In the margin of *The Notebooks* manuscript Malte has written, "To be loved means to be consumed. . . . To be loved is to pass away" (250). He imagines that the Prodigal Son often thought of the troubadours as men who feared more than anything else that the woman they longed for might reciprocate their love (255). Malte seems to project onto them his fantasy that any woman who loved him would engulf him. His illness and isolation recall the fate of Dostoevsky's narrator in *Notes from Underground,* who sends away the prostitute Liza when she comes to his apartment, in the fear that her love will suffocate him, and thus compulsively and helplessly seals himself in his hole, cut off from everyone but a servant, living on daydreams which turn to nothingness, as his precursor, the narrator of Dostoevsky's earlier novella, *White Nights,* tells us.

The Notebooks closes on a curiously negative note of hope. In concluding his version of the story of the Prodigal Son, Malte comes up with a notion of how a prodigal returned might continue to live with his family while defending himself against the threat of engulfment. This defense might work just as well in any human community. The selfish, egocentric nature of the love surrounding the Prodigal Son, which at first seems so menacing, provides a defense against itself. Those who threaten to reshape his face so that it will resemble theirs tend to see him through the colored lenses of their egocentric love, their fears, their hopes, their mistrust, their needs and desires. In brief, they see what they want to see and are blind to what frightens or displeases them.

Their distorted perceptions and their lack of understanding protect him against them. Their denial of what they do not want to see and their tendency to see what they desire mask him. Behind the masks they unconsciously create for him, he will have the freedom to develop inwardly, secretly, in accord with his distinctive needs, desires, and gifts. This part of *The Notebooks* brings to mind Nietzsche's argument in *Beyond Good and Evil* that false interpretations of everything a "profound spirit" does and says create a mask around him. Evading communication, he makes certain that "a mask of him roams in his place" in the minds of other people.[3] J. R. von Salis reports in his book on Rilke's years in Switzerland that the poet told him he had never read Nietzsche. But, as Erich Heller has shown in *The Disinherited Mind*, there are many affinities between the ideas of the two. At least it is likely that Rilke acquired some knowledge of Nietzsche's thought through Lou Andreas-Salomé, whose brief relationship with the philosopher had a major impact on her thinking.[4]

Malte imagines the actress Eleonora Duse using the parts she played on the stage as masks which defended her inwardness against the threat of engulfment by the audience that was "gnawing on" her face. For Duse, he believes, acting became a camouflage so effective in hiding her from the psychological cannibals around her that she could let herself live with unrestrained emotional intensity and vitality behind the roles she performed (234–35). Rilke saw Duse in Ibsen's *Rosmersholm* in Berlin during November 1906 before writing about her in *The Notebooks*. She was also the subject of his poem, "Bildnis" (Portrait). After talking with her for the first time in Venice at the beginning of July 1912, he declared that this meeting had been "almost my greatest wish" for years (*Letters* 2:64).

II

The *Notebooks* entry on Duse reflects Malte's weak ego boundaries, his poor capacity for differentiation, and his insecure sense of self and identity. But the passage points beyond Malte's illness to the idea that a thoughtful, creative person—philosopher, poet, or actress—feeling threatened by engulfment, might use masks to defend growing inward strength. Duse's fear of having her face devoured by her audience motivates her to hide behind the play and her role. Hiding, she becomes so powerful that the audience which, she feels, has been "gnawing on" her face, breaks into applause "as if to ward off . . . something that would force them to change their life." Her fellow actors feel as if they are in a cage with a lioness (235).

Malte imagines her holding up a poem as a mask. Were Rilke's poems and his fiction masks behind which he defended his strength and singular gifts from being drained away by the people around him? Did these masks become, paradoxically, powerful, if indirect, expressions of the inwardness which they were hiding? A poet expresses himself selectively in his poems. If we compare the more objective *New Poems* with his contemporaneous novel, which is sometimes autobiographical, and his letters, we can see that many of his poems, which do not seem to tell us anything about their author, were indirectly self-expressive. In writing about Eleanora Duse, who seemed to him to be very much like himself, was Rilke revealing obliquely that his poems, his novel, and Malte himself, as a fictional surrogate, concealed and expressed him at the same time? Here, too, I wonder if Nietzsche influenced the poet's thinking. In *Beyond Good and Evil*, he asks if one does not write in order to hide what is within oneself.[1] Kierkegaard, who interested Rilke as early as 1904, argued that all genuinely expressive and original writing is elusive and oblique (as figurative language and irony are indirect), concealing as much as or more than it communicates because the individual is and must remain essentially secret, incommunicable. According to the Danish philosopher, whenever "the process of communication is a work of art," it is shaped by the underlying sense "that personalities must be held devoutly apart from one another, and not permitted to fuse or coagulate into objectivity."[2]

I have mentioned Winnicott's comment in *The Maturational Processes and the Facilitating Environment* that artists often experience both "the urgent need to communicate and the still more urgent need not to be found."[3] Surely this observation fits Duse, as Malte imagines her. But does it describe Rilke?

Rilke's prose piece entitled "An Experience" tells us that in 1913 he felt he was protected from psychological parasites and cannibals by an invisible barrier which "absorbed any relationship into itself and . . . intervened like a dark, deceptive vapor between himself and others," giving him "for the first time, a certain freedom" toward others and "a peculiar ease of movement amongst these others, whose hopes were set on one another, who were burdened with cares and bound together in death and life." His inner life, defended by this "intermediate space," had "so little reference to human conditions, that [most people] would only have called it 'emptiness.' " But this would have been a radical misunderstanding. His "freedom" brought the poet not "emptiness" or illness but "joy" and "converse with Nature" (*WSR*, 37–38).

Recurrently Rilke saw masking as a defense of inner freedom, power, and creativity. Behind the mask the face was free to grow. This was as true for himself as it was for Eleonora Duse and the Prodigal Son. But, as we have noted, often the use of such a defense is compulsive, and the freedom it affords may be quite limited. At least in Rilke's imagination Duse was *compelled* to use her role as a mask by her fear that the audience was devouring her face. In the Prodigal Son episode masking becomes a necessary defense against having one's face and inner self altered through and through under pressures from one's family. Still worse, a mask can swallow the face it is meant to protect. I have mentioned the *Notebooks* entry in which a mask obliterates the child who tries it on. In January 1912, not long before the first Duino Elegy came to him, describing his involuntary identification with people he met, Rilke says that he could step out of his room in an amorphous state of mind approaching chaos, and, suddenly finding himself an object of another person's awareness, automatically assume the other's poise. On such occasions he was amazed to hear himself expressing "well-formed things." His assumption of a poise belonging to the person he met and his involuntary compliance with the other's expectations of social behavior, masking the "lifelessness" and "chaos" he had felt in himself before these encounters, tended to engulf him, if only temporarily (*Letters* 2:37).

Reading Rilke's letters and his biographers, one can see how he developed a persona out of the vocation which was central to his innermost sense of self. He played the role of the poet so well that it helped to win him the acclaim and support of many powerful and wealthy people. This is not to say that they were unaffected by his writings, only that the role the poet played among them made them all the more eager to have him with them, often in their homes, and to become his patrons. It was a mask which obviously reflected, to some extent, Rilke's sense of himself, but also enabled him to veil and protect his inner life from the admirers who, he felt, were constantly draining his limited vitality and energy away, devouring the distinctive features of his face, the singular man and poet he was. In November 1907, for example, he described his mother's friends in Vienna as eager to eat him up—though once they'd heard him read, they lost their hunger (see *Letters* 1:325).

The biographer Wolfgang Leppmann suggests that Rilke's social personality, manners, and clothes were a protective camouflage which the poet developed to defend his inner freedom against impingements. Leppmann quotes Wilhelm Hausenstein's sketch of Rilke in 1915: "The poet went about in a navy-blue suit and wore light gray spats. His delicate frame was somewhat stooped. ... His hands moved cautiously, without expansive gestures, in light-colored deerskin gloves. He carried a walking-stick. The presence of a distinguished figure was thus disguised beneath the conventional appearance of a man of the world."[4] Like the role of the poet, this social persona may have functioned in alliance with the "intermediate space," the "dark deceptive vapor," which, Rilke felt, defended him from the people around him.

Rilke's fears of being devoured by those who loved and admired him lead me to wonder if his personas resemble the "false self" which, psychologists tell us, people plagued by such anxieties often develop to conceal and protect their innermost self against such dangers. The question is important because the "false self," which I shall define more fully, is a self-defeating defense, which ultimately encourages feelings of futility and emptiness and the sense that self and world are insubstantial and unreal.[5] Recurrently, at least until 1922, when he completed the *Duino Elegies* and wrote *The Sonnets to Orpheus,* Rilke was haunted by such feelings.

Winnicott observes that the false self usually originates in the failure of a mother to adapt herself with sufficient sensitivity and empathy to an infant's needs. The mother intrudes her own needs and fears into the child's consciousness long before he is mature enough to cope with them. Distracted, disconnected from the spontaneous flow of his own feelings and "thoughts" by these impingements, he may split himself into an inner core and a personality or personalities preoccupied with giving compliant reactions to his mother's pressures and, eventually, to pressures from other people. This outwardly directed part of the infant psyche becomes a false self, governed by the need to gratify and placate other people. While appeasing them, it conceals and protects the inner core, the "true self," which is as completely divorced as possible from the false self's need to react to external pressures.[6]

Compliance is motivated by fear of engulfment, impingement, and depersonalization if one reveals one's inner self, one's true thoughts and feelings. But this defensive front may bleed, squeeze, corrupt, or swallow the inner self it is meant to protect. According to R. D. Laing in *The Divided Self,* the false self is experienced as being governed by "an alien will" or wills. Initially this is a parent's will, however much it may be disguised. It may control one's behavior, one's body, one's speech, even one's thoughts, feelings, and perceptions.[7] The false self may be compulsively impersonating as well as identifying with the person whose expectations exact compliance. This concept recalls Rilke's unhappiness about his tendency to assume the poise of someone else, when, suddenly, he found himself "expressing well-formed things" which had nothing to do with his inner chaos and which completely concealed it. Were his aristocratic persona and the public role of the poet also examples of the schizoid false self, as Winnicott and Laing define it?

If we can say that Rilke did develop the kind of false self that analysts find in schizoid illness, we can discover its roots in the poet's relationships with his parents during childhood. Rilke felt that Phia saw him entirely in terms of her preconceptions. He willingly complied when she insisted that her little boy play the role of a girl to replace the daughter who had died before he was born. As an adult he recalled that she had exhibited him to her friends as if he were a doll. While trying to satisfy her need for a daughter, he encouraged his father's hope that his little son would grow up to be an army officer and thus fulfill Josef's frustrated ambitions vicariously. Josef Rilke had been forced out of the army after ten years of service. He had little René doing military exercises and receiving medals. The boy did his best to please him, too.

Phia Rilke wrote verse. She read Schiller's ballads to her son, persuaded him to memorize and to recite them, and did everything she could to foster in René the desire and the ambition to be a great poet.[8] In *Ewald Tragy,* an early autobiographical novella, Ewald, Rilke's surrogate, thinks of the mother who has left him as a sick woman who wants to be called "Fräulein," sitting in a train compartment letting her fellow passengers know that her son is a poet.[9] In his letters about his "unreal," "ghostly" mother, Rilke expressed the fear that he was too closely identified with her, though he had been trying to separate and distance himself from her all his life (*Letters* 1:147). His devotion to a vocation that conformed to his mother's wishes and his nearness as a poet to her conception of herself must have troubled him.

Malte's retelling of the parable of the Prodigal Son reflects Rilke's sense of the ways in which a false self may engulf one as it develops under pressures from one's parents. Malte imagines that the mask of the false self which grows in response to the expectations, fears, hopes, and relentless scrutiny of a family threatens to become the son's face. If that were to happen, all distinction between the outer false self and the inner true one would collapse; the former would replace the latter (251–54). A schizoid person lives in uncertainty and danger as he tries to detach and divorce his hidden "true self" from the false one, which increasingly absorbs it.

If a large part of one's social experience is pervaded by the sense that what one says and does is controlled and shaped by other people and is false to one's "true self," relationships and contacts are likely to encourage feelings of paralysis and formlessness. The false self acts as a barrier protecting the inner self from engulfment, but it also confines the inner self, cutting it off from nurturing contacts with other people.[10] There are a number of intimations in Rilke's letters that the roles he played among his aristocratic hosts involved him in deception and self-deception, which were painful and debilitating. The letters suggest that his attempts to exist in harmony with his aristocratic friends forced him to live a dispiriting lie, to enact a false self. He longed to escape from them: "The good,

generous asylums, such as Duino was and immediately thereafter Venice
. . . require so much adaptation each time . . . and when at last one has
got to the point of belonging to them, the only thing accomplished is
the lie that one belongs" (To Lou Andreas-Salomé, December 19, 1912;
Letters 2:81).

As for the aristocratic persona, caught in William Hausenstein's description, it may well have originated in the pretensions of Rilke's parents
and those of his father's older brother, Jaroslav, a paternalistic uncle, who
paid for René's studies in a commercial high school and then at the University of Munich, and gave his nephew an allowance which lasted until
after Jaroslav's death. This uncle put much time and effort into an attempt to link the family with old nobility. Though he failed to gain legal
recognition of any such connection, his nephew, the poet, maintained all
his life the myth of noble descent. Phia Rilke, whose father was wealthy
and held the title of imperial counselor, no doubt thought she was marrying into a family descended from aristocrats. In her photos she often
appears in long black dresses, which give her a rather absurd resemblance
to some great lady of an earlier decade, and her striking expression of
loftiness fits in with this impression. Josef Rilke was bitterly disappointed
when he did not succeed in following the career of a military officer,
once the exclusive privilege of the nobility. Later he also failed to obtain
a job as the manager of a count's estate, which would have enabled him
and his family to live in the kind of proximity to a noble heritage which
his son later found in the castles and palaces of his patrons. Josef's career
as a railway inspector decisively defeated all such hopes.[11]

Rilke's need to be a gentleman probably expressed an identification
with his parents' aspirations and a desire to escape from the tawdry reality of their bourgeois life. In this respect he made himself in their image
of themselves. He tried to fulfill their hopes for themselves and for him
and to give some reality to their illusions, despite his scorn for their self-
deceptiveness. His descriptions of his own life during his childhood, so
different in its external circumstances from Malte's, point toward these
conclusions: "My childhood home was a cramped rented apartment in
Prague; it was very sad. . . . our little household, which was in reality
middle class, was supposed to have the appearance of plenty, our clothes
were supposed to deceive people, and certain lies passed as a matter of
course" (Letter to Ellen Key, April 3, 1903; *Letters* 1:98).

In *René Rilke: Die Jugend Rainer Maria Rilkes* (René Rilke: The

Youth of Rainer Maria Rilke), the poet's son-in-law, Carl Sieber, reports that Rainer's parents pasted high-sounding labels on bottles containing cheap table wine. Drawing upon Sieber, Leppmann says that when company came, there was so little room that René sometimes had to sleep behind "a black folding screen decorated with gold birds."[12] Leppmann's inventory of their belongings gives us the picture: "Together with various lacquered Japanese fans, views of Vesuvius and other Italian motifs, and a vast number of knickknacks, this bamboo screen formed part of the inventory of an apartment that most differed from hundreds of others, if at all, through its sitting room which was done in blue silk."[13]

Did the aristocratic persona begin as a false self, developed by the child, René, in response to his parents' aspirations? Did it continue to serve unconsciously as a response to those aspirations, while at the same time complying with the tastes and values of parental surrogates among the aristocratic patrons who offered Rilke their homes, financial support, admiration, and even, in some cases, warm affection? If this was a false self, did the poet experience it, consciously or unconsciously, as a masquerade, hence unreal, hollow, futile, unfulfilling?

Early in *The Notebooks* Malte, who, unlike Rilke, is descended from high-ranking nobility, becomes anxious about his cleanliness and the appearance of his clothes, because they distinguish him from the poor "outcasts" who seem to feel that he belongs to them:

Even though the jacket I wear every day has begun to get threadbare in certain spots ... True, my collar is clean, my underwear too, and I could, just as I am, walk into any café I felt like, possibly even on the grands boulevards, and confidently reach out my hand to a plate full of pastries and help myself. No one would find that surprising; no one would shout at me or throw me out, for it is after all a genteel hand, a hand that is washed four or five times a day. There is no dirt under the nails, the index finger isn't ink-stained, and the wrists especially are irreproachable. (38–39)

What precedes and follows this shows that Malte's anxiety about his clothes and cleanliness, about his ability to walk into shops without being thrown out, is not normal middle class anxiety concerning respectable appearances. In the homelessness of the Parisian "outcasts" and in their apparent dehumanization, Rilke found what he suspected, with fear and revulsion, were mirror images of his own existence. He imagined that they were "living on nothing, on dust, on soot" (*Letters* 1:109). In *The Notebooks* he elaborates this conception of the "outcasts." They are "trash, husks of men that fate has spewed out," "[w]et with the spittle of fate," stuck to a wall, a lamppost, a billboard, or trickling like dung down a street (40).

One source of Malte's desire to sustain the look and fastidiousness of the gentleman in the streets of Paris is the fear of being reduced to something like this—less than human, degraded, repulsive, and unselved. This was at least part of the motivation behind the development and duration of the style and manners which Hausenstein found incongruous. Rilke's portrait of Malte reflects the fact that he was not entirely deceived by this persona. Late in the novel Malte thinks, "I know that if I am destined for the worst, it won't help me at all to disguise myself in my better clothes" (214).

Malte also comes to recognize the harmful consequences of such disguises. A brief entry in *The Notebooks,* preceding the passage on Duse by a few pages, acknowledges his despair of ever being able to "rub off the make-up and remove everything that is artificial. . . . we go around, a laughingstock and a half-truth: neither real beings nor actors" (231). Malte's thoughts here purport to take in all of us. "We" and "our" in this passage refer to human beings in general. But in the context of the novel, if we consider his illness and his anxieties, this entry describes the consequences of developing a false self or selves in an attempt to defend what he calls elsewhere "the hard core of a personality" beneath "the mask," to defend what a person feels is his true self. Eventually this defense may result in an inability to separate mask from face, false self from true, as parts of the false self or selves get mixed up with the individual's innermost being, pervading feelings and thoughts, governing gestures, words, and acts, despite his best efforts to liberate himself from them. In schizoid illness the false self or selves seem to take up more and more of the mind's energy and space. In schizophrenia the true self may disappear in a welter of false selves and fragments.

In *The Maturational Processes and the Facilitating Environment,* Winnicott distinguishes between "the False Self" in schizoid illness and the healthy use of social adaptability and pliancy to create a "compliant [social] self" that defends the inner self against discovery and intrusion.

Winnicott maintains that in health, as in sickness, we feel the inner self must be defended, not only against pressures to conform, but against being discovered and known. He argues that even in health an individual must keep his innermost self secret, inaccessible to everyone else, and that all of us feel its exposure threatens us with obliteration, with being converted into a usable thing, a danger exemplified in the results of brain-washing and in science fiction about people being reprogrammed or changed into robots.

Winnicott's conclusions, drawn from his work with patients, provide support for Rilke's evolving thoughts about the dangers inherent in human relationships and the need to protect his imaginative and emotional freedom by means of something like a "dark deceptive vapor." Winnicott theorizes that "in health there is a core to the personality that corresponds to the true self of the split personality; . . . this core never communicates with the world of perceived objects, and the individual person knows that it must never be communicated with or influenced by external reality."[14]

I do not know whether Winnicott read Kierkegaard, but the psychologist's argument that all of us are *permanently unknown*" reads like a paraphrase of the Danish philosopher's thinking about the nature of the individual, which almost surely confirmed Rilke's sense of himself and helped him to articulate it. Winnicott's analysis of normal fears of intrusive influence on what he calls "the secret self" would have found ready assent in Rilke at the height of his powers. Nothing can be more frightening and painful than changes in the core of the self as a result of a failure or breakdown in the defenses that protect it against communication.[15]

Winnicott distinguishes the false self in schizoid illness from the public self in a state of health. The first may be debilitating and destructive, and often leads a person to feel that he is "a collection of reactions to impingement." The second appeases the world by complying with its demands and expectations, hiding and defending the inner life of the "true self," while the latter is able in its strength and health to express itself and to find fulfillment and sources of new energy and vitality.

Surely we can accept Rilke's assertion in "An Experience" that his hidden inner life, defended by a "dark, deceptive vapor," was not empty, despite its "freedom" from ordinary human concerns and relationships, that it was joyful and rich in "converse with Nature." His resurgent creativity at the time justifies this claim, though we also know that during the years 1911–22 he often lapsed into states of despair, emptiness, and emotional paralysis. It seems likely that his social personas (his aristocratic manners and his public role as a poet among admirers), his fantasy of an "intermediate space," the "dark, deceptive vapor" around him, and his belief that poems and other writings might serve as masks were rooted in schizoid defenses against fantastical threats and anxieties, such as those I have described, but that he developed sufficient strength of ego and imagination to convert them into something more closely akin to the adaptable, "compliant [social] self" and the artfully shaped masks of behavior which Winnicott sees as the healthy psyche's means of concealing and protecting its secret inner life, its creative depths, from disturbing scrutiny and pressures.

III

In *The Divided Self,* Laing says that people suffering from the dread of engulfment often defend their identity by means of isolation.[1] In this respect Malte's behavior is typical. Unlike the Prodigal Son, he does not return to his home except at the time of his father's death. Unlike Rilke when he was newly arrived in Paris, Malte does not write long, almost daily letters to a wife and friends he has left behind. None of his encounters with other people in Paris relieve his isolation. He goes to see doctors in a hospital, but this encounter is impersonal. He thinks that some of the Parisian outcasts look at him as if they sensed an affinity, but his notes do not show that he exchanged one word with them.

Rilke's repeated insistence that solitude was necessary to his creativity must be understood at least partly as an outgrowth of his anxieties about having his inner life and self involuntarily changed, corrupted, taken over, or absorbed by other persons or alien external phenomena. Two pages after describing his fantasy of being invaded, filled up, and driven out of himself by what is "horrible" in the world, Malte meditates on Beethoven's death mask, thinking of the great composer as "a man whose hearing a god had closed up, so that there might be no sounds but his own; so that he might not be led astray by what is turbid and ephemeral in noises" (73–74 and 76). In 1903, probably near the time he began his work on *The Notebooks,* Rilke wrote to the young poet Franz Kappus, saying that anyone who wished to write poetry needed to be alone within himself much of the time.[2] Even among other people this might be possible, if one could look upon their lives "from out of the depth" and "expanse" of "one's own world," with the sense of distance and strangeness a child feels watching adults.

To Baladine Klossowska he wrote in December 1920, arguing that Malte could never "have penetrated so far into the confidence of things" if he had been diverted and distracted by human relationships. He had to be able to devote himself completely to "the things whose essential life" he wanted to express in his work. Rilke must have been thinking about his own *New Poems,* which were contemporaneous with *The Notebooks:*"Der Panther," "Die Gazelle," "Römische Sarkophage," "Der Schwan," "Die Spitze" (The Lace), "Die Treppe der Orangerie" (The Steps of the Orangery), "Das Karussell," and "Die Rosenschale" (The Bowl of Roses).[3] An earlier letter to Klossowska reveals underlying reasons for Rilke's need to get away from other persons, including Baladine herself. He did not like to have people looking at him, guessing what was troubling him, forcing him to be aware of them, inhibiting his freedom to shape his own life.[4]

Reading the parts of *The Notebooks* concerned with Malte's lonely boyhood and passages in Rilke's diaries and letters, one can see how difficult and painful solitude was for him. It often brought severe anxiety, frightening fantasies, and even delusions. Recurrently from 1911 to 1914 Rilke felt so barren and impotent in his comparatively solitary life that he longed for a companion. But this yearning dismayed him. It seemed a reflection of a diminished capacity for creative work. The following is from a letter to Salomé written on December 28, 1911, little more than two weeks before the First Elegy came to him:

Dear Lou, I am in a bad way when I wait for people, need people, look around for people. . . . So it is a bad sign that since Malte I have often hoped for someone who would be there for me, how does that happen? I had a ceaseless longing to bring my solitude under shelter with someone, to put it in someone's protection; you can imagine that in those conditions nothing made any progress. . . . How is it possible that now, prepared and schooled for expression, I am left in fact without a vocation, superfluous? (*Letters* 2:34)

The companion he imagined would have to be his perfect complement and utterly unintrusive. She must make no demands, expect nothing from him. She must in no way confront him with a distinctive, independent, self-assertive personality or with needs of her own, as he says in a letter to Salomé written on January 10, 1912, two days before the First Elegy came to him (*Letters* 2:38–39).

In December 1913, not long after completing the Third Elegy, writing to his maternal patron and friend, the princess Marie von Thurn und Taxis, in whose castle at Duino he had penned the First and Second Elegies, he expressed his longing for a place in the country with a house-keeper, who either would feel no love or would show an extraordinary love that made no demands, while protecting the poet in his vulnerable openness to "the invisible" (*Letters* 2:102). Rilke's fantasy of a perfectly empathetic, selflessly responsive, undemanding woman was a dream of the impossible. Reading an earlier version of this chapter, some colleagues were distressed to find such weakness in a poet whose writings often express deeply felt admiration and genuine understanding of the strengths shown by many women in history and literature. The fantasy of the perfect companion makes him seem antipathetic, a man possessed by ideas and attitudes which have often led to the oppression of women. Only a mother attuned to her infant, completely identified with him, expecting nothing for herself, an ideal parent created by a narcissistic mind, could fulfill such needs.

We can find other dimensions of the maternal figure that almost certainly underlies his longings for a woman whose love would protect him "at the border of the invisible" in *The Notebooks.* One entry praises and celebrates the incomparable power of the mother who can calm the terror of a child lost among the phantoms he himself has created in a dark room when he is left alone at night. Lighting a match, she becomes in her child's mind the source of all the real or imagined noises that have been frightening him, as she urges him to feel no fear now that she is with him. At the sound of something moving in the wall or creaking in the floor, her smile reassures him, as if she "knew the secret of every half-sound, and everything were agreed and understood between you." The passage ends with the question, "Does any power equal your power among the lords of the earth?" (75).

The companion who could do this for the poet would shelter his solitude and free it from the anxieties which often grew unbearably intense when he was alone. His fantasy of a housekeeper who would not expect anything from him reflects his dread at the prospect of having his internal freedom and his sense of a separate, distinctive self overwhelmed by intimacy with an assertive friend or lover. This fear was rooted in his relationship with his mother. If the unconscious fantasy underlying his longing for a "perfect" woman was the yearning for the kind of parent imagined in the passage quoted above from *The Notebooks,* this desire was strengthened by the poet's feeling that his emotional illness had originated in Phia's blind, smothering narcissism. To protect himself against a repetition of his childhood relationship with Phia, he must have her extreme opposite as his companion. Ironically, he seems to have longed for the freedom to be as blindly narcissistic as Phia in his relationship with the woman who would care for him. Nothing caused him more distress than his awareness that he had taken on some of his mother's worst qualities.

In an essay entitled "The Fantasy of the Perfect Mother," Nancy Chodorow and Susan Contratto analyze this widespread fantasy and its adult derivatives. They are particularly interested in the closely related assumption in many cultures that mothers have incomparable power to shape their children's lives and the consequences of the fantasy and this assumption: the tendency to blame mothers for all the ills that befall their children and the ubiquitous idealization of mothers which often reinforces, not only exaggerated expectations, but also negative ideas and feelings about maternal failure and destructiveness. Chodorow and Contratto conclude that infantile fantasies of maternal perfection and omnipotence and the ideas of maternal responsibility resulting from them in a number of cultures have encouraged the oppression of mothers and much of the anger felt toward women.

Chodorow and Contratto trace current ideas about mothering to the evolution of parental roles in the nineteenth century. They argue that as men among the bourgeoisie became increasingly absorbed in urban commerce and industry, responsibility for, and control over, the rearing of children was assumed to be almost entirely in the mother's hands. These conditions and assumptions fostered the isolation of mother and child. They also encouraged conceptions of the ideal mothering which would produce the best possible children and thus the best of all possible worlds. The notion that the mother and the child are isolated in a protected sphere, which is reflected in Rilke's fantasy about a life apart with a protective, nurturing, selfless woman, becomes, as Chodorow and Contratto show, one focus of recent feminist writings. A number of feminists whose works they discuss have explored the ways in which the fantasy or the reality of mothers' aloneness with their children exacerbates their sense of oppression, their rage, and their fears that their separate identities will be obliterated. Children often react with fear, anger, and aggression to these feelings in their mothers, all the more so because of their fantasies of maternal omnipotence. Such reactions continue, later in life, to have an unconscious influence on adults' feelings and ideas about mothers. They fuel men's antagonism toward women, as well as the doubts and tensions in women's attitudes toward themselves.

This essay helps to place Rilke's ideas and feelings about his mother and other women against a larger cultural and social background. It also indicates the tendency of psychological theorists in recent times to share the cultural assumptions which have grown out of the fantasy of the perfect mother, as they have moved away from the triangular oedipal paradigm to focus upon the power of the mother to shape the child.[5]

Later I shall examine Rilke's brief relationship with Magda von Hattingberg during the early months of 1914, when he thought he had at last found the companion he had described in his letters to the princess Marie and Lou Andreas-Salomé. This relationship, falling dismally short of the fantastical hopes which filled the poet's letters to von Hattingberg in the month before they met (she started the correspondence by writing to him after coming across his *Stories of God*), ended all too swiftly, leaving Rilke in anguish. Shortly afterward, in June 1914, he wrote to Salomé a letter revealing that this failure had brought him to painfully clear self-understanding. "For I no longer doubt that I am sick, and my sickness has gained a lot of ground and is also lodged in that which heretofore I called my work, so that for the present there is no refuge there" (*Letters* 2:113–14).

But relationships with other women, who had not been sent by heaven to play the part of the angelic housekeeper, were essential to Rilke's emotional strength and vitality. In chapters five and six I consider the poet's love affair and long friendship with Lou Andreas-Salomé and his marriage and friendship with Clara Westhoff, two women who, for many years, helped to allay his fears and fostered his creativity, often from a distance, through letters.

The seclusion which Rilke sought sometimes intensified his illness. But no student of his life is likely to disagree with his belief that it nurtured his genius. In an essay on Rilke, Robert Hass notes the poet's loathing for the superficiality and falseness which he saw in the everyday social life of most human beings and observes that his evocative power seems to have come from a lonely inner depth. His poems can awaken in us a corresponding depth of inwardness and a responsiveness that creates something like the perspective of the child's distance evoked in the letter to Franz Kappus mentioned above. Hass argues that Rilke's greatest poetry strips away many layers of apparent richness and complexity within us, enabling us to discover a solitary self in all its strangeness, a dimension of the psyche which Hass associates with "the huge nakedness and poverty of human longing."[6]

CHAPTER 4

This Lost, Unreal Woman

Phia Rilke and the Maternal Figures in *The Notebooks*

I

In April 1904, at the age of twenty-eight, two months after beginning the book that was to become his novel, Rilke wrote a letter to Salomé which more fully and precisely than anything else he left us reveals his adult conceptions of his mother and her effect on him. Phia had come to Rome, where her son was staying, and he was forced to meet her from time to time, though he felt that "every meeting with her [was] a kind of setback." He found her "lost" and "unreal," "connected with nothing," determined to remain young. The sight of her brought back memories (who can say if they were accurate?) of his struggle as a child to escape her. Their meetings intensified his fear that after years of trying to separate himself and distance her he was still deeply identified with her, "fear . . . that somewhere inwardly I still make movements that are the other half of her embittered gestures, bits of memories that she carries broken within her." His sense of still carrying in himself, somewhere hidden, her false, "distraught pieties," narcissistic religiosity, and pretentious affectations of manner and dress, "all those distorted and perverted things to which she has clung," horrified him. And he could not help wondering if he shared her ghostly unreality and emptiness. If his "entrance into the world" was like a "wallpaper door" in a "faded wall that doesn't belong to anything," that helped to explain why he sometimes felt he had no place and was not at home in the world (*Letters* 1:147).

I have mentioned the letter which Rilke wrote in November 1907 from Prague about Phia's effect on him. For a reading he was giving she had assembled an audience of old women who seemed hungry for him but quickly lost their hunger when they heard him read (*Letters* 1:325). No doubt, his sense of these women, his mother's friends and contemporaries, his fantasy of their desire to devour him and his feelings about the sudden rejection and indifference which abruptly replaced it were partly transferred from Phia herself. At the same time he wrote to Clara that his mother had little or no understanding of the man her son had become. She saw him almost entirely through her preconceptions. He was unable to make her see any of his real nature or character. Such was the power of this blindness that after being with her he had a strong sense of the hole, the void, her perceptions left in him: "in relation to her nothing remains valid."[1]

Every time he met her, Rilke felt his mother defended herself against taking in the strange, very different man who long ago had been René and transformed him into an embodiment of images and ideas that satisfied her needs and did not arouse her fears, just as she had done in his childhood. Meeting her for the last time in October 1915, in Munich, he wrote a poem which utters its complaint against Phia's blind, self-absorbed destructiveness with naked simplicity. In this poem he compares himself to a small house, which he has built, stone by stone, until it is able to stand on its own. But his mother demolishes him. Looking at her son, she cannot see that he has been building. Blindly, she goes through his stone wall. Dogs recognize him. Only his mother does not know his face, which has been slowly growing. He never feels a warm breath of air coming from Phia and ironically imagines her lying in a lofty compartment of her heart, where Christ comes to wash her daily.

Ach wehe, meine Mutter reisst mich ein.
Da hab ich Stein auf Stein zu mir gelegt,
und stand schon wie kleines Haus, um das sich
sogar allein. [gross der Tag bewegt,
Nun kommt die Mutter, kommt und reisst mich ein.

Sie reisst mich ein, indem sie kommt und schaut.
Sie sieht es nicht, dass einer baut.
Sie geht mir mitten durch die Wand von Stein
Ach wehe, meine Mutter reisst mich ein.

Die Vögel fliegen leichter um mich her.
Die fremden Hunde wissen: das ist *der*.
Nur einzig meine Mutter kennt es nicht,
mein langsam mehr gewordenes Gesicht.

Von ihr zu mir war nie ein warmer Wind.
Sie lebt nicht dorten, wo die Lüfte sind.
Sie liegt in einem hohen Herz-Verschlag
und Christus kommt und wäscht sie jeden Tag.
(*WDB* 2:101)

The poem is so clear it needs little explication. Among all creatures only the poet's mother cannot see the individual her son has made of himself. She has no warmth or life to give him. Her deadness, her blindness to his work of self-creation, her self-absorption in egocentric, narcissistic fantasies of a Savior devoted to her are extremely destructive, despite the strength he has struggled to develop in himself. The poet's fantasy that he has built himself up stone by stone brings to mind his relationship with Rodin and his tendency to think of artistic work in terms of sculpture. He has developed his sense of himself through the writing of his poems and the mastery of his art. The stone represents the strength and permanence of the self, the life, and the body of work he has created. In telling us that his mother goes through his stone wall, the poem suggests that his unsuccessful defense against her devastating imperviousness was to try to make himself impervious.

Stone is unfeeling; it's dead. Did he suspect that in protecting himself against Phia, in trying to make himself impervious and indestructible, he had deadened himself? In a 1913 letter to Princess Marie von Thurn und Taxis-Hohenlohe, the poet says that he is not a lover, that no one has ever "shaken" him "utterly," possibly because he is unable to love his mother (*Letters* 2:90). Parts of the poem express an opposing, positive sense of self, as creatures of air and earth recognize the poet's distinctive face and its steady growth and change.

A number of times Rilke retold the story of his childhood in letters to sympathetic women. The earliest of these which has survived was addressed in 1894 to Valerie von David-Rhonfeld, one of his early loves, who wrote novellas and painted porcelain, dressed in red, Empire style gowns, and carried a shepherdess's crook.[2] To "Vally" he wrote on his nineteenth birthday that his mother had entrusted him to a servant and that she had loved him only when she could exhibit him to her friends in a little dress (*Letters* 1:18). Years later, during the troubling spring of 1903, three months before he felt he could appeal to Salomé for help, he described the mother of his childhood in a letter to the Swedish feminist Ellen Key, who had read his *Stories of God* with much excitement. This long self-introduction focused upon memories or fantasies of himself as a child "infinitely forsaken" and "utterly astray in an alien world," played with by his mother as if he were a doll, treated by her as a girl, and otherwise neglected by that nervous woman who wanted to be called "Fräulein" and "to pass for young, sickly, and unhappy." Haunted by such memories or fantasies of Phia in his childhood, the poet yearns for "a mother who is greatness, kindness, quietude, and beneficence." And he imagines that in this reply to Ellen Key's praise of his stories he may be writing to such a mother (*Letters* 1:98–104).

In *The Notebooks* and the Third Elegy he developed his conception of such a parent. Yet one cannot help wondering if Malte's Maman is an unconscious retrieval of Phia from Rilke's early childhood, a maternal figure that at least partly belies the bitter accusations of early neglect in his letters. Or is Maman largely invention, a fantasy of the benevolent, devoted, empathetic protectress long wished-for by the son who felt he had not had one?

One of the earliest recollections from Malte's childhood takes us back to Urnekloster, the home of Maman's father, Count Brahe. At the age of twelve or thirteen Malte is staying there with his father, years after Maman's death. The motherless boy keenly feels the absence of any sense of "family" in the group of relatives who gather for dinner at his grandfather's table. Even his relationship with his father is "cool." Malte is in a "state of annihilation." The high, dark banquet hall "sucked all images out of you" until you "sat there as if you had disintegrated—totally without will, without consciousness ... without defense ... like an empty space" (26).

"Annihilation," "disintegration," emptiness, lack of will, and defenselessness are central and recurrent elements of Malte's experience as a child and as an adult. The child experiences the "vaulted room" as if it were a living thing. Its "darkening height and its never fully illuminated corners" forcibly draw his thoughts and feelings, his will, his consciousness of world and self, all his insides, out of him. The images suggest, ambig-

uously, irresistible vacuums and voracious mouths. Psychoanalytic studies reveal that unconscious infantile fantasies and fears of cannibalism
often underlie such thoughts. The infant projects his desire to devour the
breast or the mother onto her, and is then terrified of being eaten. In
schizoid and schizophrenic illness these fantasies surface again in many
forms, often involving displacement from the mother to other objects,
as, for example, the dining hall in the home of Maman's father. Malte's
fantasy here suggests weakness of ego defenses and boundaries, impairment of integration and differentiation.

If Malte were "a real person" rather than a character in a book, one
could say without fear of troubling a commonsensical mind that his
mother's illness and early death, his father's remoteness, and the absence
in the boy of any sense of family and home after Maman's death must
have undermined his fragile sense of personal identity and integrity. And
one could see that these factors in Malte's childhood must have encouraged the fears of engulfment and implosion which resurfaced in Paris.

In the childhood scenes at Urnekloster, Malte's mother is associated
with two other members of her family—Mathilde, a distant cousin, and
Christine, whose ghost walks through the dining hall during dinner.
Malte discovers his mother's features in Mathilde's face. The connection
between the two women is even more tightly drawn. Malte is unable to
remember Maman, but the time spent with Mathilde Brahe brings together in his mind "hundreds and hundreds of details" which "form an
image of my dead mother." And from then on this image "accompanies
me everywhere I go" (28).

Yet Mathilde Brahe's face differs from Maman's in one important respect. Looking at this cousin, he sees his mother's features "forced apart,
distorted, no longer connected to one another, as if a stranger's face had
thrust itself among them." The "as if" is curiously out of place. In fact
this *is* a "stranger's" face. Rilke's comments about his own mother make
one wonder if Mathilde Brahe obliquely reflects the poet's adult perception that Phia, the mother whom he came to detest as disconnected,
lacking coherence, was a grotesquely distorted incarnation of the one he
had loved as a young child.

The first time Malte sees Christine Brahe at dinner in Urnekloster he
does not realize that she is a ghost. Mathilde has stayed away from the
meal. When Malte's grandfather, Count Brahe, explains that she is absent
because she does not want to encounter Christine, his uncle, a retired

army major, leaves the room, beckoning Malte and his young cousin, Erik, to follow him. Later, when they have been served dessert, a door which Malte thought was always locked opens, and "a slender woman in a light-colored dress" moves slowly in their direction (33). Malte's father jumps up from the table and starts walking toward her, but the count grabs his arm and drags him back. The woman exits through another door, which Erik closes with a bow. Furious, shouting, Malte's father demands that the count tell him who the visitor was. When the old man, whose face is like a mask, smiling, identifies her as Christine Brahe, a member of the family, Chamberlain Brigge rushes out of the dining hall, leaving his son behind. Long afterward Malte learns the story of Christine's death in childbirth ages ago.

Rilke implicitly associates Christine's ghost with Malte's dead mother when he has Count Brahe speak to the boy's father about Maman as if she were a girl, dressed in white, who might be about to come into the dining hall. Not long after, the dead woman "in a light-colored dress" does enter the room, and the next morning Malte wakes up and his bones freeze when he sees "something white" sitting on his bed (31, 33, 35). The novel strengthens one's sense that Mathilde and Christine represent Maman in Malte's unconscious mind. All three women seem to become confused with one another, if only momentarily, when his horror at the ghostly image on his bed changes as he hears the voice of Mathilde speaking to him and tries to "assemble" his mother's features in the living cousin's face, while asking her about the strange woman who came into the dining hall the night before.

With her "warm, sweetish breath" that touches his face and her voice that immediately calms him, putting an end to his horror in the morning, Mathilde embodies a fantasy of the mother as a comforter and protector. Curiously, she seems to have acquired some distasteful associations with Phia Rilke as well. Apart from the disconnectedness and incoherence of the mother's features in her face, her interest in an Austrian spiritualist recalls Phia's "distraught pieties," which probably influenced her son at an early age, though later he found them repulsive. Perhaps, Mathilde reflects elements of the poet's ambivalence about his mother and his sense that Phia could be seen as a somewhat ridiculous figure. If the poet did, consciously or unconsciously, associate her with Phia, he may have defended himself against this association by making her harmless and only "a distant cousin" (27).

The reactions Christine's ghost arouses in various members of the family point to an underlying fantasy that contact with the dead is deadly and to the feeling that they can exert a dangerous power over the living. Count Brahe grabs Malte's father, pulls him back to his chair, and holds him there when he tries to approach Christine.

Later in the novel Malte recalls a story Maman once told about the return of another member of the household, Ingeborg, shortly after her death. Though Ingeborg is invisible, the members of the family realize that she is there because Cavalier, their dog, runs to meet her as he always did during her lifetime, when she came at tea time, bringing the mail. He jumps up "to lick her. . . . whimpering with joy." Suddenly he howls, whirls, falls back, and lies "stretched out before us, strange and flat on the ground, not moving a muscle" (90). This story suggests that the touch of ghosts is lethal. Ingeborg's relationship with Malte's mother, Maman's fascination with her behavior during her last illness and her return after death, and the context of this story (Malte's account of his mother's last illness) form a web of associations between the two women.

Hence, Maman is associated with two menacing Brahe ghosts, at least one of whom is deadly, though she has been benevolent, comforting, lovely, and beloved during her lifetime. Indirectly, through latent displacement in these stories, *The Notebooks* suggests that the dead mother is a threatening figure, capable of killing if one cannot overcome the power of her magnetism.

Unconscious dread of the mother as a destroyer may begin in infancy as a fear of being swallowed or smothered by her. In clinical work psychologists also find the unconscious fantasy of a mother sucking up all one's life, energy, and feeling. Such fantasies may be transferred to other figures, as they are in *The Notebooks* and in D. H. Lawrence's novels *Sons and Lovers* and *Women in Love*. Such fantasies are sometimes lumped together under the psychological term "engulfment." If a dead or absent mother is a lively ghost in the mind, and if one feels unable to separate oneself from her, one may feel swallowed up in a kind of living death, emotionally dependent on someone who can no longer actively reciprocate, no longer give much nurture or support. Too close an attachment to a dead, absent, or distant mother may sustain a symbiotic relationship which should have ended with early childhood. And this can result in a continuing sense of being trapped among the dead, among ghosts, unable to make vital contact with the living.

Maurice Betz, who worked with Rilke on the French translation of *The Notebooks*, recalls in *Rilke vivant* that, as the poet tried to describe Malte's mother telling her ghost story, he seemed to confuse her with his own.[3] Curiously, in her last illness Malte's benevolent mother does come to resemble Phia Rilke, as the poet saw her. In his biographical account of the young Rilke, Carl Sieber confirms his father-in-law's description of Phia as "unreal," offering details of her appearance and behavior to support this, such as her long black dresses, which had been out of fashion for many years, her extreme thinness, and her diet. She seemed to eat almost nothing but biscuits, and Sieber wondered how she could exist on such fare.[4] During the last years of her life, Maman has a strainer to filter what she drinks. Biscuits and bread are her only solid food. She tells her son she is unable to digest anything any more. Her hand is weightless and feels like an ivory crucifix, and she comes alive only when she is absorbed in the story of Ingeborg's death and her return as a ghost who seems to kill the dog that runs to her in love and joy.

Toward the end Maman "began to die, slowly and hopelessly, over the whole surface of her body" (111). This is to say, her senses die, her connection with the external world and the source of her sense of her separateness from it. At this point she recalls Rilke's description of Phia, as "lost," "ghostly," "connected with nothing" (*Letters* 1:147).

The connection between Rilke's mother and Malte's is most obvious in a scene based on Phia's insistence that René transform himself into a girl during the first several years of his life. Carl Sieber, in his book about the poet's childhood and youth, confirms that this scene in *The Notebooks* is autobiographical.[5] Magda von Hattingberg testifies that Rilke told her Phia had encouraged him, as a child, to play the part of a girl, dressing him as one and making him dust around the house and do other chores ordinarily performed by daughters at that time.[6] Rilke's self-introductory letter of April 1903 to Ellen Key confirms the assertion that he was treated like a girl before going to school (*Letters* 1:99). As Sieber suggests, by drawing little René into this game, Phia provided herself with a substitute for the daughter who had died before René was born.

In the episode of the novel based on this experience, Maman calls Malte "Sophie," the name of Rilke's mother and his dead sister. But

Malte's memory of the time "when Maman wished I had been a little girl and not the boy that I undeniably was" is free from the distaste implicit when Rilke mentions in his letters his transformation into a little girl. Perhaps, in his novel, Rilke is recapturing the pleasure he felt as a small child "in the little girlish house-dress," in playing this game which gave such pleasure to his mother: "Then, when she asked who was there, I would delightedly answer 'Sophie,' making my voice so dainty that it tickled my throat" (99).

This is not just a game. The boy's sense of himself as a little girl is quite real. "I really was Sophie, not just Maman's little Sophie . . . whose hair Maman had to braid, so that she wouldn't be mistaken for that naughty Malte, if he should ever come back." If this section of the novel emphasizes the intimate rapport between mother and son and the boy's delight in becoming Sophie for his mother, it also suggests another, very different sense of that early relationship. Increasingly it concentrates on Maman's rejection of the little boy and her son's identification with her in this rejection. "[Malte's return] was not at all desirable; Maman was as pleased at his absence as Sophie was, and their conversations (which Sophie always carried on in the same high-pitched voice) consisted mainly in enumerating Malte's misdeeds and complaining about him. 'Oh dear, that Malte,' Maman would sigh. And Sophie would go on and on about the naughtiness of boys in general" (100).

This sounds like good fun. The tone is humorous, teasing. One might think that, perhaps, the mother is ambivalent. When she chatters about Malte's naughtiness, one might suspect that Maman finds this rather appealing as well as off-putting. But the pleasure Maman takes in Malte's absence is the feeling that stands out.

If Rilke's memory that his mother converted him into a little girl and played with him as if he were a doll was accurate, it seems likely that she was depersonalizing him in order to defend herself against the male in her son and his separate individuality (*Letters* 1:99). If the poet's letters and poems about Phia give a true picture of her, her need to do this must have come from a lack of a strong sense of self, of her own distinctive reality.

One can easily see what the consequences of such childhood games might be: doubt and confusion about one's identity, and in particular one's sexual identity, confusion about body image, guilt at being male and an inclination to reject one's masculinity, fear of women, difficulty in staying with a woman. Above all, the mother's game would draw her son into a collaboration which would entail at least a partial rejection of himself, of his value and worth and right to exist in harmony with his own nature, character, and sexual identity.

Maman's choice of Rilke's mother's name for her little boy-girl in the game may be memory or invention on Rilke's part. Sieber says that the girl's name Phia used for René was Ismene, but Magda von Hattingberg reports that Rilke told her in one of his letters that his mother had called him Sophie as a child.[7] In either case the choice of the name Sophie in *The Notebooks* reflects Rilke's sense of Phia's desire to identify her son with herself and not to allow him a separate existence.

Maman's death in *The Notebooks* may have helped Rilke to defend her in his own imagination from association with the destructiveness, unreality, and emptiness he loathed in his own mother. Often death enables surviving children to purify their parents of negative qualities, to idealize them, and to isolate love from hate, fear, anger, and guilt, repressing negative feelings.

II

In *The Restoration of the Self,* Heinz Kohut defines the harmful effects of a narcissistic mother on her child. When such a mother supports and encourages her child's displays of his grandiose sense of himself, he understands very well that he must conform to her idealized image of him, shaped by her own narcissistic grandiosity, in order to keep her love. One can see the narcissistic nature of Phia's love for René in her insistence that he become a daughter, a girl, hence closer to a mirror image of herself; in her playing with him as if he were a doll and exhibiting him to her friends; in her blindness to all that he really was and her tendency to see him through her own preconceptions.

Kohut argues that the sense of the self's reality, its cohesion and continuity, grows out of adequate early maternal mirroring. This also enables an infant to merge with a parent whom he experiences as omnipotent and secure and thus to internalize her capacity for mastering anxiety. Thus, failures in maternal empathy, resulting from the kind of narcissism that Rilke attributes to Phia, tend to prevent a child from developing an adequate sense of his coherence and reality and an ability to control his fears. Because of her sense of her own unreality, disconnectedness, and unworthiness, a mother may be unable to give her child the emotional support that fosters self-acceptance and security.

Kohut explores the ramifications of these failures. A child of a narcissistic mother, one who responds selectively out of her own needs and fears, and is often withdrawn, may be vulnerable to fragmentation and is likely to lack self-esteem. As an adult he will probably experience emotional impoverishment and fear of love because it has proven so unstable and manipulative in his childhood. The kind of fragmentation which we have found in *The Notebooks,* and which Kohut traces to the weakness or perversity of maternal mirroring, often gives rise to hypochondria. According to Kohut, fears, such as Malte's, about illness and disease in parts of the body may be a way of attempting to "maintain control of the totality of [the] body by focusing ... attention on the parts that [are] becoming estranged from [oneself]" as the "body-self" seems to be coming apart. The fantasies that accompany such anxieties may arise from a need to give physical form to a sense of impending mental disintegration, which is all the more terrifying because it is vague, not visible, not tangible, and thus eludes efforts at comprehension, defense, and mastery.[1]

Can we say that Rilke's writing of *The Notebooks* had a similar defensive function? Did Rilke use the concrete imagery of *The Notebooks* and Malte's experiences to give tangible form to "the deeper unnameable dread experienced when a person feels that his self is becoming seriously enfeebled or disintegrating. ... the dread of the loss of his self—the fragmentation of and the estrangement from his body and mind ... and the breakup of the sense of his continuity"?[2]

In *Collected Papers on Schizophrenia and Related Subjects,* Harold Searles observes that in many cases the mother of a mentally ill patient is unable, because of her own ego-fragmentation, feelings of unreality, and high anxiety, to respond to her child, with the result that the child finds himself "completely shut out of his mother's awareness, out in the cold, with a highly anxious sense of non-existence, of not being really alive."[3] Such a mother's perceptions of her child in terms of her own preconceptions, Searles notes, may be experienced as tantamount to annihilation. The dependent mother may be attempting to keep her son tightly bound in the symbiotic relationship which he is trying to escape.

She may project her sense of herself onto him, motivated by her need to see him as part of her.

Rilke's vocation as a poet was inextricably enmeshed with his mother's ideal image of him. Nothing could have been more intolerable to him than the feeling that by following his vocation he was involving himself in the narcissism of the mother he portrays in his early novella *Ewald Tragy,* the woman who has abandoned her child and has become a homeless traveler, like the young author of the novella. Rilke's fictional surrogate, Ewald, tells a French girl at a family gathering that his mother, who has left her husband and son, is sick. He has not heard from her for quite a while. They have not even written to each other for a year. Nonetheless, he imagines, she likes to mention to other people in her train compartment that her son is a poet.[4]

Phia fostered her son's desire to be a poet. As the biographers tell us, she recited Schiller's ballads for René's benefit, got him to memorize poems, and encouraged his early efforts to write verse. In 1900 she published, through a vanity press, a book of aphorisms entitled *Ephemeriden.* It was dedicated to her son.[5] If she had any ambitions to prove herself as a writer, this was the closest they came to fulfillment. The poet may have sensed that his own achievements fed his mother's narcissistic grandiosity.

One cannot help wondering if Rilke had to contend with a probably unconscious feeling that, in writing poetry and in achieving recognition and fame, he was displaying his grandiose sense of self exhibitionistically before his self-loving mother, cutting himself to her design to win her love, much as he loathed her. Substitutes, markedly different from her— among them Lou Andreas-Salomé, Clara Rilke, Auguste Rodin, the princess Marie von Thurn und Taxis-Hohenlohe, and Nanny Wunderly-Volkart—helped him to defend himself against this feeling. They afforded him a more genuine mirroring, which gradually brought healing, strength, and confidence. But one suspects the narcissistic mother was always there with him. She outlived him.

III

Malte's most romantic memory of a loving, enchanting Maman accompanies a recollection of one of his worst bouts of terror as a child. After he has been "screaming and screaming" while servants try to calm him, his mother arrives at last. We are told that "Maman never came at night," except this one time (96). Two pages later Malte says, "Maman sometimes came for a half hour and read me fairy tales," but "the real readings, the long ones, Sieversen did" (98). Even in this entry where the small boy's romantic image of his mother is the focus, there are intimations of neglect, muted, veiled echoes of Rilke's complaints against his mother and his bitter assertion that he was often left in the care of a servant. In the next entry Malte describes how he allowed himself to be converted into Sophie to please his mother.

Yet on that one night, when Malte "screamed and screamed" in his fever and terror, his mother did come home from "a great ball, at the Crown Prince's." Wearing "her magnificent court gown," she let her "white fur fall behind her and took me in her bare arms."

And I, astonished and enchanted as I had never been before, touched her hair and her little smooth face and the cold jewels in her ears and the silk at the edge of her shoulders, which smelled of flowers. And we stayed like that and cried tenderly and kissed each other, until we felt that Father was there and that we had to separate. . . . "What nonsense to send for us," he said. . . . They had promised to go back if it was nothing serious. And certainly it was nothing serious. But on my blanket I found Maman's dance-card and white camellias, which I had never seen before and which I placed on my eyes when I felt how cool they were. (96–97)

The phrasing—"astonished and enchanted as I had never been before" and "Maman's dance-card and white camellias, which I had never seen before"—reinforces the intimations of distance and absence which frame the passage. Nonetheless, this entry brings into clear focus the tenderness, tinged with erotic feeling, which Malte feels for his mother. This is also one of several parts of The Notebooks which call to mind the essay "Family Romances," in which Freud analyzes the significance of fantasies that we are descended from high-ranking persons, arguing that they reflect the struggle to break free from parents by whom we feel neglected or toward whom we feel hostile. But Freud, at length, concludes that such fantasies "preserve, under a slight disguise, the child's original affection for his parents." Fantasies of aristocratic fathers and mothers, he finds, often reproduce traits of the real ones. The replacement of the child's real parents by the ones in the fantasy recaptures earlier idealizations of the former.[1]

Rilke took over his uncle Jaroslav's myth that the family ancestry was aristocratic. Though neither the uncle nor his nephew could prove their connection with an ancient noble family, the poet never abandoned this belief. Giving his fictional surrogate in *The Notebooks* aristocratic parents obviously involved displacement of this fantasy. Through Malte's noble heritage he can, if only in his imagination, escape the tawdriness of his parent's thoroughly bourgeois life in Prague. Perhaps, also, his creation of such a life for Malte and his parents was, through unconscious transference, a disguised way of rescuing his own parents from the seediness of their lives and giving them the aristocratic status for which they longed.

If we think of Maman on her return from the crown prince's ball in terms of "Family Romances" we can see that this passage may well have arisen from Rilke's desire to recover or invent a mother of early childhood whom he could love and adore.

In *Rainer Maria Rilke: Legende und Mythos,* Erich Simenauer, discussing this entry in *The Notebooks,* cites the opinion of Otto Rank and other psychoanalytic writers that Malte reveals a neurotic fixation in the oedipal stage with its incestuous desire for the mother.[2] Simenauer argues that in Rilke an unconscious "infantile fixation on the mother held [the writer] in chains during his lifetime and determined the direction of his unconscious longing, which lay at the foundation of his artistic creativity."[3] Drawing upon an analysis of Gottfried Keller by E. Hitschmann, Simenauer implies that Rilke's need to distance his mother and his apparent lack of love for her were elements of "a reaction formation," covering up the forbidden yearning.[4]

Simenauer also mentions Rilke's story "Die Letzten" (The Last Ones) as evidence of incestuous feelings in its author. In her biography of Rilke, E. M. Butler calls this story "a Freudian situation played out to the death between a mother and son."[5] In "Die Letzten" a sick son abandons his girlfriend and his work and gives himself up entirely to his mother. Then, as Leppmann says, "in the feverish imagination of her dying son" the mother becomes "a mysterious girl dressed in white." "The conclusion of this short work," says Leppmann, "is drenched in sultry eroticism and barely manages to skirt incest."[6]

Rilke's passionate affair with Lou Andreas-Salomé, who was fourteen years older than himself and an acknowledged second mother, also supports the thesis that Rilke's feelings for Phia were governed by a powerful oedipal attachment and the need to repress it.

In a fascinating and richly insightful chapter, entitled "Mutter und Urphantasien," Simenauer goes through the voluminous evidence of Rilke's "fixation." Although he emphasizes the argument that Rilke's loathing for his mother can be explained as "a reaction formation," an attempt to reinforce his repression of the incestuous love which leaks through some passages in his writing, Simenauer acknowledges that the poet's ambivalent relationship with Phia was determined by a variety of unconscious and conflicting feelings.[7]

Searles offers another perspective on the relationship between the child's tenderness and enchantment, so beautifully evoked in *The Notebooks,* and the poet's flight from Phia. A child's love for an emotionally ill mother may give rise to the fear of being sucked into her sickness or to the loathing which results from his awareness that his feelings for her have mired him in an illness from which he cannot escape. Such love, though repressed and denied, may remain very much alive in later years, sustaining his identification with her in her illness.

If we accept the argument that Malte's love for Maman obliquely reflects Rilke's early love for his own mother—and, as I shall show, there is much evidence in Rilke's poems and letters to support this conclusion—and if we accept Rilke's portrait of Phia, we can see more clearly how the poet's illness may have begun in his relationship with his mother. Searles argues that a child who "detects in *his* mother ... a tragically unintegrated and incomplete person" often reacts with intense "compassion, loyalty, solicitude, and dedication." These feelings, he observes, keep the child trapped in a "disastrous" "symbiotic" relation with the mother.[8]

Worse still, the child identifies with his mother, making her "ego-fragmented" existence a part of himself. "He introjects her not primarily out of hatred or anxiety but out of genuine love and solicitude for his mother ... primarily in an effort to save her by taking her difficulties ... upon himself." From long experience as a psychotherapist with the children of such mothers and from observing their transference behavior toward himself as a surrogate mother, Searles notes that usually they deny this disastrous and extremely dangerous and painful love and cover it up with antagonism, hatred, and loathing, in useless efforts to defend themselves against it.[9] This helps us to reconcile Rilke's portrayal of Malte's love for Maman with the poet's professed aversion to Phia.

Malte's offering of all his strength to the victim of St. Vitus' dance, the dissolution of his ego boundaries, and his near-engulfment by the man's anxiety, struggle, and convulsions bring to mind Searles's analysis of the origins of schizophrenia in a child's loving offer of himself as a sacrifice to help a schizoid or schizophrenic mother hold herself together and the child's absorption by her illness as, out of love and sympathy, he gladly gives himself up to the mutual parasitism encouraged by the mother in her desperate need.

Rilke's descriptions of Phia suggest that as a child, loving and adoring her much as Malte does Maman, he may well have suffered from the sense of her ego-fragmentation. Such a situation, Searles argues, impels the child to identify with his mother out of "genuine love and solicitude" and through his identification to introject her, with "disastrous results," namely, the kind of illness which one finds in Malte and in Rilke's letters about himself.

From the perspective offered us by Searles, Malte's experiences identification with the man suffering from St. Vitus' dance, with the medical student, with the stranger dying in the crémerie, with the patients in the hospital, and with the outcasts of Paris appear to be the result of unconscious transference in the poet-novelist for whom Malte is a surrogate. In psychoanalytic texts "transference" means "*displacement* of patterns of feeling and behavior, originally experienced with significant figures of one's childhood, to individuals in one's current relationships."[10] In Rilke's Parisian experiences and in his novel, this would include a redirecting of an inclination to identify with an emotionally ill and crippled mother to other needy persons.

In sum, Rilke's long-lasting flight from his mother, his loathing for her, and his efforts to separate himself from her may be seen as originating in a struggle against the consequences of the child's early love which he evokes in *The Notebooks*. Although there are good reasons for accepting Simenauer's argument concerning "the reaction formation" against oedipal feelings, this defense may be regarded as a secondary cause, a reinforcement of the poet's more deeply rooted negative feelings toward Phia. "Deeply" here signifies depth in the past, an earlier stage of development in the child's life. Searles's analysis leads to the conclusion that the resolution of the "Oedipus complex" cannot free someone from such an illness, in which oedipal feelings often play a comparatively unimportant role.

IV

Recurrently Rilke suggests Malte's identification with Maman. At times this has positive consequences: her storytelling and her fascination with lace play a role in shaping his inclination to be a poet, an artist. But other entries bring to mind Searles's argument concerning the origins of schizoid and schizophrenic illness.

At the end of her life Maman becomes "dominated by her fear of needles": " 'What a lot of needles there are, Malte; they are lying around everywhere . . . ' . . . [H]orror shook her at the thought of all the poorly fastened needles, which could fall down anywhere, at any moment" (85). Time and again in *The Notebooks* one finds echoes of Maman's fear of needles, direct and indirect, transparent and disguised, in Malte's anxieties. He describes the recovery of his childhood as the reemergence of "[a]ll the lost fears" (63). Among them are the "fear that a small woolen thread sticking out of the hem of my blanket may be hard, hard and sharp as a steel-needle . . . that this little button on my night shirt may be bigger than my head, bigger and heavier . . . that some number may begin to grow in my brain until there is no more room for it inside me" (63–64).

Such fantasies, like the fantasy of "the Big Thing," express displacement of feelings about the phallus, which grows hard like a needle and swells like a tumor. As everyone knows, the phallus has a will of its own. In a boy or a man it is a focus of sexual feelings which take over mind and body, until it seems that there is no room for anything else inside oneself. The fear of the phallus is closely related to the apprehension that one's sexuality may become uncontrollable and overwhelm one.

In part 2 of *The Notebooks,* where Malte's meditations on legendary and historical figures indirectly reflect his sense of his body, mind, and self and allow him to externalize and distance it, an entry expressing his fascination with Bosch's painting *Temptation of Saint Anthony,* or something very similar, plays with the tendency to find a willful, autonomous phallus in multifarious objects and with the almost irresistible power of sexual desire over body and mind:

How well I now understand those strange pictures in which Things meant for limited and ordinary uses stretch out and stroke one another, lewd and curious, quivering in the random lechery of distraction. Those kettles that walk around steaming, those pistons that start to think, and the indolent funnel that squeezes into a hole for its pleasure. . . .

And the saint writhes and pulls back into himself. . . . His prayer is already losing its leaves and stands up out of his mouth like a withered shrub. . . . His sex is once again in one place only, and when a woman comes toward him, upright through the huddle, with her naked bosom full of breasts, it points at her like a finger. (184–85)

Malte's fear of needles and "the Big Thing" and the other anxieties described in the passage quoted from pages 63 and 64 of *The Notebooks* suggest that he is drawn into his mother's fear of male sexuality. But Maman's fears, which become focused in the passage about the needles, obviously infect Malte in a more complex way. Her needle phobia is described in an entry which also tells us that toward the end of her life she did not want to see people and felt she could no longer digest food (84–85). Taken together, these memories of Maman reveal wide-ranging fears of penetration by objects and other persons, by anything outside the self. Such anxieties originate in childhood at a time preceding the focus on the genitals, when the boundaries of the body-self and the security they afford the individual are weak. If this weakness persists into adult years, it may encourage frightening fantasies of impingement and invasion such as the ones we have discovered in *The Notebooks* (see 73–74).

Searles observes that the mother whose psychic integration is precarious may unwittingly bind her child more closely to her by creating in him the sense that the world around them is a fearful place, full of dangers, so that he will continue to seek safety within the tight nexus of the symbiotic relationship, which the mother needs to preserve as a source of support and nurture for herself. As a result he may become closely identified with her in her anxieties.[1]

In *René Rilke: Die Jugend Rainer Maria Rilkes*, Sieber describes the ways in which both parents filled their small son's existence with their anxieties about the state of his health:

Fear that the youth might catch cold, that he might be exposed to a draft, that his bed was hard, that his glands were swollen, was the constant thought of his dear parents. ... Although the doctor found nothing, for the sake of prevention René had to gargle salt water three times a day, and when late in the evening, he traveled in a carriage, he was put on the floor of the coach and so tightly bundled up that only his head was exposed. In summer he had to lie on a rug in the garden so that he wouldn't catch cold.[2]

And we are told that Josef Rilke changed his son's nurses twenty-four times during the first year of René's life.[3]

Is it any wonder that the poet was beset by anxiety for much of his life and was particularly prey to fears about his health? In *The Restoration of the Self*, Kohut says that a mother's hypochondriacal reactions to a child's fears at an early stage of his life, when he is still closely identified with her, tend to become part of his mental existence, persisting as he grows older.[4] In contrast, closeness to a mentally healthier parent eventually permits internalization of his or her capacity for calming one's fears.

V

Malte's version of the end of Grishka Otrepyov, the false czar Dmitri, explicitly reveals the fantasy of the mother as a destroyer. It is clear that this episode obliquely refers to Malte and to Rilke. The poet explained to his Polish translator, Witold von Hulewicz, that the historical figures in part 2 of the novel may be seen as "the *vocabula* of [Malte's] distress" (*Letters* 2:371).

In 1606 this false czar, faced with an uprising led by Prince Shuisky and a number of boyars, summoned Maria Nagoi, the real Dmitri's mother, the seventh wife of the late czar, Ivan the Terrible, from her convent to Moscow. Dmitri had been killed mysteriously in 1591. The pretender wanted her to acknowledge that he, Grishka, was her son. Malte speculates, "[H]e believed in himself so strongly that he actually thought he was summoning his mother" (188–189). Maria Nagoi did what he wished, supporting his claim that he was the rightful successor to the throne. What makes this account of Grishka strangely interesting and revealing is Malte's fantasy about the czar's reaction to Maria's lie:

But the mother's declaration, even if it was a conscious deception, still had the power to diminish him; it lifted him out of this magnificent self that he had invented; it confined him to a tired imitation; it reduced him to the individual he wasn't; it made him an imposter. (189)

Malte has already asked himself if Grishka's uncertainty did not arise from Maria's confirming that he was her son. He answers his own question with the thought that "the strength of his transformation lay in his no longer being anybody's son" (189).

In the margin of the notebook he jots down his belief that all young men who left their families gain their strength from this sense of themselves. This marginal note connects Malte's conceptions of Grishka and the Prodigal Son. In Malte's mind, as in Rilke's, having a mother diminishes an individual, reduces him to someone he is not, "a tired imitation" of her image of him, an inauthentic person who cannot be "the magnificent self" he has it in him to create, hence, "an imposter."

After Grishka jumped from a window, fleeing Shuisky and the boyars, who invaded his palace, Maria Nagoi disavowed him. The effect of this disavowal at the moment of Grishka's ruin is the main point Malte focuses upon in the conclusion of his brief narrative: "you must be ready to swear that between voice [of the Tsarina Mother disavowing him] and pistol shot [which killed him], infinitely compressed, there was once again inside him the will and the power to be everything" (191). Freed from this mother and all mothers, Grishka felt, if only for a few moments, the freedom, power, and strength of will to avail himself once more of all the gifted creativity which had manifested itself in his remarkable conquest of the Russian throne. Implicitly, Grishka's realization that he was about to die makes this reawakening all the more remarkable in Malte's eyes and emphasizes the importance of the freedom from mothers, from parents, which is the main theme of Malte's interpretation of this moment in history.

One should not forget that Malte is Rilke's fantasy of a young man who is "no longer ... anybody's son." The deaths of his mother and father, as well as his having left home and having no home to return to, are essential elements of this fantasy.

CHAPTER 5

Take Me, Give Me Form, Finish Me
Lou Andreas-Salomé

I

"Now there is still time—" he writes, "now I am still soft, and I can be like wax in your hands. Take me, give me a form, finish me ... "
  It is a cry for motherliness.[1]

This is from the early autobiographical novella *Ewald Tragy.* Ewald is a transparent self-portrait of Rilke during 1896 and 1897, both before he left his family and native city, Prague, and after he settled in Munich and began to lead an independent life as an artist. If scholars are correct in their dating of the novella, Rilke began writing *Ewald Tragy* more than a year after he had attached himself to a woman who had generously responded to the need for mothering, forming, and finishing expressed in Ewald's "cry."[2] On May 12, 1897 in Munich he met Lou Andreas-Salomé, author of books on Nietzsche and Ibsen as well as several novels. The daughter of a Russian general and his German wife, Salomé was fourteen years older than the poet. She was married to Friedrich Carl Andreas, professor of Persian at the Berlin Institute for Oriental Languages, but had kept the marriage sexless.

Fifteen years before Rilke met her, in her early twenties, Lou had received a marriage proposal from Friedrich Nietzsche, who had thought her "sharp as an eagle and brave as a lion, yet a very girlish child." Nietzsche also called her "the *most intelligent of all women*," and told

his friend Overbeck, "Our mentalities and tastes are most deeply akin—
and yet there are so many contrasts too that we are for each other the
most instructive of subjects. . . . I should like to know whether there has
ever before been such philosophical openness as between the two of us."
Trying to reassure Lou that he was not interested in using her as a secretary, he wrote to her that he was looking for "heirs," "the finest, most
fertile soil" for that "something" "I carry . . . around with me absolutely
not to be read in my books."[3] Fiercely jealous and prudishly offended
by Salomé, the philosopher's sister, Elizabeth, did everything she could
to turn him against her. At the end of 1882, Lou went off to Berlin with
their mutual friend Paul Ree, and Nietzsche realized that he had lost her.
Deeply hurt and angry, influenced by his sister's vilifications of the girl,
he wrote in response to letters from Lou, that she was "giving free rein
to everything contemptible" in her nature, transforming her own "sacred
self-seeking" into "the predatory pleasure-lust of a cat." He described
her as "that scraggy, dirty, smelly she-monkey with her false breasts."[4]
But he came to regret his denunciations. In 1884 he wrote from Nice,
expressing his hope that Ree and Salomé would visit him and the wish
"to make amends for some of the evil things my sister did." Later he
said he thought Lou was "by far the *smartest* person I ever knew."[5] This
echoes the extraordinary assessment of the twenty-two year old Salomé
offered in a September 1882 letter from Nietzsche to Overbeck, at a time
when all was going well with her: "I have never known anyone who
could draw from their experiences so many *objective insights,* or anyone
who knew how to derive so much from everything they'd learnt."[6]

By the time she met Rilke, Salomé's studies of Ibsen and Nietzsche
and her extraordinary intelligence as an essayist and conversationalist had
earned her a widespread reputation among European intellectuals and
artists. She was to become, in 1912, a friend and disciple of Freud, who
wrote to her after reading her essay "Anal and Sexual," "Your incredible
subtlety of understanding as well as the greatness of your bent for syn-
thesizing what has come apart through investigation find beautiful
expression in it." The father of psychoanalysis also called her "My dear
inexhaustible friend," praised her for her "authenticity and harmony"
and her "modesty and discretion," and expressed gratitude for her comments on his essays and books ("You always give more than you
receive").[7]

Salomé's study of Rilke, written just after his death, makes idiosyncratic use of psychoanalytic ideas, mixing them with intuitions which are sometimes shrewd. She is now remembered primarily for her friendships with Nietzsche, Rilke, and Freud. But the publication of several biographies reflects continuing interest in her thinking and writing.[8] In his portrait of Salomé, Kurt Wolff measured her stature in terms which may be suspected of male condescension but which, nonetheless, clearly place her among the Olympians in the German world of letters: "No woman has radiated a stronger or more direct influence in German-speaking lands in the last 150 years."[9] As for her importance to Rilke, it can be summed up in his own words, addressed to the princess Marie in 1924: "my entire development without the influence of this exceptional woman . . . could never have been on the lines that have led to so many achievements." [10]

Having recently left his family and native city for Munich, Rilke, at twenty-one, was rapturous over this meeting with "the famous writer," as he wrote to his mother.[11] He had read Salomé's essay "Jesus the Jew" and been excited by its affinities of thought and feeling with his own poems *Visions of Christ*. He told her so in a letter sent after their first meeting, at the home of the novelist Jakob Wasserman, that evening in May 1897 which was to bring such a change in his life. Within less than a month they were lovers. In her posthumously published memoir, *A Look Back at Life (Lebensrückblick)*, she recalled her relationship with Rilke at this time as a unique experience in her long life. "If I belonged to you for some years it was because you represented absolute reality for me for the first time, body and person indistinguishably one and the same, an unquestionable element of life itself."[12] In retrospect she saw the young poet and herself at the time of their lovemaking as closer than husband and wife, "like brother and sister, but from primeval times before incest became sacrilege."[13]

From the beginning of their relationship Salomé offered a creative response to the young poet's appeal for a mother who would give him a form. Her maternal, shaping influence in those early days was reflected in the fact that she persuaded him to change his name from René to Rainer. Biographers have pointed to the noticeable change in his penmanship in the summer of 1897, from a careless, often almost illegible hand to the clear, elegant, graceful script he used for the rest of his life, as evidence of Salomé's influence. Leppmann notes the similarity between this script and Lou's.[14] Biographers have also argued that she was responsible for significant changes in the style of his work and was the source of many of his ideas. [15]

In saying that Lou Andreas-Salomé was a mother to Rilke, I am subscribing to their explicit, shared conception of the relationship. Obviously the difference of fourteen years between them shaped this conception. In the Florentine diary which he kept for her in 1898, at her suggestion, he wrote, "Once I came to you so very destitute, almost like a child did I come to you, the bountiful lady. And you took my soul in your arms and cradled it."[16] In a letter written during January 1904, after they had lived apart for years, Rilke calls himself "your somehow lost son" (*Letters* 1:140).

After Rilke's decision, in February 1901, to marry the sculptor Clara Westhoff, having decided to break off all contact with him, at least until some future time when he would be in dire need of her help, Salomé wrote to the poet, saying, "[A] final duty devolves on me out of the memory still dear to both of us that in Wolfratshausen I came to you as a mother. So let me tell you like a mother of the pledge I made to Zemek [her friend and lover Heinrich Pineles, a physician and a student of psychoanalysis] some years ago after a long talk." "Zemek" had pre dicted that Rilke, caught in the snares of emotional illness, might be inclined to commit suicide. In her sense of her "duty" as a mother, Salomé promised the poet, "[T]here is always refuge for you with us for the worst hour Pineles spoke of."[17] He was to turn to her for maternal succor and advice a number of times in the years that followed, from 1903, when he first took advantage of this promise, until the end of 1926, when he was dying.

A poem written about Salomé after their last talk in February 1901 describes her as "the most motherly of women." The poet calls her "the tenderest" person he has met and "the cruelest" one with whom he has struggled. She was "the height that blessed" him and "the chasm that devoured" him. The poem also expresses Rilke's fantasy that Salomé "clung" to him, as "the hand with the creator's power" clings to the clay which it shapes, and then, having grown weary, let him drop and smash to pieces:

II
Du schmiegtest Dich an mich, doch nicht zum Hohn,
nur so, wie die formende Hand sich schmiegt an den Ton,

Die hand mit des Schöpfers Gewalt.

. . . .

da wurde sie müde, da liess sie nach,
da liess sie mich fallen, und ich zerbrach.

III
Warst mir die mütterlichste der Frauen

. . . .

Du warst das Zarteste, das mir begegnet,
das Härteste warst Du, damit ich rang.
Du warst das Hohe, das mich gesegnet—
und wurdest der Abgrund, der mich verschlang.[18]

These lines bring us full cycle from the appeal for a mother who would take him, form him, and complete him, which we found in Ewald's letter. The fantasy that the powerful creator clung to the clay may reflect an accurate perception of ambivalence in Lou. But it also seems to express Rainer's clinging, unconsciously projected onto her, at a time when she was happy to see him go. The poem shows that Rilke's childlike sense of dependence on Salomé was closely connected with infantile fantasies of a mother that could destroy and devour her child. The fantasy of the mother who had the Creator's power to give form as well as a desire to cling to her creation, but who then, like a chasm, devoured him, surely did not originate in the relationship with Lou. The devouring chasm calls to mind the dining hall at Urnekloster, which threatens to suck Malte's mind and self out of him not long before the slim figure of a woman in a light dress, implicitly associated with Malte's dead Maman, terrifies the family at dinner.

Rilke did not publish the poems which he wrote for Salomé from May 1897 through May 1898, though he thought of them as having the collective title "Dir zur Feier" (A Festival for You).[19] They provide us with rich impressions of the young poet's feelings about her at this time. In one of these poems, asking Salomé to give him direction, Rilke says that after much suffering, he is now following her lead with blind steps:

Ich habe viel gelitten,
vieles starb and brach,—
jetzt geh ich mit blinden Schritten
deinem Leben nach.
(*Sämtliche Werke* 3:173)

I have suffered a great deal
died and broken often,—
now with blind steps
I follow your life.

In another poem, written for Salomé at this time, the phrase "Ich geh
dir nach" ("I follow you") echoes time and again. Out of his gloomy
cell he follows her with outstretched hands, in deep confidence, as out
of the horrors of fever frightened children go to bright women, who
soothe them and understand their fear. He does not ask where her heart
may be leading him:

Ich geh dir nach, wie aus der dumpfen Zelle
. . . .
Ich geh dir nach in tiefem Dirvertrauen.
Ich weiss deine Gestalt durch diese Auen
vor meinen ausgestreckten Händen gehn.
Ich geh dir nach, wie aus der Fiebers Grauen
erschreckte Kinder gehn zu lichten Frauen,
die sie besänftigen und Furcht verstehn.

Ich geh dir nach. Wohin dein Herz mich führe
frag ich nicht nach. . . .
(Sämtliche Werke 3:176)

In a third poem Rilke reflects that before meeting Salomé his blind
goal was to get away from the many people who play at life, while now
he knows that he was moving on a thousand paths toward her. He calls
her his deliverance, his salvation, saying that in feverish anxiety he cried
out to her and that in grateful recognition of her help his ripest thoughts
sank like children to their knees:

Nur fort von allen vielen,
welche das Leben spielen:
Das war mein blindes Zielen,
war ohne Sinn und Saum.
Jetzt weiss ich: Dir entgegen
trieb ich auf tausend Wegen
am Tage und im Traum.

Und du bist das Erlösen,
nach welchem ich in bösen,

bangen Fiebern schrie;
im Dicherkennen sanken
meine reisigen reifsten Gedanken
wie Kinder in die Knie.
(*Sämtliche Werke* 3:185)

Late in June 1903, after a breach of more than two years, Rilke wrote to
Salomé from Paris, saying that he was going to spend some time in Ger-
many and wanted to see her. She replied, suggesting that they first resume
contact by correspondence. Rilke's answer was the long letter largely
devoted to descriptions of his severe anxieties in Paris.

Imploring Salomé for help, Rilke wrote, "[Y]ou alone know who
I am. You can help me, and I feel already in your first letter the
power which your calm words have over me. You can clarify for me
what I don't understand, you can tell me what I shall do; you know
what I must fear and what I need not fear—: must I be afraid? ...
every word from you means a great deal to me and vibrates and lives
a long time for me."[20] In this response to Lou's offer to correspond
with him, he seems to have sunk back into infantile dependence on
this highly idealized mother figure. But important advances from the
old relationship soon became apparent: Salomé recognized not only
the familiar signs of anguish, illness, and infantile dependence which
had caused her to try to detach and distance herself from Rilke in
1900 and 1901 but also the maturing strength of a gifted writer. She
realized that she could play an active part, from a distance, in encouraging and shaping his work.

In 1903 and 1904, at times when he was deeply troubled and full of
self-doubt, Salomé encouraged his self-confidence with repeated affir-
mations of his gifts as a writer and a thinker. He trusted her judgment
completely. Her effect on Rilke at this time can be seen by comparing
two successive letters which the poet sent her in August 1903. In the
first, written on August 8, he laments, "[T]here is nothing real about me;
and I divide again and again and flow apart." In his next letter, written
two days later, after he had received Salomé's response to his book on
Rodin, he says, "Nothing could fill me so with certainty and with hope
as this yea-saying of yours to the most full-grown of my works. Now
for the first time it *stands* for me, now for the first time it is completed,
acknowledged by reality, upright and good" (*Letters* 1:122–23).

Read together, the two letters suggest that Salomé's enthusiasm about his Rodin book, her assurance that it "[meant] much" to her, gave him a sense of his own "reality" and value. Her response to the new work glowed with loving praise. She called it "great in a thousand respects" and told him that it was "the dearest of all your published books."[21]

On July 22 of the same year Salomé had sent the poet her reaction to his accounts of the frightening experiences he had endured in Paris, telling him that he had misunderstood himself in thinking that he had been helpless in the grip of his anxieties. It seemed to her that he had given these things a new existence in his prose, through a "higher" mental process of artistic transformation. That was very different from mere passive suffering. Now that she had read his portrayals of his "fears," they existed in her mind as well and had an independent living reality, like all fine works of art.[22]

She sensed that he had become capable of going through such experiences without being alienated from himself. As the younger man she remembered all too well, he would have described someone suffering from St. Vitus' dance in a soulful, densely metaphoric, conventional language, defensively distancing himself from the victim. His portrait of the St. Vitus dancer in the July letter had an authenticity that was new in his writing. Although he had felt identified with the other man in his agony, his portrait revealed a fine artist's clarity of insight. His ability to empathize with the human subjects of his art and, at the same time, to observe them sharply, had made it possible for the artist in him to resurrect the *misérables* who suffered helplessly and without much comprehension. This was the gist of her argument against his belief that he was in danger of losing himself, as it seemed many of the Parisians he encountered had done.[23]

Salomé tried to put to rest his belief that that there was "nothing real about" him and the fantasy that he had "been pressed out of the world in which all is familiar and near and meaningful, into another uncertain, nameless, fearful environment," as if he were completely alien, "like one who has died in strange lands, alone, superfluous, a fragment of another unity." He felt he was lost there in the other world, unable to approach anybody in this one. Suspended in fear over an abyss of nothingness, he found nothing to hold fast to. As he looked around for something solid to grasp, everything grew distant, gave him up, moved away. In danger of losing all contact with the reality of this world, he thought that he might be lost forever, in unreality, in madness.

In November 1903 he wrote to Salomé about closely related fantasies and feelings, saying that he could not become real ("wirklichwerden"), that there were always things and events which, having more actuality and presence than he did, went right through him as if he did not exist. The house which he had built in Westerwede and his little family had not made him more tangibly present to himself, as he had hoped they would. That house and everything in it had seemed alien to him. Even having a daughter (who lived far away from him most of the time) did not help him now to attain to the vital feeling of his own existence ("Wirklichkeitsgefühl") which he longed for, the sense of being someone real in a real world ("Wirklicher unter Wirklichem zu sein").[24]

Turning this self-assessment on its head, Salomé argued that his fears and the frightening experiences in Paris had become part of the most genuine reality ("Wirklichste") now growing within him as germinating seeds of his genius, of his future work. She drew this conclusion from the strength of his recent writing. The extraordinary nature of his gifts as an artist had become apparent in the Rodin book and in the letters about the experiences in Paris. Despite his doubts about his mental condition, in her view he had never before been so close to mental health as he was now.[25]

Her praise of the Rodin book and her response to Rilke's account of his near-madness in Paris almost surely helped to give him the strength to resist his fears and the confidence to work. We have noticed how his mood changed when he received the letter she sent him after reading his study of the sculptor. No doubt, Salomé's encouragement provided impetus the following February, when Rilke started working on *The Notebooks of Malte Laurids Brigge* without knowing what it would turn out to be. At the beginning of August 1903 Salomé promised the poet that henceforth he could rely upon her.[26]

II

The letters Salomé sent Rilke in the summer of 1903 show that she fulfilled for him something like the mirroring function which a benevolent mother performs for a young child. Kohut defines one type of psychotherapeutic transference as a "reinstatement" of a phase of the self's development "in which the gleam in the mother's eye, which mirrors the child's exhibitionistic display," confirms "the child's self-esteem."[1] By mirroring (in this sense of the metaphor) Rilke's "exhibitionistic display" in the Rodin book and in his powerfully evocative accounts of his Paris experiences, Salomé enabled him to satisfy the childlike "need to confirm the reality of the self" which he revealed in his letters.[2] Rilke had sought this kind of mirroring from Salomé with his gifts of poems and the diary which he had kept for her in Italy in the spring of 1898.

The poet's reaction to Salomé's empathetic responsiveness resembles the reactions of Kohut's patients when he attempted to give them the maternal mirroring whose absence or dearth in infancy and early childhood had crippled them emotionally and made them ill. The illness which he describes closely resembles the illness which Rilke portrays in his letters to Salomé and in *The Notebooks.*

Kohut observes that at first a good mother ardently mirrors her infant's narcissistic grandiosity. Then, gradually and sensitively, she frustrates his demand for this response and thus slowly tames his grandiosity, directing the energies fostered by self-esteem and self-love toward more realistic goals and achievements. But he notes that in highly talented men and women the survival of primitive grandiosity may provide the high octane of motivating energy necessary for achievements commensurate with their gifts. By strongly encouraging a heightening of self-esteem in Rilke, Salomé's empathetic responses to the poet's need for a mirroring mother helped to liberate the energy and to nurture the ambition which made possible his major works, beginning with *The Book of Hours.* These poems were dedicated to her with the words "Placed in the Hands of Lou" ("Gelegt in die Hände von Lou").

Naked expressions of primitive grandiosity appear in Rilke's early diaries. In an entry written at Zoppot on the Baltic in July 1898, Rilke sees artists as precursors of a godlike, all-powerful, solitary Creator who will understand that all things which have appeared to be outside him "have been merely symbols of those realities which he finds in himself. Everything has flowed together in him, and all powers, which, formerly scattered, opposed one another, tremble under his will. . . . He no longer prays. He is. And when he makes a gesture, he will create . . . many millions of worlds."[3] The young poet who wrote this identified the all-powerful solitary whom he envisioned in the future with himself, though he may not have been clearly conscious of this identification.

Reading the diary written in Italy at Zoppot, Lou failed to show the admiration Rilke had been been expecting. She received his display of intelligence and style with indulgence, forbearance, and condescending generosity, Her too obvious endeavor to give him courage had the opposite effect. His reaction was shame and anger.[4] Then, in his need to rebuild his shattered grandiosity, he developed the argument that artists of his own time were "ancestors" and foreshadowings of the divine, solitary Creator in the future, possibly modeled on Nietzsche's *Übermensch*. One of his letters to a young poet would echo the central theme of this passage, but that letter, written six years later, would emphasize the distance between the divine Creator toward whom creative artists were developing and the artists themselves: "Why do you not think of him as the coming one, imminent from all eternity, the future one, the final fruit of a tree whose leaves we are? ... As the bees bring in the honey, so do we fetch the sweetest out of everything and build Him."[5]

Some of the poems in *The Book of Hours* also reveal the young Rilke's grandiose sense of self. In the following lines, addressed to the Deity, the poet imagines himself as God's dream and His will. He claims mastery of "all grandeur," picturing himself curving "like a starry stillness/ over the strange city of time."

> Wenn du der Träumer bist, bin ich dein Traum.
> Doch wenn du wachen willst, bin ich dein Wille
> und werde mächtig aller Herrlichkeit
> und ründe mich wie eine Sternenstille
> über der wunderlichen Stadt der Zeit.
> (*WDB* 1:20)

A number of Rilke's letters to Salomé reveal in fairly precise terms what her maternal mirroring meant to him when their relationship resumed in the summer of 1903, after a breach of more than two years. Although Salomé had revolted against his infantile demands, his dependence, his bouts of neurotic anxiety in earlier years, the poet was effusive in his praise of her unique capacity for empathetic responsiveness. Despite his growth as a person and as a poet, in 1903–4 he still felt deeply dependent on her willingness to function as a maternal mirror for him. In January 1904 he wrote to say that "every path" he took could become meaningful through his return to a woman who "knows how to hear everything."

Even if he cannot speak to her in person, the thought that in his letters she can hear him gives him the feeling that he exists, that he is alive. In the same letter he expresses his belief that only her highly intelligent and empathetic "listening" to his accounts of his life in these letters can give him the sense that his existence has vital significance and vibrancy. "If my life is insignificant . . . it will *be* only when I can tell it to you." Her hearing him and her responsiveness will shape its meaning. It "will be as you hear it!" he concludes (*Letters* 1:140).

As he writes her about his daily life in his letters, just the fact that he is telling her about it and the belief that she is listening, with all her intelligence and her knowledge and understanding of him, bring order and meaning into the noise and confusion of which he has not been able to make sense. Obviously her recent letters allowed him the fantasy of her maternal presence. This must substitute for the maternal face in which the child finds confirmation of his existence and worthiness and then often finds, as well, silent intimations of who and what he is, intimations of the meaning and value of what he is doing, uttering, and experiencing. In the mother's absence the child, of course, comes to rely on memory images of her. But Salomé was speaking to her "lost son" through her letters. No doubt, despite her long absence, he could hear her voice creating a refuge from the chaotic noise around him.

Rilke's fantasy of his potential power as a writer involved an image of Salomé's receptive listening. He saw his mouth "become a great river" flowing "into your hearing and into the stillness of your opened depths" (*Letters* 1:140). The "displacement upward" is rather obvious. The fantasy fuses creative utterance with a sexual act. For Rilke, several years after their love affair had ended, writing prose and poetry was associated with making love to Lou. The displacement suggests a desire to return to their love-making and an awareness that it could be retrieved only in a sublimated form.

In this passage he does not see himself merely as the needy child (dependent on her listening), but also as powerful, aggressive, giving. In the Zoppot diary entry, he recalls that he had come to Salomé "[a]lmost as a child . . . to a rich woman. And you took my soul in your arms and cradled it." He adds, "Then you kissed me on the forehead, and you had to bend low." But since then, he says, he has grown, so that there is a shorter distance from her eyes to his. He asks her if she understands that, and says that he wants to bend down to her lips, as her soul once bent to his brow. He wants her to be able to lean on him, if she is weary. He no longer wants to feel her comforting him; instead, he needs to be confident of the power that he would have in himself to comfort her, if she needed to be comforted. In bringing her his Florentine diary he had wanted to be the rich one, the one who gave, the master, and he had hoped that she would be guided by his care and love and would indulge herself in his "hospitality."[6]

Returning to her from his sojourn in Italy, he had assumed that he had traveled a great distance and, with his diaries, had risen "to the peak" of imaginative perception and thought. But at Zoppot she flew over his insights with ease and was far above and ahead of him intellectually. He imagined her waiting in clarity and "radiance" beyond his still cloudy altitude.[7]

Her indulgence and forbearance, her condescending kindness, and her flights of intellect made him feel like a beggar on the outermost peripheries of her existence, deeply humiliated. He felt that he had become ridiculous in his "masquerade"; "the dark wish awakened in me to creep away into a deep nowhere. . . . Every reunion made me feel ashamed. I was always saying to myself: 'I can give nothing to you, nothing at all.' "[8]

Paradoxically, the Zoppot entry reveals the poet's need to have this mother affirm his independent strength and creativity, and, in particular, his ability to support and sustain her and to give her intellectual and imaginative work which she can value and esteem. His reaction to her failure to do this shows that he is not in the least independent of her, though he needs to feel free and powerful and male. Her failure to collaborate with his "masquerade" plunges him into uncertainty and despair. He feels that he has lost or cast away all his riches and is miserably poor. Above all, he feels a desperate need to escape the degrading encirclement of her goodness.[9] While it expresses infantile dependence and vulnerability, this entry also brings to mind an adolescent's humiliation and anger over his dependence on a powerful mother, whose benevolence he cannot, but badly needs to, escape.

Reading the correspondence between Rilke and Salomé, I am struck by the fact that so many of his letters show *comparatively* little interest in her life, though he is eager to have her response to his accounts of his own experience. (I should emphasize the word *comparatively*, because at times he does show interest and concern; but these times are the exceptions.) More often than not her letters focus upon *his* experience, thought, and work.

In 1900 Rilke's narcissism and egocentrism, combined with his high anxiety and smothering dependence on Lou, impelled her to try to distance him. She was especially put off by his behavior in the summer of 1900. After they traveled in Russia together, she left him to spend several weeks with her brother and his family in Finland. The poet wrote her an anguished letter out of his loneliness, appealing to her to hurry back to him, emphasizing his anxiety in her absence and his preoccupation with the prospect of her return.[10]

Years later, recalling his response to her brief absence, she remembered that he had seemed almost depraved in the arrogance and presumption of his importunities. The fact that she might be having a lovely reunion in Finland with her brother and his family had mattered not at all to Rainer in his infantile need of her. The memory of Rilke's extreme egocentrism and anxiety at that time brought back the strength of her own reaction, her need to be free of him.[11]

Despite Rilke's greater maturity in 1903, his letters to Salomé then and in 1904 continue to approximate what Alice Balint labels the "naive egoism" of a child's love for a mother. Balint is describing "an archaic, egotistic way of loving, originally directed exclusively to the mother," and characterized above all by "the . . . lack of reality sense in regard to the [libidinal and ego] interests of the love object." The "fundamental condition" of such "archaic love" is the child's assumption of "the complete harmony of interests" between his mother and himself.[12]

Obviously, Salomé's strength of mind and will prevented the young poet from losing all sense of her separate needs even during the early years of their relationship. But he was much inclined to see her largely in terms of an identity of interests. His attitude toward her calls to mind the blindness of which he accused Phia. No doubt, the attitude was rooted in close identification, at an early age, with his narcissistic, egocentric mother. Eventually the egocentrism which grew out of this identification must have been reinforced by the need to fence out Phia's separate needs and interests in order to defend himself, in his dependence, against Phia's desire for separateness and distance. No doubt, the tendency to fence, if not wall, out Lou's separate life originated also in the poet's need to defend himself against Phia's destructive, alien preconception of him. Furious with both women for their inclination to separate themselves from him and for their egoism, he denigrated his mother's life and interests and, to a large extent, refused to give mental space and energy to Salomé's, while at the same time idealizing and overestimating her. In his letters to Lou, the fury, the hostility, had to be repressed; the idealization dominated conscious thought.

Michael Balint suggests that naive, infantile, egoistic love in adults reflects a desire to recover the primary "ego-object identity." The fantasy of complete fusion with the mother may be transferred to a maternal figure, such as Salomé, with whom Rilke longed for "final unity."[13] Alice Balint argues that all of us (some far more than others, of course) continue, throughout our lives, to retain the "naive egotistic attitude" toward mothers, the expectation that "the interests of the mother and child are identical," with the result that "one hates the mother [as Rilke loathed Phia] because she is no longer what she used to be." Such hatred for the maternal therapist in psychoanalytic transference reveals "the preservation of the attachment but with a negative sign."[14] Psychoanalytic transference reflects the fact that an adult in whom this primitive attachment remains strong often seeks a perfect surrogate. When, almost inevitably, any such surrogate fails to maintain the harmony demanded by naive, archaic, infantile egoism, she is likely to reawaken the hatred originally felt for the mother. When Mother Lou failed to give the required response to the Florentine diary presented to her at Zoppot in the summer of 1898, Rilke wrote in his dairy, "I hated you as something *too big*."[15]

Quickly the young poet's hatred yielded to his earlier idealization of Salomé as the embodiment and image of all the goals he was striving toward. His need of her was so strong that he could not break away. Shattered by her failure to continue to give him the mirroring gleam, by her unwillingness to provide a joyful affirmation of his grandiose conception of what he had done, in his despair and his poverty he felt all the more intensely dependent. "But then, in this state of shock, I became aware . . . that all motion in me wants to go to you." Several paragraphs later he reflects that she is not one goal for him, but a thousand. She is everything, and he knows her in everything.[16]

Eventually, Rilke's dependence, along with his narcissism, volatility, and anxiety, made Salomé want to send him packing. But this did not happen until more than two years after their meeting at Zoppot. The high points of the relationship during those two years were their trips to Russia together in the spring of 1899 and the spring of 1900. They spent months together preparing for these trips, studying Russian history and culture. These two journeys were among the poet's most memorable and pleasurable experiences. I have described their visits to Tolstoy. They were welcomed by aristocracy, artists, intelligentsia, and peasants, including a peasant poet, S. D. Drozhzhin. Like Salomé, Rilke was deeply moved by the religious devotion of the people. Their first Russian Easter, the ringing of the bells and the joyous responses of the masses of celebrants at the news of Christ's resurrection, left memories which remained vibrant for years. Rilke's impressions of the Russian idea of God became a central theme of *The Book of Hours.* Writing to the painter Leonid Pasternak (father of Boris) a quarter of a century later, Rilke said that Russia was "forever embedded in the foundations of my life."[17] His thinking and feeling about this adopted spiritual "homeland," which he never again visited, were inseparable from his attachment to Salomé.

Their second trip ended with her leaving him in St. Petersburg, while she journeyed to Finland to see her brother and his family. Her absence set off the fit of anxiety which I have described above. He sent her the letter begging her to return to him, then apologized in a second letter. Reading his first letter, she recalled earlier times when he had been deeply disturbed, plagued by fears, and childishly dependent on her for maternal support, and this made her think of putting distance between the two of them. But even before this episode, while they were traveling through Russia together, thinking that she would like to have some time away from him after their trip, she had persuaded him to accept an invitation from Heinrich Vogeler, a young painter, book illustrator, and designer whom Rilke had visited in his home at Worpswede, near Bremen, for Christmas in 1898.

Salomé was delighted when he went off to Worpswede at the end of August 1900. Rilke was soon spending much of his time with members of the artists' colony there, especially two attractive young women: the painter Paula Becker, whose work was to earn her lasting distinction, and the sculptor Clara Westhoff, whose work had been critiqued by Rodin when she attended his school in Paris the year before. He was to marry Clara the following spring. On October 5 he left Worpswede to return to Berlin and Schmargendorf, where he resumed his Russian studies with Salomé. But fairly soon he must have realized that she no longer wanted their old intimacy. On October 18 he began to write glowing letters to

Clara and Paula, and he continued to do so during the rest of the fall, though his letters to Paula were affected by the news of her engagement to the painter, Otto Modersohn. During that fall and winter Salomé's determination to get rid of Rilke apparently intensified, to the point where, on January 20, 1901, she was writing in her diary, "Outside rainy weather. Let R. go away with it, *far* away. ... "[18]

In mid-December, probably because he sensed that she would no longer play the part of the benevolent mother for him, Rilke was plunged into a depression, which he described at length in his diary, recording that he felt buried, hopeless, frightened at everything that was happening around him, confused, and sometimes insane.[19]

Salomé's rejection of the poet must have brought back with great force the anguish which had followed his mother's withdrawal. It must also have swept away the defenses which Salomé had helped him to build against that trauma at the center of his psychic life. Or, to use Rilke's own metaphor, it tore wide open again the wound that ran all through him and his life, the wound which the relationship with Lou had been helping to heal.

After the resumption of the friendship by way of correspondence in 1903 Lou's letters show a sober, well-considered enthusiasm for his writing, which must have pleased him more than any reaction he had dreamed of winning from her at Zoppot in 1898. In January 1904 he imagined that he would become a great river which might flow into her, a sign of his new confidence that he had successfully attained the right to the powerful, penetrating, and giving masculine role in their relationship, the role which he had longed for in bitter frustration at Zoppot.

Yet this letter also expresses his feeling that his power as a writer and a poet is dependent upon her maternal mirroring, her empathetic hearing, her capacity for "stillness" so that nothing, in particular no egocentric interest of her own, may distract her as she listens to him. His grandiose, infantile narcissism dreams of maternal silence as the most perfectly attuned and receptive response (*Letters* 1:140). In April 1904, after the shock of a meeting with his disconnected mother in Rome had made him feel like "a convalescent ... weightless, tottering," Rilke wrote to Salomé to say, "A help it would be to talk to you ... and to see you listening and keeping silent ... " (*Letters* 1:147 and 149). Such receptive silence would defend him against the threat of her egotism, reinforced by a powerful intellect, which had shattered him at Zoppot six years before.

Deprived of the opportunity to talk with her, he finds that just writing his letters gives him the feeling of having a "refuge" in her. His mother makes him feel that he shares her unreality and disconnectedness, whenever he sees her. In contrast, even a dream of Salomé is "more real than all daily reality" and has the power to restore his sense of his own reality and cohesion. Her "presence," created by the dream, "makes me peaceful, patient, and good" (*Letters* 1:146).

Psychological theory would suggest that Rilke's sense of his own unreality arose at least partly from early identification with a mother he felt was ghostly and from the inadequacy of her responsiveness to him as a child, her inability or unwillingness to make him feel that he was physically and mentally and emotionally there for her by the ways in which she saw him, listened, touched, and talked to him. A good mother enables her child to experience the world around him as having a comparatively stable and dependable reality. Like the protector who comes to the frightened child at night in *The Notebooks* and the Third Elegy, she gives form to the chaos around him by her reactions to it, by explaining it to him, by helping him distinguish illusion from objective reality. Selfabsorbed in illusions, pretensions, and narcissistic religiosity, Phia apparently failed to do this for her son. The consequences of her failure may be found in the letters and *The Notebooks*.

Rilke's letters to Lou reveal that during his twenties he found in her a mother who could shape his experience of the world and make it real for him. Reading them, one can see that she may have been a model for the mother in *The Notebooks* and the Third Elegy, who confers solidity, form, and benevolence on the chaotic, frightening darkness. In November 1903 Rilke wrote saying,

[T]he experience of formlessness, which, at that time, seized me in a hundred places at once, that was ended by the inexpressible reality which you were. . . . [Y]ou bore witness to the existence of all things you [touched] . . . and [saw]. The world lost its cloudiness for me, this fluid taking and abandoning of form, which was my first verse and poverty; things emerged, animals, one distinguished, flowers. . . . And all this happened, because I was permitted to meet you . . . when I was . . . in danger of dissolving into formlessness. . . . In Paris, . . . when all things drew back from me, as if from a man gone blind, when I trembled with fear that I would no longer recognize the face of the person closest to me, then I healed myself with the thought that I still recognized you within myself, that your image had not become strange to me ... but had remained standing alone in the alien void in which I had to live.[20]

III

In essential respects the two mothers—Phia and Salomé—are diametrically opposed in Rilke's mind. He could not convey to Phia "the least thing that is real for [or about] me," for she saw him in the mirror of her preconceptions. When she looked at him, he felt the gap in her perceptions as a hole, a void, in himself. Her blindness tore him down. When he felt that he was disintegrating or feared that he had become emotionally dead and his imagination barren, he appealed to Salomé for help. Her answers gave him a sense of clarity and confidence. "You are so wonderfully right. ... the way you feel it [the anguish he has described to her in an earlier letter] and clarify it with your great knowledge of the human: you prophetess" (*Letters* 1:123).

Most biographers agree that Rilke probably never underwent analysis or that, if he did, it was for a very brief time. He said that expelling his devils might well mean expelling his angels. He did not want some analyst bringing the mysterious processes and contents of the unconscious to light before the poems germinating there were ready to be born and subjecting them to alien systems of classification before they arranged themselves, and were re-formed by him in his poetry and prose (see *Letters* 2:44–45).

But Salomé became an unofficial, informal, geographically distant mother-therapist, as their correspondence continued both the transference (projection of maternal images upon her, displacement of feelings for a mother to her) and the insights which he would not seek in an official, formal relationship with a psychoanalyst such as her friend Gebsattel.

As he turned to her for help again early in the summer of 1903, after a breach of more than two years, Rilke's letters showed the infantile nature of what Kohut might have called his "idealizing transference." His language calls to mind Kohut's observations about patients prevented in childhood, by a parent's traumatic withdrawal, from going through

the normal gradual process of shrinking that parent down to fairly realistic dimensions while internalizing his or her power to calm anxiety,
to clarify, and to give guidance. Never having adequately internalized
such maternal and paternal functions, these patients continued to seek
surrogates whom they could idealize and invest with the great power to
perform them which infants and small children attribute to their parents.
"[Y]ou alone know who I am. You can help me, and I feel . . . in your
first letter the power which your calm words have over me. You can
clarify for me what I don't understand, you can tell me what I shall do;
you know what I must fear and what I need not fear—: must I be afraid?
. . . every word from you means a great deal to me and vibrates and lives
a long time for me."[1]

Two main foci of Rilke's thought were an egocentric, destructive
mother and one who was idealized, all-seeing, life-giving, life-preserving.
He distanced them from each other as much as he could in his imagination, though sometimes his early love for Phia broke through his defenses, and sometimes he hated Lou and saw her as a destroyer. Such
splitting, such polarities suggest a need to isolate the love for a parent
from hatred and fear. The ego may be too weak or immature to sustain
ambivalence. Or, perhaps, as in Rilke, the negative feelings are so strong
and fierce that they must be isolated from the positive emotions in order
to sustain the child's sense of having a good, benevolent, protective
mother, to preserve his belief that he is loved, to defend him against fear
and guilt.

The fact that such splitting and extreme polarization may be found in
work of great genius makes me reluctant to see these phenomena simply
as signs of ego weakness or immaturity. *King Lear* and *Hamlet* exemplify
this tendency in Shakespeare's work. In *King Lear* the playwright himself
polarizes good and evil daughters and sons. In *Hamlet,* although the
prince sees Claudius, his uncle and stepfather, and the dead king, his
father, as extreme opposites, Shakespeare has the ghost of old King Hamlet acknowledge that he has been sinful, and Claudius is given some
redeeming qualities. To some extent, in other words, the playwright qualifies Hamlet's polarizing of these two fathers. In both plays the splitting
and polarizing calls to mind the small child's and the adolescent's tendency to divide parents and parental figures into good and evil, benevolent and destructive, protective and frightening, and the child's
comparative incapacity for ambivalence. In *Hamlet,* as psychoanalytic

criticism has shown, the splitting and polarizing enable the prince and the audience to isolate hatred and the desire to kill a father from love and idealization of a father: hateful Claudius is so distanced from the ghost of the dead king that neither Hamlet nor the audience consciously associates the two, though they are brothers, husbands of Hamlet's mother, and rulers of Denmark. In this way Hamlet and the audience, insofar as they identify with him, can defend themselves against the guilt arising from unconscious negative feelings (the desire to kill the father and possess the mother) and against the fear of a vengeful, punishing parent.

In Rilke the mind's maneuvering took another course, because it was guided by other motives. The memory or fantasy that his mother had withdrawn from him and eventually abandoned him for a time made him see her as hateful, a destroyer. He defended himself against Phia and from his loathing for her, his fear and despair, by devoting a great deal of energy to creating her opposite in Salomé. Having done so, he immersed himself in his love for Lou, returning to her with devotion unabated after the breach of more than two years and sustaining his idealization of her as a saving, all-knowing, benevolent mother for most of his life, though she successfully managed to avoid seeing him after their break in February 1901, except on a few occasions. The fact that when they parted in February 1901 she left the door open to him, should he really need her, and the extraordinary generosity of her response when he took advantage of this offer in 1903, obviously strengthened his inclination to maintain the polarization of these two maternal figures. He used this maneuver and Salomé's renewed willingness to collaborate with him to provide himself with a sense of maternal love strong enough to heal, at least temporarily, the self-doubt, the sense of unreality and vulnerability with which, he felt, Phia had infected him, and to defend himself against the maternal destroyer he feared he had within him.

For many years Rilke thought of himself as a traveler seeking a home and a mother (the two were associated in his mind; see *Letters* 1:46). Early in the summer of 1903, deeply disturbed and depressed, he imagined Salomé holding in her hands all the experiences which, if he had been stronger, he might have transformed into the work that would have been a home to him (see *Letters* 1:116). Six months later, in January 1904, he wrote to Lou about an ancient mural he had seen in a Paris art dealer's shop, implicitly identifying himself with the traveler in the painting and her with the woman listening as the traveler spoke both to himself and to her. The woman in the mural seemed "home-filled." Given the refuge she offered, the traveler would find "a final unity that was slowly closing like a healing wound" (*Letters* 1:139–40). In the same letter his mouth, his song, his being flow into the "stillness" of Lou's maternal "depths."

"To Lou Andreas-Salomé," a poem written in the autumn of 1911, reaffirms and develops his conception of the kind of shelter he can find in her. Only when his face has sunk into Lou is it not exposed; it grows into her and together with her, as it "settles darkly,/ infinitely [farther] into [her] protected heart."

> ... Ach nur zu dir gestürzt,
> ist mein Gesicht nicht ausgestellt, verwächst
> in dich und setzt sich dunkel
> unendlich fort in dein geschütztes Herz.
> (*WDB* 2:39)

The home to which the poet longs to return, which will guard him against exposure, is the heart or the womb of this mother. To grow into her "depths," her protected and protecting heart and womb, would be to retrieve the original unity of mother and child "in a final unity," so that the "wound" of division between them could close and heal. Not exposed, completely defended, his face would continue to grow, as would the self and the work which he was building.

CHAPTER 6

To Fill All the Rooms of Your Soul
Clara Rilke

I

If Rilke was unhappy about his separation from Salomé in September 1900, his diaries do not show it. Soon after his arrival in the artists' community at Worpswede, he became infatuated with two young women: the painter Paula Becker and her friend, the sculptor Clara Westhoff. Paula was close to him in age, Clara almost three years younger. In his diary he noted that the painter's hair was golden. He compared her voice to silk.[1] Her eyes seemed to unfold "like double roses."[2] His diary is full of their times together, images of Paula, and intimations of platonic intimacy but it shows no interest in her work. When he wrote his monograph about the Worpswede artists (1902), Rilke left her out of it. Not until years later, when he saw Becker's paintings at Christmas in 1905, did he discover that she was a gifted, highly original artist. But during those heady days of September 1900, he must have sensed the imaginative responsiveness which eventually helped to make her an extraordinary painter. "In her joyful brown eyes" he saw "much of the agitated, shifting land to which [he] had turned [his] back, and also every feeling which connected her to this land."[3] When he returned to Berlin at the beginning of October 1900, he left a notebook full of poems for her, and continued to send her poems in the weeks that followed.

On October 28 the news of Becker's engagement to the Worpswede painter Otto Modersohn was announced. In mid-November she wrote to the poet to tell him about her love for Modersohn. There is no clear evidence that Rilke had made a decisive choice between Paula Becker and Clara Westhoff before receiving this letter. Biographers have speculated that his abrupt departure from Worpswede on October 5 may have been motivated by his realization, while spending the previous evening with her, that Becker would not have him. And they have wondered if the despair expressed in his December diary entries may have come from the loss of Paula.[4] But no one really knows.

The diaries the poet kept at Worpswede and the letters which he began to send to Becker and Westhoff on October 18, two weeks after returning to Berlin-Schmargendorf, show an equally lively interest in Westhoff, whom he married on April 28 of the following year. If he was much taken with Paula's eyes, what struck him about Clara was the sculptor's strength in her hands and her gifts as a vivid storyteller. These gifts were evident in her account of her sojourn with a family from Bremen while she was living in France: a deaf mother, whose attempts to communicate seem powerfully self-expressive as they come to us through Rilke's rendering of Clara's narrative; the woman's embittered daughter; her contemptuous son—all estranged and distanced from one another in the small house at Joinville, where Clara had hoped to find refuge from the noisy, bewildering disorder of Paris. Fascinated with the storyteller and her tale, Rainer made a detailed record of it in his diary.[5] The fact that Clara had studied in Rodin's school and received instruction from the master must have interested him. He was attracted by her "fine dark face." At a gathering she seemed "mistress among us." Everything in the room adapted itself to her good taste.[6]

When he first met them in Worpswede, Clara and Paula appealed to him as "*Mädchen*," as virginal women. In his diaries he described Paula as "delicate and slim in her white maidenliness."[7] Delighting in their apparent innocence and simplicity, he also found in them the developing intelligence of young artists working hard at learning to see the world around them. As artists they were "half-knowing," and as "girls" "half-unaware": "the artist in them takes control and looks and looks, and if it is deep enough in its looking, they are again at the limit of their being and their capacity for wonder and slip gently back into their girlish simplicity."[8]

They brought back to mind the "Lieder der Mädchen" which he had written probably in the spring and early summer of 1898,[9] and they inspired "Von den Mädchen."[10] In these two latter poems, written in September 1900 soon after Rilke met Paula and Clara, he imagines that poets learn from maidens to *say* in their poems what the young women express in their existence: "Mädchen, Dichter sind, die von euch lernen/ das zu *sagen,* was ihr einsam *seid.*"[11]

A true poet can think of the women who inspire him only as "Mädchen." Hearing the two young women in the distance among people whom he avoids, he feels that their participation in the merriment of these tiresome acquaintances threatens their virginal beauty. He is miserable at the thought that they are happy to let themselves be looked over by men who are attracted to "the woman" in them.

The poet who wrote "Von den Mädchen" had enjoyed a passionate love affair with Lou Andreas-Salomé. No doubt, Rilke's fascination with the virginal qualities of Clara and Paula was intensified by the recent deterioration of his relationship with a lover who was also a surrogate mother, by a need to distance himself from the mix of incestuous desire and childish dependence which had not lost its hold on him.

If Rilke now turned to these young women, rejoicing in their virginal beauty, it must have been out of a desire to avoid the anxiety, painful humiliation, and shame associated with that old love. Perhaps he feared the complications and the entanglement which had come with the sexual relationship and also the kind of power that his passion for Lou had given her over him. When he became attached to Clara and Paula, he was suffering once again from a deeply wounding rejection by a mother, and this may have encouraged his veering away from the search for another older woman, another surrogate.

"Von den Mädchen," anticipates a passage in *The Notebooks.* Having watched some girls drawing the unicorn tapestries in the Cluny Museum in Paris, Malte imagines them finding in the images of the medieval woman with the unicorn and other animals "a quiet life . . . of slow, never quite clarified gestures," which "for a time they even thought . . . would be their own." But these girls in the museum, he suspects, are trying to forget the sheltered, protected life in the family home they left "rather violently" when they came to Paris. In their desire to change, to keep up with the times, they think of themselves "as men might speak of them when *they* aren't there." Searching for pleasures, they suppress in themselves "the unalterable life" that in the unicorn tapestries "radiantly opened in front of them" (131–33).

Like "Von den Mädchen," this passage makes one wonder if Rilke's attraction to maidenliness arose from the split which Freud analyzes as "the Universal Tendency to Debasement in the Sphere of Love," the tendency of men to separate women idealized as asexual, and thus lovable, from the objects of sexual desire (women degraded by their sexuality). Freud explains this split as an attempt to disassociate objects of lust from objects of affection and tenderness, because the latter are too closely associated with mothers, and many men must defend themselves against the surfacing of a strong, unconscious, incestuous attachment to their mothers.

Rilke's marriage to a woman he had idealized in a virginal image was unexceptional at first. Clara gave birth to a daughter, Ruth, on December 12, 1901. Rilke left the domesticity of his small family in Westerwede, near Worpswede, the following summer, little more than a year after marrying, and the marriage evolved into an affectionate friendship. As for the isolation of sexuality from idealizing love which Freud describes, the poet's passionate and loving, if relatively brief, affairs with a number of women in subsequent years suggest that he did not precisely fit Freud's conceptual model. He never got over his incestuous relationship with Salomé. The brevity of most of his other affairs, often followed by long affectionate letters for months or even years, may have been rooted partly in his need to defend himself against an unconscious incestuous attachment to Phia. But his frequent flight from women was also motivated by the fear of being changed in his innermost being, of being drained or overpowered, engulfed and annihilated. Such anxieties originated in his relationship with his mother, as I have shown. In any event, he did not spend his life dividing women into Freud's two categories (idealized and degraded) in order to reinforce the repression of an incestuous attachment.

The association of poetry with maidenly purity in "Von den Mädchen" is closely related to the argument of Rilke's requiem for Paula Becker, written in 1908, after her death. The requiem laments her having given up her devotion to art for motherhood. It contrasts her objective detachment as an artist and the resulting purity of her painting with her subjection to her body, to sexual desire and to all the demands made by pregnancy and motherhood. Ironically, when Paula Becker came to Paris in 1906, escaping from her marriage to devote herself to painting, Rilke

may have been partly responsible for her surrender to her family's desire
that she return to her husband. His letters show that, after sitting a number of times for a portrait by her, he stopped before the portrait was
finished, began to avoid her, and refused to let her join him, Clara, and
their daughter Ruth on a holiday trip to Belgium.[12] Paula went back to
her husband, gave birth to a child, and died shortly afterward of an
embolism in November 1907. One can only guess the reasons for Rilke's
reaction to Paula Modersohn-Becker in Paris. Perhaps the old attraction
remained. Possibly he was wary of becoming involved in an affair with
her. Here are the lines from the "Requiem for a Friend" which develop
the lament over Paula's diversion from her painting to pregnancy and
motherhood:

Da riss ein Zufall dich, dein letzter Zufall
riss dich zurück aus deinem fernsten Fortschritt
in eine Welt zurück, wo Säfte *wollen*.
. . . .
    O lass uns klagen. Weisst du, wie dein Blut
aus einem Kreisen ohnegleichen zögernd
und ungern wiederkam, da du es abriefst?
Wie es verwirrt des Leibes kleinen Kreislauf
noch einemal aufnahm; wie es voller Misstraun
und Staunen eintrat in den Mutterkuchen
und von dem weiten Rückweg plötzlich müd war.

Then, for the last time, chance came in and tore you
back, from the last step forward on your path,
into a world where bodies have their will.
. . . .
    Ah let us lament. Do you know how hesitantly,
how reluctantly your blood, when you called it back,
returned from its incomparable circuit?
How confused it was to take up once again
the body's narrow circulation; how,
full of mistrust and astonishment, it came
flowing into the placenta and suddenly
was exhausted by the long journey home.[13]

Earlier in the poem Rilke praises Paula's painting, arguing that it was
masterful because it was a purely objective mirror, free from all self-
assertion and egotism, even when the subject was her own body. She did

not say, "I am that" ("das bin ich"); her gaze had become "so unpos-
sessive" ("so besitzlos") that "it had no desire even/for you yourself"
("es dich selbst nicht mehr begehrte"). She transformed even her own
naked body into the abstract form of fine art:

> Und sahst dich selbst zuletzt wie eine Frucht,
> nahmst dich heraus aus deinen Kleidern, trugst
> dich vor den Spiegel, liessest dich hinein
> bis auf dein Shauen; das blieb gross davor
> und sagte nicht: das bin ich; nein: dies ist.
> So ohne Neugier war zulezt dein Shaun
> und so besitzlos, von so wahrer Armut,
> dass es dich selbst nicht mehr begehrte: heilig.

> And at last, you saw yourself as a fruit, you stepped
> out of your clothes and brought your naked body
> before the mirror, you let yourself inside
> down to your gaze; which stayed in front, immense,
> and didn't say: I am that; no: this is.
> So free of curiosity your gaze
> had become, so unpossessive, of such true
> poverty, it had no desire even
> for you yourself; it wanted nothing: holy.
> (*SP* 76–77)

This view of art would have appealed to Kant, Schopenhauer, and
Stephen Dedalus (see the culminating chapter of *A Portrait of the Artist
as a Young Man*), but Nietzsche and Freud have argued persuasively
against it. And the poet of the Third and Sixth Elegies, the writer of the
Letters to a Young Poet, shows a strong sense of the rich and essential
influence of the body, human sexuality, and the libidinous unconscious
upon great art. For most of his life Rilke did not suppress his own sexuality, though there were dedications to pure spirituality from time to
time, as in his letters, written early in 1914, to Magda von Hattingberg,
"Benvenuta," the Welcome One, the Beloved for whom he imagined he
had been waiting all his life. His love for her lasted a few months. Ordinarily he did not find that his sexuality conflicted with his creativity.
As for the distractions of parenting, he fathered a daughter but saw relatively little of her. He sometimes argued that he had broken up his
marriage to free Clara as well as himself, so that both of them could
devote their lives to their art. But his letters show he thought that she

had a mother's responsibility to care for their child, while, implicitly, he was free to be elsewhere (see *Letters* 1:74). To give him the slim credit he deserves, he did write to his daughter Ruth from time to time, and he provided some financial support, when he could find the money.

In October 1900, after returning to Schmargendorf, the Berlin suburb where Salomé lived, he wrote to her friend Frieda von Bülow, explaining that he had left Worpswede because he had been "too far away from all the helpers and helps which my labors need (particularly the Russian ones)" (*Letters* I, 49). The "helpers" with his Russian labors were really one person—Lou. Yet in the same letter he admitted to being homesick for "the dear people [in Worpswede] to whom I must seem faithless" (*Letters* 1:50). Obviously he had conflicting feelings and was drawn in opposite directions.

Two weeks after returning to Schmargendorf he began writing Clara and Paula long affectionate letters. In November Paula wrote to him about herself and Modersohn, narrowing the field of choice.[14] In February Clara came to visit him. It was at this time that they decided to marry and Lou decided to break off her relationship with him, while promising that she would not close the door to an appeal in the future for refuge and help, in his "worst hour." Considering his emotional condition at the time, she thought it folly for him to marry. His diaries show the desolation he had felt during the winter of 1900–1901, probably because Salomé was making it clear that she did not want him around.

In this state of mind he turned to Clara, hoping that she would resolve his uncertainty, restore his sense of reality, quiet his anxieties, and bring him happiness. On February 15, 1901 after her departure, he wrote to her, "Behind it all I am calm ... and somehow comforted in all my former anxieties. ... Give me strength for everything that has to be done now. ... Beginner of my joys!"[15] On the following day he sent another letter, saying, "My life till now was something uncertain, but now all is reality around me."[16] Clara seems to have taken over essential maternal functions from Lou, if these letters are truly indicative of Rilke's expectations. But she was not to become a mother surrogate to the extent that Lou had been. One can see signs of the very different role she would play for him in the poem, dedicated to Clara, which he wrote while he was in Arco in March 1901, visiting his mother. The poem implicitly describes his fiancée:

Du schöne dunkle Laute, mir gegeben,
damit ich prüfe meine Meisterschaft,—
   spielen will ich auf dir das Leben!
. . . .
jetzt ist das Instrument mein eigen
auf dem sich *meine* Klänge zeigen[17]

You beautiful dark lute, given to me,
that I may prove my mastery,
I want to play life on you!
. . . .
now the instrument is mine,
on which *my* tones emerge

Reading this poem, I am reminded of Rilke's reaction to Salomé's cool reception of the diary that he brought her from Italy, her condescending response to the effusions which he offered her in hopes of winning an enthusiastic, affectionate confirmation of his sense of his own young genius. In his bitterness he had written in his diary, "This time, *I* wanted to be the wealthy one, the giver, the one offering invitations, the master. . . . And now, face to face with you, I was again only the most insignificant beggar, at the last threshold of your being. . . . I felt myself becoming ever more ridiculous in my masquerade. Everything in me was shame, shame. Every encounter [with you] made me feel ashamed. Do you understand that? Always I said to myself: 'I can give you nothing, nothing at all. . . . ' "[18] With this second mother—herself brilliant, self-confident, much-published, inclined to analysis of his psychological weaknesses—he suffered from the sense of a lack of mastery, though Lou's dominance was also appealing. With Clara, who was three years younger and was still struggling in her development as a person and an artist, he was to find the mastery he desired. The poem Rilke wrote in February 1901, after Salomé broke off their relationship, attributing to her the power to shatter and swallow as well as to shape him, could not have been written about Clara. The young poet's delight in the possession of a wife who would be the instrument on which he played *his* music contrasts with his later condemnation of possessive love in *The Notebooks* and in letters, where he insists that genuine love gives the beloved utmost freedom, protecting and guarding his or her separate individuality (see *The Notebooks,* 251–58).

Was Clara so malleable? Angered by her apparent withdrawal from their friendship after her marriage to Rilke, Paula Becker wrote to her, complaining that she had transformed herself into an imitation of Rilke.[19] In many respects Clara did reflect her husband's attitudes, values, and beliefs. But these included an emphasis on their independence and differences from each other. Above all, she was dedicated to her own art. The combination of sameness and separateness helped to make their marriage and long, close friendship possible.

Rilke was not a fool, and he was not so vulnerable and weak that he felt compelled to choose a wife merely because she was not threatening and could be manipulated. Clara Westhoff appealed to him at least partly because of her strengths. Leppmann observes that her face was "strong and full of character" and that she appeared "robust" and "vibrant" in contrast to her husband.[20] Another biographer, E. M. Butler, mentions "her vitality, exuberance and strength."[21] Friends and acquaintances remarked that she was taller, larger than the poet. One can see this in photographs of the two standing together.

I have mentioned that Rilke admired the sculptor's vigor in her hands.[22] Writing about Rodin, Rilke expressed the feeling that the sculptor has incomparable means of establishing a connection with the world around him and control over it. The poet, who often felt disconnected from his world and threatened by it, longed for this ability. The modest work that Clara produced never awakened anything like the awe and immense admiration and longing which Rilke felt in response to Rodin. Yet one can see that her evolving skill and talent as a sculptor must have encouraged in the young poet the belief that he could turn to her, unthreatening as she was, at a time when Salomé wanted to be rid of him, with the needs and expectations expressed in the letters from which I have quoted.

In late November 1900 Clara sent Rilke a photograph of the small sculpture of a boy. He was impressed by "the simplicity and largeness of his bearing." Though the figure was small, the poet imagined the boy as gigantic, observing, "He is Clara Westhoff through and through."[23] He finds in her the distinctive qualities of "the sculptural." He also associates the boy with the softness and love which he hears when she speaks. Her voice becomes multidimensional. Choirs sing in it and landscapes open.

Rilke's feelings about the creative vitality and power of sculptors are reflected in his poems and stories about Michelangelo. In "The Book of the Monastic Life," the first part of *The Book of Hours,* the Renaissance master is called "the man, gigantic beyond measure, who forgot the immeasurable." Unlike those who came before him, who were possessed by pain and pleasure, "he feels only life's mass" and "can encompass it all as *one* thing":

Das waren Tage Michelangelo's,
von denen ich in fremden Büchern las.
Das war der Mann, der über einem Mass,
gigantengross,
die Unermesslichkeit vergass.
. . . .
Die vor ihm hatten Leid und Lust;
er aber fühlt nur noch des Lebens Masse,
und dass er Alles wie *ein* Ding umfasse. . . . [24]

Rilke's fascination with sculpture can be understood more fully in the light of the whimsically humorous story "Of One Who Listened to the Stones." This is one of the *Stories of God.* It was written in November 1899 (soon after the poem quoted above) and revised during February and March 1904. Michelangelo was the one who listened to the stones. The sense of the sculptor's incomparable strength makes God anxious. The Deity asks the sculptor, "Who is in that stone?" The answer: "Thou, my God, who else? But I cannot reach Thee." Hearing this, recognizing that "he was indeed *in the stone,*" God "felt fearful and confined" and longed "for the hands of Michelangelo to deliver him."[25]

The implied argument of the story, prominent in *The Book of Hours,* as well, is that God is created by artists, and that as they develop through their work, He evolves in them and in their art. As Michelangelo contemplates his monument for Pope Julius II and thinks of the mountain he will build "over the Iron Pope," "the newly broken surfaces of stone [appear] like a great pale face under aging hair," and then he sees "two enormous eyes of stone, watching him." The sculptor feels his own stature grow "under the influence of that look," which he has created. "Now he too towered over the land; it seemed to him that since the beginning of time he and this mountain had been brothers." These discoveries bring him to the realization which is the central idea of the story: "Thee will I complete, thou art my task." He is speaking to "the great face of rock under its white stone veils," but one cannot help feeling that he means

God. Afterward a voice comes to him, saying, "Michelangelo, who is in thee?" He answers, "Thou, my God, who else?"[26]

Obviously Rilke did not credit Clara Westhoff with such genius or anything like it. Nonetheless, these feelings about sculpture and sculptors, which had long been growing in him, must have played some part in his attraction to the young artist whose strong, shaping hands caught his eye and whose work he admired and encouraged.

II

Rilke's reaffirmations of his faith in Clara's abilities as a sculptor outlasted his marriage by many years, as he tried time and again, even after their friendship had dwindled, to obtain commissions and funds for her. In June 1902, living away from Clara and Ruth for a month at Haseldorf Castle as a guest of the poet, Prince Emil von Schönaich-Carolath, he wrote to Julie Weinmann, asking for help. The letter expresses his expectations of his wife, describing her as "a girl full of power and artistic ability, an artist, from whose growth I expect the greatest conceivable results" (*Letters* 1:69).

Then Rilke makes a statement about women which contrasts with his argument in the requiem for Paula Becker, that mothering was a tragic diversion from her painting. Here he says that having a child frees a woman from insecurity and brings her to maturity. Thus, raising children may foster her development as an artist. A woman, in particular a mother, can achieve just as much as a man in the arts, he thinks, assuring Frau Weinmann that "the meaning of my marriage lies in helping this dear young person to find herself, her greatness and depths, insofar as one person can help another." She is "no beginner," and "can be seen beside the best" (*Letters* 1:70).

Rilke's language in this letter reflects the assumption of superior knowledge in the young husband and master and his belief that his expectations of growth in his girl-wife will carry authority with Frau Weinmann because the lady knows that he is a fine poet, knowledgeable in the arts and gifted with critical discrimination.

The letters which he wrote to prospective patrons on Clara's behalf suggest a continuing attempt to bank up the fire of his own faith in her art out of a need to protect his belief in the fruitfulness of her separation from him, to justify in his own mind the breakup of the marriage. Yet some of them also show that he did not expect his wife to follow his course in separating himself from their child in order to be completely free for his work. Writing to the novelist Friedrich Huch in July 1902 as he contemplated new freedom, he says that Clara will have to "think of Ruth as well as of herself" (*Letters* 1:74). She must be bound by conventional attitudes about parents and children, while he may remain completely free from them. In fleeing from parental responsibilities and marriage, Rilke must have experienced some sense of identification with his mother. At the same time he must have felt qualms about subjecting his child to the kind of anguish which he had suffered when Phia withdrew from her marriage. He also needed to believe that Clara's burden as a mother, resulting from their marriage and his desertion, would not be so oppressive as to prevent her from developing as an artist. His attempts to find her clients and other sources of financial support, his long, frequent letters to her, and his willingness to spend periods of time with her during the next few years, often with Ruth conveniently left in the care of her grandparents, were motivated at least partly by his need to resolve the tensions arising from these conflicting pressures.

Rilke chose a wife whose devotion to her own art would enable her to empathize with him in his dedication to the writing of poetry. She would be able to understand all the sacrifices he would demand of her as of himself. These expectations were amply fulfilled by Clara's readiness to cooperate with him when he broke up their family and for years afterward when they carried on their frequent correspondence and lived intermittently together or near each other in separate domiciles. There is little evidence that she complained, in the early years, about their recurrent separations.

In December 1906 Clara wrote to Rilke, telling him about a conversation with Salomé in which his old friend had advised her "that if her absentee husband presumed to sacrifice his family to his poetry, the police should teach him where his duty lay." (This is Rudolph Binion's reading of the letter in his biography of Salomé, *Frau Lou, Nietzsche's Wayward Disciple*.)[1] Rilke's reply indicates that Clara had struggled against an inclination to be drawn into righteous anger. He acknowledges that he has given her ample cause for indignation, confessing that Lou's accusations against him echo his own thoughts. And then he defends his behavior, saying that he and Clara are only postponing their life together and that his world grows out from the house they shared, which remains its center. He insists that, despite the geographical distance between them, mentally and emotionally Ruth and she and he live in the same house, though it is invisible to other people (*Letters* 1:245).

For a few more years Clara accepted these conditions, and their correspondence continued. He sent her some of his most extraordinary letters, including the ones on Cézanne, written during October 1907. In his foreword to the published collection, *Letters on Cézanne*, Heinrich Wiegand Petzet observes that Clara's "presence and silent participation are sensible" throughout these remarkable expressions of the poet's intelligence and imagination, and that they bear witness to Rilke's awareness that his wife "possessed a quality which the poet only very rarely encountered . . . : she was his equal."[2]

Reading Rilke's letters to Clara from 1900 to 1911, one realizes that his respect for his wife grew during this time, although in no way could he see her as his equal in artistic achievement and genius. His respect depended upon her willingness to protect his freedom and distance, to care for their child without complaining, and at the same time, despite her failure to achieve eminent success, to sustain her dedication to her sculpture. Her long, friendly letters, which, from time to time, he would admire with enthusiasm, may have helped him to maintain his illusion that, as he pushed infinitely out into the periphery of their imaginary existence as a family, the center held: their marriage and friendship, his life as husband and father. She did that for him for years, largely without complaining. No wonder he was grateful. No doubt his respect was genuine.

The fact that Clara was not a poet, not even a writer by profession, may have been important to Rilke. She was not a competitor. She was much less likely to become a threat as a judge and a critic. In these respects she differed from Salomé. When Rilke chose a master in 1902, he too was a sculptor rather than another poet. Knowing little or no German, Rodin could not read Rilke's poetry, let alone judge it.

Yet Rilke's wife was far from inarticulate. Reading his responses to her letters side by side with Paula Becker's prose, I suspect that Clara's thinking and her use of language must have been more interesting and appealing to the young poet than her friend's. In his first letter written to

Clara after he left Worpswede to return to Lou, in October 1900, he recalls her extraordinary powers of evocation as she told him the story of her experience modeling her father's mother and credits her memory with having given him a "wonderfully beautiful picture" of her grandmother and her own responses to the old lady's face (*Letters* 1:42–44). He is delighted that she can create people with her pen as well as her sculptor's tools.

The admiration of her letters echoes time and again in his. Writing her from Capri in March 1907, he replies to a letter from Egypt with ardent praise of her descriptions, noting especially "the keenness" of her language and the sureness and richness of her notes (*Letters* 1:265). Yet here, as elsewhere, one finds the poet talking down to his wife, offering her instruction and encouragement as well as a master's approval to a talented person who is still in the process of a promising but uncertain evolution. His commendation may be objective and discriminating. No doubt he was being generous, as he so often was to his correspondents. It was easy to be generous in his letters, as Clara willingly collaborated with his efforts to defend his life as a poet against any sense that he was not sufficiently meeting his obligations as a husband and a father. Often the letters reveal the sources of the poet's power over his wife. As the letter from Capri continues, Rilke's instructions to Clara have the originality and the wisdom of a true master. Any aspiring artist on such a trip would benefit from them. They have enduring value:

Only collect many more impressions; don't think of letters that have to give information and be easily understood; keep taking in with swift capturing gestures one thing and another: something that passes quickly by, glimpses, brief flashing revelations that last a second in you under the influence of some occurrence; all the unimportant that often becomes significant through a passing intensity of our vision or because it happens at a place where it is perfected in all its fortuity and perpetually valid and of deep import for some personal insight which, appearing in us at the same moment, coincides meaningfully with that image. Gazing is such a wonderful thing, of which we still know so little; with it we are turned completely outward but just when we are most so, things seem to be going on in us that have waited longingly to be unobserved, and while they, untouched and curiously anonymous, achieve themselves in us *without us*,—their meaning is growing up in the object outside.... [O]ne has already had lots of sun very early, an abundance of brightness, and if then suddenly in the shade of a street a face is held out to one, under influence of the contrast one sees its character with such distinctness (distinctness of nuance) that the momentary impression is spontaneously heightened to the symbolic. (*Letters* 1:265–66)

One can see why Clara might want to go on corresponding and conversing with the poet who offered such insights concerning the arts and the creative process. He looks forward to the time approaching when she will again be with him and he will be able to help her to re-create her visit to Egypt in an incomparable piece of writing. Without any apparent vanity he fondly dwells upon the prospect of this joint effort, reminding her and himself of what he can do for her.

In Rilke's responses to Clara one finds a delicate balancing act, as he is poised among three endeavors—keeping her in a subordinate role, subject to his power, charming and pleasing her, and generously encouraging in her a sense of her own gifts. He is not hypocritical. He truly believes that her "letters are beautiful and remarkable," as he wrote to Paula Becker on March 17, 1907.

There are a number of salient differences between Rilke's correspondence with Salomé and that with Clara. Often in writing to Salomé he sounds like a child complaining to his mother-lover of anguish, illness, paralysis, and barrenness, and asking for help, clarification, and advice. Writing to his wife, he rarely shows any weakness. The correspondence with Clara seems to have been governed by the desire to remain the master, the lute player, with his wife. He needed to assure her that the sacrifices he was asking her to make were justified by the strength of his creative genius, displayed in the sharp, clear, vivid perceptions, the verbal energy, and the originality of thought which distinguish him as one of the great letter writers of modern times. He attempted to compensate her for her sacrifices with these frequent splendid offerings, as if to prove that he could give her such richness from a distance. This generosity would contrast in her mind with his sullen behavior as her obliging housemate, when "there still was . . . always much of me that only reproachfully stood by, that . . . would gladly have been alone, far away, God knows where" (*Letters* 1:248).

III

On October 18, 1900 Rilke wrote to Paula Becker, saying that he had "no little house," and that he must seek a home. He associated a home with a mother: "Every home has a warm and good influence, like every mother. Only I must seek my mother, mustn't I?" (*Letters* 1:46). Earlier in the same letter, explaining his abrupt departure from Worpswede, he says, "To me Russia has really become . . . home and heaven." He had returned to Schmargendorf, near Berlin, to resume his Russian studies with Salomé (*Letters* 1:45). What a contrast is his letter to Clara Westhoff, written the same day! In this one he says he has found a home in hers: "Your home was for me . . . simply home, *the first home in which I saw people living* (otherwise everyone lives abroad, but all homes stand empty . . .). . . . your home is rich enough to love me too and to uphold me, and you are so kind and take me in as a real member of the family" (*Letters* 1:43). How strange to find such opposing feelings on the same subject in two letters written the same day to women who might show them to each other! If they did so, what must they have thought?

Obviously the poet was expressing division and conflict. Home was with maternal Lou and Russia. Home was with Clara, though he did not think of her as maternal. "I wanted . . . to be a brother beside you all" (*Letters* 1:43).

I have argued that Clara was not comparable to Salomé as a maternal surrogate. Nonetheless, she too appealed to the poet in his need of a woman who would mirror him. Her mirroring calls to mind the passage in *The Notebooks* in which Malte imagines the lady in the unicorn tapestries holding the looking glass up to the unicorn, showing him his image. Contemplating the tapestries, Malte imagines that Abelone, his mother's younger sister, second only to Maman in his love, is there. He is confident that she "must understand" his response to the lady in the tapestries. It is hard to escape the conclusion that Rilke found in his wife the fulfillment of a desire to have a beloved woman show him his image. By the time he met Clara probably he had come to feel that Salomé's mirroring was flawed because of her egotism, expressed in her reaction to the diary he had brought her from Italy. She no longer wanted to perform this selfless maternal function for him. She wanted him gone.

Rilke's diaries and his letters to Clara suggest that he sought in her a woman whose mirroring would be more perfect and more patient than Lou's. Her great gift to the poet was to embody something like the fantasy in Rilke's 1913 "Narcissus" poem, of the woman in whose face he might find himself so that he might never lose himself in his own self-absorbed gaze.

Curiously, in his early letters to Clara he showed her her own image, as if to demonstrate that he truly had seen and heard her. On October 18, 1900 he recalled in vivid detail for her the story she had told him about her attempt to sculpt her grandmother. A month later, on November 18, he wrote to her to say that he was trying to render back to her her own pictures, almost in her own words, "as if I wanted to present you with your own possessions. But so it is, Clara Westhoff, we receive many of our riches only when they come to meet us borne by the voice of another." He imagined himself loading his "speeches" with her possessions, sending his sentences to her like caravans "to fill all the rooms of your soul with the beauties and treasures of your unopened mines and treasure chambers" (*Letters* 1:51–52).

He was in Schmargendorf near Berlin, Salomé's village, when he wrote these letters. With Clara Westhoff he seems to be playing the mirroring role that Lou had played for him, at a time when she was trying to separate and distance herself from him. Perhaps this was a way of identifying himself with Lou in order to keep her with him, within him, even as he felt he was being forced to give her up. (I am thinking of Freud's theory, formulated in "Mourning and Melancholia" (1916), that we tend to identify with objects of love whom we feel we are losing or have lost.)[1]

But Rilke's rhetoric in this letter is suspect. The desire underlying his expressed intention is scarcely hidden. His sentences would fill Clara with his thoughts, and he would discover that the still unopened treasure chambers of her psyche are full of just such thoughts. He would find himself in her as he opens her up? The passage recalls the image in Sonnet II.3, of Narcissus penetrating the face of the lovely woman in the mirror and finding himself in the mirror and in her.

The letters reflect confusion in the young poet's mind between the one who is mirroring and the one who is being mirrored. And this confusion points to the longing for a wife who would at least partly blend or merge with him. Obviously this desire and its fantasy fulfillment run counter to his often expressed doctrine that those who truly love express their love by allowing the beloved freedom and separateness. Both the fantasy and the opposing doctrine, as we have seen, expressed themselves in his marriage. Both grew out of the same fear of being overwhelmed, smashed, or devoured by the other person and particularly by the beloved woman. The converse mirroring fantasies which we have just examined were defenses against this anxiety and the fear of becoming totally cut off from human intimacy because of it. When Salomé would no longer sustain the young poet in this network of anxieties and defenses, Clara proved able to do so.

Clara was able to help him maintain his much needed con-fusion of two fantasies: that he was presenting her with her own possessions and that his sentences were filling all the rooms of her soul. Was she intuitively letting him feel that he was bewitching her? Or was she truly confused by his rhetoric? There is no evidence that she clearly understood what was going on.

IV

Rilke's response to the angry letter in which Paula Becker chided Clara for turning herself into an imitation of her husband may have confirmed Paula's fears for her friend.[1] He reminds Paula that Clara had seemed strange and unlike anyone else in the early days of their relationship, a solitary even then, whose inner seclusion she could not enter. Wasn't that what had made Paula love her? If so, she ought to be willing to accept Clara's discovery of "a new solitude" (*Letters* 1:65). His answer makes one wonder if he was encapsulating his wife in his own preoccupation with separateness, shaping her as the perfect collaborator in a marriage which "can consist only in the strengthening of two neighboring solitudes" (*Letters* 1:150). In an answer to a March 1907 letter from Clara in Egypt, the poet focuses on her expressed desire to be alone and the origins of his own similar yearning for solitude (*Letters* 1:267). But we do not hear from Clara. Her letters are not available to us. We cannot say to what extent she allowed herself to be reshaped into a mirror image of her husband, to what extent these were her own original predilections, to what extent she resisted and he ignored or blinded himself to her resistance. Perhaps she had come to him at twenty-one with such matching inclinations already well defined. Perhaps he persuaded her that such a way of life would foster her independent creativity. It is possible her own experience convinced her that he was right and that their marital arrangements and this singular friendship with her husband were more conducive to her development as an artist than living together full time would have been.

We shall probably never know the answers to the questions raised here. But we do have Rilke's ultimate judgment that his wife was not truly independent and strong in herself. He thought of her as a lute he could play his own tunes upon, a young, relatively unformed person whom he could shape to a large extent in his own image, the perfect responder, someone who would not threaten his autonomy, his separate identity, or his sense of his mastery, but would support and nurture them from close by or far away, just as he wished. These qualities, real or imagined, which had drawn him to Clara, became the grounds for his disappointment in her.

She did not have the strength or force of mind and personality to give Rilke the intellectual and emotional nurture and support he needed. He was caught in a dilemma common among persons suffering from the kind of illness reflected in his letters, *The Notebooks,* and some of his poems. They seek close relationships with people who will not overpower them, threaten their autonomy, or engulf them. But such individuals may lack sufficient personal strength and development to give them the maternal responsiveness, reassurance, and guidance they need to feel real and vital.

A letter to Rilke's friend Sidonie Nádherný von Borutin delineates the nature of his disappointment in Clara. The girl in her, he says, still longs for a conventional married life. He finds her subjugated to himself, "more a disciple than a wife," an imitator. How ironic it is to hear him echoing the complaints Paula Becker had made years earlier, about his relationship with Clara, when probably he did not remember them! Clara cannot stand beside him in her own independent strength. She mirrors him "instead of forming a counterpart."[2]

A 1912 letter to Salomé reveals Rilke's belief that, apart from her sense of herself as a mother, Clara was a living mirror, at times filled with his image, at others struggling to empty herself of it. But he does not seem to understand that he is portraying his wife as afflicted with a form of his own illness, suffering from a weak, undeveloped sense of identity, dependent upon another person for self-definition, troubled by the fear of engulfment by that person.

Clara's tendency to become identified with her husband was in Rilke's mind a kind of devouring. And this was all the more threatening, he says in the self-contradictory letter to Salomé, because, when she did identify herself with him, she was too strong for him. But when she tried to purge herself of Rilke, her willful negation of him distressed the poet.

At such times she may have been reminiscent of the mother who had turned all that he was in his own mind to nothing with her defensive blindness. Clara had a weapon which pierced his defenses. Her look of reproach reminded him that she was unloved, and that his inability to love her must deprive her of the fulfillment which, he believed, "the woman" in her longed for. This expression brought to mind a disconcerting memory, the extraordinary power of the *"unloved* look" he had seen on the face of Rose Beuret, Rodin's longtime companion, whom he married in the year of his death (1917).[3]

Eventually, the friendship which had replaced marriage wore thin. Perhaps it was because Rilke's sense of Clara's inadequacies grew. It is not hard to guess the reasons Clara must have had for finding the relationship unsatisfactory, as the years went on with infrequent contacts and, at the end of the decade, dwindling correspondence. Clara consulted a lawyer about a divorce in 1911. For the next two to three years the Rilkes made inquiries, but, as the biographers tell us, bureaucratic and legal difficulties, arising from such matters as nationality, legal residence, and differences in religion, as well as the time and effort and money required, kept them from going through the process.[4]

Nearly a year after marrying Clara, uncharacteristically searching for means to support his wife and newborn daughter, Rilke penned an explanation of his having married without a job. He had done it, he said, because as a bachelor he had felt "abandoned to every wind, unprotected" (*Letters* 1:61). He had thought that marriage would offer shelter from external pressures and distractions without violating his inwardness. These expectations faded all too swiftly. Within little more than a year of his wedding, the poet knew that he had made a mistake, that he could not feel at home with Clara and Ruth. The household he had created seemed alien, nothing but a drain on his time and energy. Wife and daughter were like unwelcome visitors.[5]

He had assumed that a house, a wife, and a child would enable him to feel more certain of his own existence. With them, he would become more visible and palpable ("sichtbarer," "greifbarer"). Things would no longer go through him as if he were not there. The little house in Westerwede had been undeniably there. But he had not felt that it was connected with him or that he could begin to live and grow in it.[6] Not even his relationship with his daughter could bring him the "feeling of reality"

("Wirklichkeitsgefühl"), the experience of what it was like to be someone real in a real world ("Wirklicher unter Wirklichem zu sein").[7] I am interpreting the language of the November 1903 letter to Lou cited in chapter 5.

Marriage with Clara, his role as a parent, and their little household were no substitute for the lost home of childhood, which he often believed he had never had. They were alien to him because they did not correspond to any conscious or unconscious memory or fantasy of that early home. Escaping from them, he sought the "feeling of reality" from a second powerful parental figure, who had, he felt, a unique gift for conferring solidity and certainty on everything and everyone around him—Rodin (see *Letters* 1:123).

CHAPTER 7

This Always Secret Influence

The Poet's Changing Relationship with His Father

I

Rilke's relationship with his father was far more complex than a narrow "orthodox" Freudian analysis, such as Erich Simenauer's, would have it. Reduced by Simenauer to oedipal phase antagonism, with expressions of love and esteem defined as "nothing more than 'cant'," camouflage created under the dictates of the superego, their relationship becomes a simplistic cartoon.[1] In this chapter I delineate the poet's multilayered feelings about Josef, his ambivalences, the conflicts and tensions between opposing emotions and attitudes, their origins in his pre-oedipal childhood, and their development during his adolescent and adult years.

It is hard to imagine a less likely father for this great poet than the railway inspector whose ambition to be an army officer was defeated after ten years of service, this absurdly old-fashioned gentleman, rigidly devoted to propriety and conformity. Nonetheless, to argue, as Simenauer does, that Rilke's discoveries of redeeming qualities in his father are simply defensive "reaction formations," covering up his oedipal hostility, is to miss by a mile the fascinating complexity of this relationship and the father's pervasive influence on the poet, whose vocation Josef could not begin to understand or value.

Rilke expressed the belief that his father was "incapable of love" in a letter written early in 1914 to Magda von Hattingberg, eight years after

Josef Rilke's death. In this letter he complained that his father's concern for him had taken the destructive form of "speechless anxiety," against which Rainer had found it almost impossible to defend himself. It was, after all, the source of Josef's attentiveness and generosity.[2]

In June 1914 Rilke wrote to Lou, lamenting the "region airless and loveless" which he found in himself. He was afraid that if any benevolent and loving person came to him to try to help him, he would imprison the kind person in this region, "so that his aid, unusable, would grow overripe in him and wilted and horribly atrophied" (*Letters* 2:113). The year before, he had written to Princess Marie, explaining that he was not a lover possibly because he could not love his mother. He lamented this emotional poverty, associating it with his caution and fear of danger (see *Letters* 2:90).

Taken together, these letters suggest that in his sense of being crippled by an "incapacity for love," the poet may have felt identified with his father. One can see how the feeling that he shared his father's incapacity for love would affect his sense of himself. In this respect Rilke struggled to overcome his father in himself. In the first few months of 1914, Magda von Hattingberg raised his hopes of overcoming this emotional sterility, but the hopes soon died.

The description of the father in the letter to von Hattingberg reveals conflicting feelings in the son. To be sure, one sees affection, compassion, and gratitude, but also contempt for the old man so fearful and timid, so constricted in emotion and limited in understanding. Josef's fear is recalled again in the fourth Duino Elegy (1915), where Rilke thinks of his father as "occupied [or preoccupied] with the aftertaste of such an alien future" (his son's), and imagines that Josef has, since his death, often experienced fear within the poet, "within my hope."

> und, mit dem Nachgeschmack so fremder Zukunft
> beschäftigt . . .
> der du, mein Vater, seit du tot bist, oft
> in meiner Hoffnung, innen in mir, Angst hast. . . .
> (*WDB* 1:454)

The passage suggests that the poet has internalized and identified himself with the anxious father and thus come to share the paternal fear about his future. Even within his hope the son finds the gnawing worm of Josef's anxiety, which has become part of himself.

In a number of letters Rilke contradicts this impression of his father. In January 1923, writing to Countess Margot Sizzo, from the perspective of a man who had achieved fulfillment in his work (the final *Elegies*, the *Sonnets*), the poet remembered the strong love between him and his father in his childhood and his fear that Josef's death might mean the end of his own existence. Then, with wisdom later acquired, he reflects that death cannot negate love, that it thrusts someone we have loved intensely only more deeply into "our heart," where the dead person continues to exercise a "secret influence." These thoughts lead to the conclusion "Where can we come closer to it, where more purely celebrate it, when obey it better, than when it appears linked with our own voices, as if our heart had learned a new language, a new song, a new strength" (*Letters* 2:315–16).

Is Rilke covering up in this letter his true feelings as a child toward his father? He does remember their "extremest difficulty in understanding and accepting one another," and he emphasizes the great difference between their orientations. From what we know about his life as a child and from what we know generally about the ways in which young children experience their parents, his recollection of his fantasy that loss of his father would mean the end of his own existence is persuasive. His mother's self-absorption and withdrawal may have encouraged a transfer of such intense feelings of dependency to his father, as René began to struggle to free himself from the enmeshment with Phia which continued through much of his life. I cannot agree with Simenauer's argument that such reflections about his relationship with Josef were "nothing more than 'cant' " or a "reaction formation," reinforcing the repression of his hostility toward his father by exaggerating his love for him. The poet's linking of the "new strength" which he has found in himself with his father's "ceaseless," "secret influence" reveals a conception of Josef which is clearly opposed to the one we find in the letter to von Hattingberg and in the Fourth Elegy. Both may be partial truths, reflecting different aspects of the father and of his effect upon his son, brought to memory by different moods and states of mind in the poet.

Does Rilke idealize his father or their relationship in this letter to Margot Sizzo, written in 1923, so long after Josef's death? Rather than "cant" or cover-up, the letter may express a rediscovery of the strength of his childhood love for Josef, underlying doubt, resentment, hostility, and fear, a rediscovery arising out of the greater confidence and freedom he had attained through his fulfillment and extraordinary achievement in the *Elegies* and the *Sonnets*—above all, freedom from repression and defensiveness, and, as a result, greater access to emotional energies and to memories.

In commenting on Rilke's relationship with Phia I referred to Harold Searles's observations concerning patients whose fear of their early love for their mothers had caused them to repress it. Through analysis Searles was able to help some of his patients "de-repress" this long-unconscious love. Searles's supporting evidence for this argument is persuasive.[3] From many of the images of the father in Rilke's writings, it seems clear that the affection he expresses for Josef involved something like this retrieval of early feelings. Obviously there was ambivalence. Some of the passages expressing love for the father suggest attempts to cover up hostility. At times the retrieval of genuine affection may have become confused with the need to veil painfully negative attitudes. Such confusions and ambiguities of genuine self-expressiveness and defensive concealment may be found in all of us. The affection for the father shown in letters, poems, and *Ewald Tragy* probably had its roots in periods of Rilke's childhood preceding the "oedipal phase," which is the focus of Simenauer's analysis.

On his nineteenth birthday Rilke wrote to Valery David-Rhonfeld, his fiancée, "If in my father's house love was shown me with both care and concern only by my papa, I was in general thrown entirely upon my own resources." There is a mixed message here. The emphasis falls upon the child's neglect by everyone. Much of the letter is devoted to the young man's bitter resentment of his mother's behavior. But he distinguishes between his parents, crediting his father with "both care and concern," which at this point in his life he does not reduce to "speechless anxiety" (*Letters* 1:18–19).

While some biographers suspect that the poet's memory or imagination distorted the mother of his childhood, there is little evidence that Rilke's recollections of his father's solicitude were inaccurate. E. M. Butler tells us that Josef changed his son's nurse twenty-four times in Rainer's first year of life.[4] Obviously this piece of information has a double edge. It suggests his devotion to his infant son was fraught with the infectious anxiety which the poet found distasteful and destructive.

Psychological studies of the father's role in the pre-oedipal years make Rilke's statements about Josef's importance to him during his childhood more intelligible. Some child psychologists see the father "as a powerful and necessary support against the pull back to the primary undifferentiated symbiotic phase" during the second year of childhood.[5] They tell us that the child's attachment to the father ("establishment of a libidinally cathected object representation of the father," in their technical language) "promotes separation."[6] He is perceived more objectively and realistically than the mother during the second year. He is felt to be part of the external world at a time when the mother is still extensively confused with the self. "Some youngsters seem to turn exclusively to the father to evade the regressive pull, while others are so ambivalently enmeshed with their mothers that they do not have time for their fathers."[7] These tendencies do not end with the second year. They may influence much later stages of life, though the influence may be unconscious. Rilke seems to have been caught between these two opposing inclinations. We can find both attitudes reflected in his work.

In *Ewald Tragy* (1898), a novella which is crude and obviously autobiographical, the mother is absent, an object of longing and bitterness, while the father is central in the first part of the narrative. He is the focus of a range of conflicting feelings in his son, from humiliation and contempt to love, tender concern, admiration, and a strong sense of affinity.

Ewald Tragy is eighteen. Rilke was probably twenty-two when he wrote the story. His portrayal of Ewald's closeness to his father and of Herr von Tragy's centrality in his son's life at this time when the boy is determined to get away from Prague and his family, and his dramatizing of both positive and negative feelings toward the father in all their intensity are compelling and convincing despite or, perhaps, because of the rawness of the work.

Herr von Tragy gives "commands" to his teenage son. He is peremptory and abrupt with him, humiliating Ewald by snatching his hat off his head because he thinks the dust on the hat disgraces them in the eyes of people they meet. The "inspector" is angry with his son because Ewald is about to leave him to go to Munich. The story seems to reflect Rilke's guilt at leaving his father. Saying that he will not hold Ewald back, Herr von Tragy tries to persuade him to remain at home, asking him what he lacks, pointing out that if he remains in Prague and treats "people correctly, the best houses will be open to you" (*ET,* 8). Reacting with angry scorn to this line of persuasion, Ewald replies, "That's all you are concerned about. To lie on one's belly before ... people—that's the right way; and to crawl on one's belly to ... money—that's the goal, isn't it?" (*ET*, 9).

The material probably comes from the time when Rilke was twenty (1896) rather than eighteen, and the choice of Ewald's age suggests that the author wishes to place more distance between himself and the younger self he is writing about.[8] No doubt, as he looked back on his shame and rage, Rilke could be more objective. But, reading this novella, one can see that the younger self's contempt for the attitudes of the Prague bourgeoisie, exemplified by the father, persisted in the author.

The novella delineates the other side of Ewald's ambivalence as well, his love for his father. The "old gentleman" smiles at his son and answers "patiently," but finally the teenager's rage gets to him. "The old officer in him" "commands" his son, "Don't yell!" and for a second time "crosses, with rigid formality, to the other side of the street." Then, as Ewald watches him, "It is somewhat disquieting to see the old man so completely abandoned on the endlessly bare sidewalk. How alone he is, he thinks,—and if something should happen to him. His eyes do not leave the father any more" (*ET*, 10).

Are we to doubt the feelings expressed here? Commentators on this early story agree that it is autobiographical. Is this passage "cant"? Surely it does not reflect a cover-up, a denial, or some other form of self-deceptive defense. The son's hostility is not hidden in the story. I suspect that Rilke has recaptured his intensely ambivalent feelings rather accurately in this scene, which is both moving and funny, as in the clumsy way in which Ewald, now once more standing beside his father, tries to express his love, although he is unwavering in his determination to leave the old man to go to Munich:

Ewald begs:
"Papa!" For a moment he is confused, and then the words tumble out of his mouth: "You should turn up your collar, Papa—it is always so chilly on the staircase." (*ET*, 10–11)

Josef Rilke opposed his son's vocation. Writing in April 1903 to Ellen Key, the Swedish author, whose enthusiastic reactions to his early *Stories of God* made her seem a potential source of financial and emotional support, he says, "My whole art has grown up from its first day against opposition: against the laughter and scorn of the noncommissioned officers, against my father, against all about me" (*Letters* 1:100). Carl Sieber quotes a note Josef Rilke sent to Phia while their son was in military school, urging her not to excite René's emotions with her extravagant letters, to keep them short, and not to encourage him to write poetry.[9]

In *Ewald Tragy*, Ewald describes his father's lack of faith in his vocation in terms that emphasize the old man's bourgeois values and incomprehension. He tells a French girl that Herr von Tragy considers his desire to be a poet "simply ridiculous," because "it is no profession. It does not pay, one does not belong to any class, is not entitled to any pension, in a word: one is disconnected from life." The passage also reflects the effect of Josef Rilke's narrow, timid doubts and fears upon his son. Ewald goes on to say, "And I myself have so many doubts. Really: I spend whole nights lying awake with folded hands and torturing myself. 'Am I worthy?' " (*ET*, 21). Perhaps the young author of the story wondered if he would ever write poetry which might redeem him from the fear and doubt Josef had fostered. His father's belief that a poet "is disconnected from life" might turn out to be true in his case. Obviously this fear goes beyond superficial concerns (pay, class, pension) to something else which profoundly concerned Rainer. In Paris Malte Laurids Brigge is "disconnected" from the life around him. And Rilke's letters suggest that at times he was no better off than Malte in this respect.

Writing to Ellen Key about his father's inarticulate kindness and anxiety for him, Rilke imagined that Josef yearned to understand who he was and what he was doing. Living on the old man was doubly painful because he so completely lacked confidence in what his son was doing. Deeply troubled because he could find no other way to support himself, the poet longed to show his father "a great, great deal of love" (*Letters* 1:99). The complexity of the analysis in this letter encourages me to trust the poet's sense of his father and his account of his own feelings. At the time the old man was suggesting that Rainer take a proper job and give up this perverse, irresponsible way of life; Rilke explained to Key that such a job would be like his old military school or a jail, though he noted that Josef was not pressing him, just offering to find him employment in Prague if at last he would see that his present way of life was a failure (*Letters* 1:103). At twenty-seven the poet was aware of a range of conflicting feelings about his father. Here, as in *Ewald Tragy*, there is no reason to believe that the love, gratitude, and empathetic understanding are any more superficial or less honest than the resentment and the desire to be freed from dependence on this very limited, uncomprehending old man.

I have said that *Ewald Tragy* is raw. Yet the scene in which Ewald talks to the French girl in his aunt's home skillfully creates, with dialogue, Ewald's thoughts, and a few gestures, a many-sided relationship between father and son. After Ewald has lamented his bad luck in parents, he "remains sad and silent." In a good mood the inspector "gently taps his son on the shoulder: 'Well, old man?'" Poor Ewald "tries to smile and kisses his hand," as the old man blindly decides that his son is not going to leave him. Then the scene comes to a focus in a passage of great clarity which suggests that even in 1898 Rilke could be extraordinarily articulate in defining his feelings about others (here they are projected onto his fictional surrogate). Ewald is talking to the French girl: "You see, this is how he holds me. So gently, without force or influence, almost with nothing but a memory, as though he were saying: 'Once you were small, and every year I lit a Christmas tree for you—remember?'—With all this he makes me quite weak. His kindness has no exit, and behind his wrath there is an abyss. I am not brave enough for this leap."[10]

Herr von Tragy differs markedly from the oedipal fathers in Kafka's writings and D. H. Lawrence's *Sons and Lovers,* though there is a suspicion here of lurking wrath. Exemplary kindness and goodness in a parent can make it very hard for the child to liberate himself from the parent's wishes, fears, and pressures. The Prodigal Son episode in *The Notebooks* reaffirms this theme. Rilke's repeatedly expressed distaste for possessive love was probably rooted in the manipulations of the parents who coddled him as a youngster, as he tells Ellen Key. Parental kindness may become a prison from which, it seems, there is no exit. And the father who keeps his anger largely in reserve, while giving his son hints of it, but, for the most part, shows him benevolence and generosity, such a father may have more power to hold and manipulate his son than one who shows little kindness and a lot of anger.

Paul Morel in D. H. Lawrence's novel *Sons and Lovers,* is largely freed from his father's power by the older man's rages and bad treatment of the mother, while the mother, with her love, holds her son far too tightly for his own good. Living a life which radically goes against the wishes of a parent who shows much kindness and generosity, and continues to do so despite his doubt and fear, is likely to give one a sore conscience. We can believe that Rilke's letter to Ellen Key in 1903 truly expresses the suffering he felt when he thought of his father.

Parental kindness which has no exit and makes the child feel weak can inspire hate and even the desire to murder. I cannot argue with Simenauer's conclusion that Malte's account of the perforation of his father's heart after the old man's death and of his own reaction to this grisly ritual suggests a desire to kill his father or see him dead. Herr Brigge's death is a welcome source of freedom and independence. But the feelings in Rilke which this episode reflects were part of a larger range of conflicting emotions which developed in the poet at various stages of his life. They cannot be interpreted merely in terms of an oversimplified version of the oedipal theory.

As for the wrath with an "abyss" behind it, imagined by Ewald, we have observed that Herr von Tragy does show anger, as, for example, when he snatches off Ewald's dusty hat. But he keeps his anger under control and gives way to it infrequently. A father whose suspected rage seems to lurk behind kindness, giving only hints of itself, may be more frightening than one whose anger explodes and lets itself be seen to its full extent. Not knowing how to measure a father's anger may create the fear that it has the power to annihilate one. Yet reading this story, in which the father appears relatively mild and the son vents a harsher anger, I suspect that the danger of annihilation by the father's anger is a fantasy arising, at least in part, from unconscious projection. This is to say that young Rilke, identifying himself, to a large extent, with Ewald, unconsciously projected his own anger onto Herr von Tragy, whom he identified with his father.

Often the punishing or murderous father in the mind is invested with such projected and, thus, fantastical anger. Does the father whose wrath has the power to annihilate the son turn up in Rilke's later work? Only rarely. Later I shall discuss the poem "David Sings before Saul," in which this fantasy of the father is obliquely represented in an oedipal competition for women. Do the terrifying Angels of the First and Second Elegies represent this wrath at a later date, as they seem to menace the poet with annihilation? If so, an analyst might argue that the menacing paternal rage has gone through several stages of displacement from its original source. Originally found in the father himself or projected in the son's perceptions of the father, the analyst would say that it was then taken into the superego and projected onto these figures of the imagination, who do seem to embody projections of the superego's power to annihilate the self and of the ego ideal toward which the poet is aspiring. In the Seventh Elegy, the poet holds off the menacing Angels with the "powerful current" of his "voice," his "cry" (*SP*, 191 and 187). But the comparatively abstract Angels of the Elegies seem far removed from the highly individualized, autobiographical fantasies of the father which we find in *Ewald Tragy*.

II

About five or six years after writing *Ewald Tragy*, Rilke began to recreate earlier stages of his life in the thicker disguises of *The Notebooks of Malte Laurids Brigge*. The autobiographical material was more extensively transformed in this later work, parts of which were sheer invention. One important difference between the two books lies in the characterization of the mother and the father. Malte's Maman is far more sympathetic than his father. The master of the hunt is an unwelcome intruder on those brief, rare occasions when Maman spends time with Malte: "But we did read a little, so that we would look occupied; it was unpleasant for us when anyone came in, to have to explain what we were doing; especially toward father, we were exaggeratedly explicit" (99).

As we have seen, Malte's love and admiration of Maman are central in the novel, and he is rather distant from his father. If there are hints that Maman is not a perfect mother, the critical attitude toward the father is explicit. When the parents are called home from the crown prince's ball because Malte is feverish, badly frightened, and in a rage, the father is stern, if also gentle. "And my father ordered me to say what was the matter. It was a friendly, softened order, but it was an order nevertheless" (96). The master of the hunt here is reminiscent of Herr von Tragy. When the boy does not answer, his father becomes impatient.

The echoing of "befahl" ("ordered" or "commanded") in "Befehl" (the noun, "order" or "command") reminds one of Josef Rilke's military background and mentality. As I have indicated, Malte's father is an officer of the court, the master of the hunt. In *Ewald Tragy*, we are told Herr von Tragy is an old officer. Rilke's father served in the Austrian army, intent upon a career as an officer. Disappointed in this hope (he did not receive a commission and withdrew from active service after ten years in the army), he was determined that his son should become an officer and achieve the kind of glory which he had too briefly tasted as commander of the fortress at Brescia in the Franco-Austrian War of 1859.

The master of the hunt, ordering his raging, frightened, feverish son to explain himself, seems an indirect reflection of Rilke's distaste for his own father's association with the military life, its values and style. Yet the poetry and prose Rilke wrote from his early years until he witnessed the hideous spectacle of World War I reveal that he had internalized his father's ideals and fantasies of military glory, that he, at least partly, identified with Josef in this respect, and was fascinated by stories of heroes and battles.

Carl Sieber, the poet's son-in-law, informs us that from the first it was determined René would be an army officer. The boy received dumbbells for exercise. He had tin soldiers to deploy in imaginary skirmishes like the ones he sketched. His mother told Sieber that he was trained in making military reports. He wore medals for battles the imperial army had fought. His father's sister's husband sent René a sabre and a helmet.[1]

Though he hated the two military schools to which Josef sent him, St. Pölten and Mährisch-Weisskirchen, and finally persuaded his father to let him leave the second one in June 1891, after this release René wrote his mother, "[T]he military profession is the only profession for which I long. I have taken off the Emperor's coat to put it on again in a little while—forever; and be convinced, I will wear it with honor."[2] While studying at St. Pölten, René dreamed of gathering laurels in war and wrote eighty-one pages of a *History of the Thirty-Years War,* which shows his fascination with such military heroes as Wallenstein, Tilly, and Gustavus Adolphus.[3]

A number of Rilke's early poems reflect the extent to which Josef's preoccupation with military glory affected his son. The most famous of these is "The Lay of the Love and Death of Cornet Christoph Rilke" ("Die Weise von Liebe und Tod des Cornets Christoph Rilke"), written in the autumn of 1899, revised in 1904 and 1906. Dashed off in one night when Rilke was twenty-three, the *Cornet* tells the story of Christoph Rilke, who fought in the Imperial Austrian army against the Turks in Hungary in 1663 and died in battle. This romantic tale of old-fashioned heroism was inspired by some family papers which the poet's Uncle Jaroslav had got from the Royal Saxon State Archives in his attempt to prove that the Rilkes of Prague were closely related to the noble old Saxon family by the same name. Thousands of German soldiers carried the *Cornet* with them into battle in the First World War. At eighteen Christoph Rilke, a knight in armor in the youthful first version, a squire in the tighter, tougher, artistically more sophistocated third, is made a cornet (ensign) by the great general Count Spork. Leppmann points out that this was young Josef Rilke's highest rank in the Imperial Austrian Army.[4] The cornet rescues a naked woman, tied to a tree, cutting her bloody ropes; sleeps with a countess in her castle; races out of the burning castle after the pagans who have set the castle afire, and carries the flag beyond his own army into the midst of the enemy, who kill him: "But, as they close in about him, they seem to be certainly gardens again, and the sixteen curved sabres, which leap up towards him, flash after flash, are a festival. A laughing fountain display" (*WSR*, 88).

If the original inspiration for the *Cornet* came surely from Rilke's identification with his father as the young cadet who had commanded the citadel at Brescia in 1859, and with his paternal uncle in Jaroslav's mooning over fantasies of noble warrior ancestors, the poem also shows the importance of the absent mother in Rilke's mind, even in 1899. Time and again the poem returns to the thought of a mother or mothers who have been left behind by the young men riding out to war. Contemplating a drooping young French marquis, Christoph Rilke says to him, "You have strange eyes, my Lord Marquis. You must favour your mother," at which "the youngster revives and brushes the dust from his collar and is like a new man" (*WSR*, 79).

In the next paragraph, "[s]omeone is talking about his mother." These "gentlemen" from many different countries "are all united in one common feeling," "[a]s if there were but *one* mother."

Later in the *Cornet* Christoph Rilke writes a letter to his mother:

"*Dearest Mother,*
"*be proud: I carry the flag,*
"*be undisturbed: I carry the flag,*
"*love me: I carry the flag—*"
(*WSR*, 83)

It is easy to see that the energy behind this fervently inspired work of one night, which brought Rilke long-lasting popularity, the splendid energy which also made him go back to the poem in 1904 and 1906 to

work it over very carefully, must have been fostered by the paternal ideal
which he had taken into himself and by the longing for the ideally supportive mother he felt he had never had. In the poem's last section, a
courier from Christoph's commander rides into Langenau, Christoph's
home village, with his letter to his mother. "There he beheld an old
woman weeping" (*WSR,* 88).

In writing the *Cornet,* through identification with his young hero,
Rainer may have experienced a brief, sublimated, limited fulfillment of
his father's fondest aspirations for him, after disappointing the old man
in reality. He also invented a mother who would grieve for her lost son.
In the *Cornet* the poet accomplished in sublimated form what his paternal uncle was not able to do in fact. He gave a vivid life to the vague
legend of the old Saxon Rilkes, linking them inseparably through his
authorship with the modern Prague family. And perhaps Rilke felt, as
he provided the young cornet with his marvelous adventures and glorious
death, that he was writing about that other young cornet whose adventure in the army had ended badly, re-creating his father's life in a much
more appealing form.

Rilke's poetry shows that Josef's military ideals, memories, and
dreams, which Rainer had made a part of himself as a child, continued
to influence him at least until the beginning of the First World war,
when, in August 1914, he wrote the five hymns to the war god. The
poet's continuing identification with his father's attachment to military
ideals was probably also a source of inspiration for the sixth Duino Elegy, a celebration of the hero, most of which was written in 1912 and
1913. The childhood fantasy of the young father as a commander of the
citadel at Brescia in the Franco-Austrian War of 1859 and the fantasies
of ancestral heroes, which his father and his Uncle Jaroslav fostered, may
well have played a part in inspiring and shaping this Elegy:[5]

> Wunderlich nah ist der Held doch den jugendlich Toten.
> > Dauern
> ficht ihn nicht an. Sein Aufgang ist Dasein; beständig
> nimmt er sich fort und tritt ins veränderte Sternbild
> seiner steten Gefahr. Dort fänden ihn wenige. Aber,
> das uns finster verschweigt, das plötzlich begeisterte
> > Schicksal
> singt ihn hinein in den Sturm seiner aufrauschenden Welt.
> Hör ich doch keinen wie *ihn.* Auf einmal durchgeht mich
> mit der strömenden Luft sein verdunkelter Ton.

The hero is strangely close to those who died young.
                                    Permanence
does not concern him. He lives in continual ascent,
moving on into the ever-changed constellation
of perpetual danger. Few could find him there. But
Fate, which is silent about us, suddenly grows inspired
and sings him into the storm of his onrushing world.
I hear no one like *him*. All at once I am pierced
by his darkened voice, carried on the streaming air.
(*SP*, 182–83)

The hideous realities of World War I undermined this part of Josef's
influence on Rainer. Soon after writing the five hymns, he began to express his revulsion from the war. His forced induction into the army
reserve in 1916 intensified his dislike of the military. Nonetheless, it is
hard to believe that he ever entirely lost all vestiges of his attachment to
those early images of his father as a young hero, commanding a fort
during the Franco-Austrian War of 1859. In 1916, after having been dis-
charged from military service because so many important and powerful
people had intervened on his behalf, Rilke wrote, "Somewhere there is
a strain of old soldier's blood in me that makes me ashamed to create
such a fuss and to be such a rebel."[6] He completed his celebration of the
hero, the Sixth Elegy, in 1922, adding the following lines:

War er nicht Held schon in dir, o Mutter, begann nicht
dort schon, in dir, seine herrische Auswahl?
Tausende brauten im Schooss und wollten *er* sein,
aber sieh: er egriff und liess aus—, wählte und konnte.
Und wenn er Säulen zerstiess, so wars, da er ausbrach
aus der Welt deines Leibs in die engere Welt, wo er weiter
wählte und konnte. O Mütter der Helden, o Ursprung
reissender Ströme! Ihr Schluchten, in die sich
hoch von dem Herzrand, klagend,
schon die Mädchen gestürzt, künftig die Opfer dem Sohn.

Wasn't he a hero inside you, mother? didn't
his imperious choosing already begin there, in you?
Thousands seethed in your womb, wanting to be *him*,
but look: he grasped and excluded—, chose and prevailed.
And if he demolished pillars, it was when he burst
from the world of your body into the narrower world, where

again

he chose and prevailed. O mothers of heroes, O sources
of ravaging floods! You ravines into which
virgins have plunged, lamenting,
from the highest rim of the heart, sacrifices to the son.
(*SP*, 182–85)

Thus the reality of Josef Rilke's disappointment and frustration as he grubbed his way in demeaning railway jobs did not obliterate Rainer's identification with his father in Josef's military memories, fantasies, and aspirations. Nor did Rilke's growing mastery and recognition as a poet and his relationship with Rodin, the father surrogate who provided him with an ideal model of mastery in an art.

In the scene of Malte's parents' return from the crown prince's ball, the master of the hunt's insensitivity and lack of sympathy are nuanced. The order Malte's father gives him is "friendly, softened" (96). There is at least a modicum of sensitivity and benevolence in the father at this point. But Herr Brigge takes his son's pulse and says, "What nonsense to send for us" (97).

The response of the father seems all the worse because it is motivated by his desire to get back to the crown prince's ball. "They had promised to go back if it was nothing serious" (97). Yet as an adult of twenty-eight, looking back upon his childish terrors, Malte agrees with his father in his skeptical response to the child's fears: "certainly it was nothing serious" (97). Is this irony? As an adult Malte still experiences those fears with all the child's feverish intensity. And so did Rilke, as his letters reveal. During 1902 and 1903 the reawakened anxieties of his childhood threatened to overwhelm him. Yet he also knew that if he could master them and turn them into poetry or prose, they would prove a resource for his genius. In writing the scene of the parents' return from the ball to the feverish boy, he was giving himself confirmation of his mastery. Malte's retrospective affirmation of his father's view expresses the side of Rilke that was impatient with his own weaknesses, his fears, his emotional illness, and longed to have the toughness and unyielding strength of will he had found in Rodin, the master and second father who was his model and a great source of strength during the years 1902–6.

Other interpreters have rightly found oedipal feelings in this episode of *The Notebooks*. Though there is nothing like the seething reaction of Paul Morel's father in Lawrence's *Sons and Lovers* to the physical affection between Paul and his mother, one can sense the anger lurking behind the master of the hunt's impatience and in his "What nonsense. . . . " We are told that in his fever Malte is possessed by rage. Its source and object are not named. But the scene as a whole intimates where it is coming from. Reading the passage, one feels that the child's fury arises from the father's lack of sympathy, the mother's submissiveness to the master of the hunt, and his ability to separate his son from this enchanting mother so easily when she is most needed. Maman, much as she loves her son, spends little time with him and has persuaded him to pretend to be a little girl, to deny the little boy in himself in order to please her. Thus, the novel makes one feel that the boy's rage arises partly from his mother's behavior and that Rilke transferred the anger aroused by her to the father. This latent transference helps him to isolate and distance, and thus to defend, the love Malte feels for his enchanting Maman from his rage. The idea that Malte might be angry with Maman is never expressed in the novel.

III

Elsewhere in *The Notebooks* the father evokes little sympathy, except, perhaps, when Malte sees him laid out after his death. In comparison with Herr von Tragy, the master of the hunt seems relatively flat, simplified. He is an aristocrat, but he makes one think of Kokoschka's portraits of the Viennese bourgeoisie and of Grosz's satiric sketches and lithographs of German civilian and military bureaucrats.

Malte remembers his father's stiffness and rigid concern for social propriety and contrasts Maman with him in this respect. "As for my father, his attitude toward God was perfectly correct and irreproachably courteous. . . . Maman, on the other hand, thought it almost offensive that anyone's relationship with God could be merely polite" (109–10). Here, as elsewhere, the hard, sharp edge of Malte's (Rilke's) irony makes the haughty father a contemptible figure. The contrast between the parents emphasizes the deadness of the one, the vitality of the other. The artist-son's hostile destructiveness is all the more damaging because in the years since he had written *Ewald Tragy* Rilke had developed distance and restraint, greater skill in indirection and irony, and the ability to simplify his live model into this relatively abstract and highly integrated figure of fine art.

One can see Malte's comments on the master of the hunt's attitude toward God as an oblique attack on Josef Rilke's devotion to conventional correctness and propriety in general. Sieber tells us that when Rilke and Clara wanted to visit Josef in Marienbad, he wrote to them, expressing his concern that they might not be properly dressed, and he made it a condition of his consenting to see them that they should provide themselves with "respectable clothes for traveling," underlining the words. In his next letter he returned to the same theme, expressing the wish that they be well dressed, without eccentricity. He advised René to have his (Josef's) Prague tailor make a suit for him and closed with the worried comment that, although unfortunately he could do nothing for Clara, he hoped that she would be well dressed.[1]

Sieber denies that a concern for external appearances outweighed Josef's love for Rainer. He says that the poet's father "loved his son with all the ardor of which he was capable, but his love was always adjusted by his correctness and his correctness by his love."[2] Apparently Sieber saw only a few letters and cards from Josef to Rainer. Apart from the old man's repeated adjurations about decent clothes, what struck him was the father's fears about Rainer's future. Josef wrote to the poet, urging him not to live so much from day to day, asking, "Do you think constantly, dear René, of your secure future?"[3] He worried about the couple's vegetarian diet. Sieber, whose sources included Phia and possibly Clara as well as Rainer, makes the old man, with his fussy, irritating, anxious love and concern, seem a figure in an old-fashioned stage comedy, though the author of this portrait might be surprised and dismayed to hear one say so. He too seems comically proper and stuffy.

Another passage in *The Notebooks* confirms the impression that Rilke's satire of his father's attitudes in the master of the hunt reflects scornful hostility, at times even intense dislike. Shortly after describing his parents' attitudes towards God and religion, Malte recalls his father's reaction to his mother's disfigurement near the time of her death: "Then my father said, 'She is very much disfigured.' ... [I]t was probably his pride that suffered most in making this admission" (111–12).

Could anything be worse?! Does this reflect the poet's feelings about his father? It does not recall specifically anything that we know about Josef Rilke. Phia long outlived her husband and suffered no such disfigurement through illness. But the passage brings to mind Josef Rilke's pride, which had been so badly undermined that it evidently suffered spasms of anxiety about the way members of the family looked to other people. It must have seemed fragile and rather hollow to his son.

Years after Maman's death, when Malte is twelve or thirteen (much younger than Ewald Tragy), his father takes him to Urnekloster, the home of Maman's father, Count Brahe. In the high dining hall, which produces intense fear of disintegration and annihilation in the boy, he stretches his leg until his foot touches his father's knee. This "slight contact" with his father gives him "the strength to sit through the long meal." Later he suspects that the master of the hunt has understood his attempt to make contact and to find some emotional support, but he is uncertain about this. He takes some comfort in the thought that his father "seemed to tolerate" his behavior, but sees their relationship as "almost cool" (26). Malte feels alone at Urnekloster and very fragile, as he must rely upon this tenuous relationship with a distant father to help him hold himself together. This is not the old man of *Ewald Tragy*, who touches his son affectionately on the shoulder, hoping that he won't lose him.

One can only speculate as to whether or not the distance which had grown between Rilke and his father after Rainer left Prague in 1896 is reflected in this passage. Surely Josef could not offer his son emotional support in 1902 and 1903, when Paris brought back childhood fears of disintegration with a vengeance and memories or fantasies of his loneliness as a child, of receiving relatively little help from his parents during episodes of severe anxiety. At twelve or thirteen, Malte's age at Urnekloster, René was in military school. His mother responded sympathetically to his anguished letters. His father seems to have been relatively unresponsive to his misery at St. Pölten and Mährish-Weisskirchen, until he finally let René end his military schooling after five very painful years (September 1886 to June 1891). The best evidence of Josef's attitude at this time is offered by Sieber, who quotes the following message from Josef to Phia:

I am sending you all the letters which in the course of the last difficult days I received from René. I have received a report from Weisskirchen that you overwhelmed René with, frankly, extravagant letters, which agitated his mind far more than they cheered it. Please, be brief in your letters and do not not in any way excite René, likewise do not encourage René's versifying.[4]

At Urnekloster the master of the hunt is frightened by the ghost of Christine Brahe the first time he sees her. He attempts to approach her, is dragged back to the table by Count Brahe, and finally in his terror rushes out of the dining hall. But the last time they see the ghost, the master of the hunt manages to stay in the room and, as the count raises a glass of wine toward him, is just able to raise his own glass, as if it were a great weight, a few inches off the table (37). Malte makes the meaning of his father's behavior clear. He asks himself a question concerning the master of the hunt which seems to answer itself. "Had he wanted to force himself, precisely because he was of such a passionate nature and yet so invested in logic and clarity, to endure this adventure calmly and unquestioningly?" The father's behavior and his character are intelligible to his son only in retrospect. "I saw, without comprehending, how he struggled with himself, and how, in the end, he triumphed" (36).

Malte's attempt to formulate the father's character in this passage comes early in the novel. Nowhere else does he credit the master of the hunt with "a passionate nature." Does the passage involve a brief attempt to redeem Herr Brigge, to give him admirable qualities? Does it cast light on Rilke's understanding of Josef? Sieber says that the poet got his extraordinary strength of will from his mother. Does Malte's expressed sense of his father's triumphant struggle with himself in this episode suggest that Rainer may have thought of Josef as a model for the struggle of the will to overcome inner weakness, fear, and disappointment at frustration and failure? Having given up his hopes of an officer's career, Josef worked his way up to "a fairly high post in a private railroad, which he has earned with infinite conscientiousness" (*Letters* 1:98). There is no evidence that he expressed despair or depression at his fate.

Against this argument one must set the mute fear Rilke ascribes to his father in the letter to Benvenuta, the anxiety mentioned in the Fourth Elegy. In his account of the ghost's visit at Urnekloster, Malte's description of his father's struggle for self-mastery undermines, with implicit satiric irony, any appeal which this struggle might have for us. Reading the details of the father's reactions to the first visitation, one feels that he is not admirable but ludicrous, leaping up from the table, "deathly pale," with his hands "clenched at his sides," shouting in fear and anger, his face "swollen with blood," tearing himself away and rushing out of the room, neglecting, in his fright, to take his son with him (33–34). Later, as the ghost once more walks slowly past, responding to his father-in-law's raised glass, Malte's father still seems to be shaped by the novelist's sense of the ridiculous, which is no less damaging to him than it is to the major, Malte's uncle, with his writhing tongue, his rotten teeth, his mouth fallen open, and his withered hand quivering in the faint brought on by the sight of his long-dead relative. And it is possible that in writing this scene, consciously or unconsciously, the poet-novelist split his father into the master of the hunt and the major, since the old uncle, like Josef, retired from the military at a relatively low rank (one of Josef's brothers had killed himself because he was not promoted).[5]

Malte's account of his father's behavior in his paternal grandparents' home, Ulsgaard, also satirizes the master of the hunt as the only person who takes his absurdly egocentric mother's recurrent bouts of choking seriously and seems to be "offering her his own normally functioning windpipe, placing it completely at her disposal" (121). Reading these scenes, I regret that Rilke did not do more with his talent for satiric-ironic comedy.

The father's overwrought struggle for self-possession is comic partly because he is so frightened by his own passions. His efforts produce stiffness and rigidity. Doubtless, Josef Rilke had urged René to bring his emotions under control, to strengthen his will, to work for logic and clarity. Earlier I quoted the message Josef wrote to his estranged wife, urging her not to agitate René's mind while he was in military school. He was eager to see his son master all his fears and doubts so that he could become a good officer. Rilke must have understood that such a rigorous effort at self-control as he portrayed in the master of the hunt can be deadening, can kill one's passionate nature and result in the petrification which pervades the portrait of Herr Brigge.

Malte's description of his father after his death was probably based on Rilke's experience when Josef died.[6] Malte's impressions of the corpse and the apartment in which the master of the hunt ended his life implicitly define his father's character and his life. One cannot miss Rilke's irony in the sentence, "I felt as if I had seen him dead several times before: so familiar did all this seem" (155). The late master of the hunt wears "the expression of a man who out of politeness is trying to remember something." This recalls, in contrast, the monstrous roaring of his own father, Chamberlain Brigge, as he lies dying at Ulsgaard. The image of Malte's dead father reminds us of his sterility, his stiffness, his apparent hollowness in life. The roaring of the chamberlain's dying body seems to express all the unused energy and passion the grandfather has had in reserve during his lifetime. The father's hands, which lie "obliquely crossed," look "artificial and meaningless" (155). This is what the striving of the will to overcome his passionate nature, to achieve correctness, logic, and clarity, has come to. The long endeavor to maintain self-mastery has deadened the master of the hunt many years before his death. The corpse is the symbol of this struggle and its results.

Earlier I asked if, despite his sense of these truths, Rilke identified with his father in the older man's admiration of discipline and self-mastery. Certainly he discovered a positive model of such virtues in Rodin, and I shall develop this argument in my chapter on his relationship with the sculptor. In psychoanalytic terms, one could say that early identifications were modified by later ones and that antagonistic feelings toward the father and critical attitudes toward the qualities which we have been exploring also brought about modifications in Rilke's sense of himself. The poet could resolve the contradictions between opposing attitudes toward the paternal values by finding a creative way in which to realize them without allowing them to deaden him, rejecting the kind of life exemplified by the master of the hunt.

One closely related aspect of Rainer's identification with Josef becomes apparent in the poet's clothes and manners, as described by Wilhelm Hausenstein, the art historian (quoted in chapter 3, part 2)—the cautious gestures, gray-blue suit, deerskin gloves, walking-stick, and "light gray spats," all of which gave him "the conventional appearance of a man of the world."[7]

In her *Freud Journal,* writing about a 1913 reunion with Rilke, Lou Andreas-Salomé says, "When the old ebony walking stick he had inherited broke last summer—the silver handle of which his father held at the little boy's eye level in all their walks, Rainer shuddered, and was shocked, as though it was the ominous destruction of something which had to be an organic part of him, something which infused him with the power of his father."[8] Lou reveals at least part of the motivation for Rilke's identification with his father—something we might not have suspected, if we did not realize that early impressions and fantasies of a parent continue to shape our psychic life long past the time when these impressions have been forgotten and the parent himself has changed substantially. If Salomé is to be believed, the small child's impressions and fantasies of the father's power continued to influence him long after his father's failures and disappointments became painfully clear to him and even after Josef died. Some elements of Rainer's early identification with Josef may have remained very much alive, if unconscious. In 1915 Rilke acquired a new walking stick of his own to replace the broken one.

The clothes of the "conventional" "man of the world," as Hausenstein describes them, would surely have pleased Josef. I said in chapter 3 that this conventional appearance may have shielded Rilke from intrusiveness, defending his inner life as a mask or a false self can protect those who fear that knowledge of their feelings and thoughts can give other people power to manipulate, exploit, depersonalize, or engulf them. Rilke's clothes, his manners, his walking stick, all the paraphernalia of the social persona, sustained an identification with Josef that was motivated by the desire to make his father's power a part of himself. But they may have reflected as well his need to protect himself against the railway inspector's efforts to shape him. They may have been his way of appeasing his father even after his death and of concealing the inner life which made Josef anxious and moved him to pressure his son to conform.

Lou's *Freud Journal* records one of Rilke's dreams, in which his mirror reflection seems to change into an image of his father, "grown smaller than he, a little bent and sad, holding his head to one side," as both Ewald and Herr von Tragy do in the novella. The feelings experienced in the dream were "horror and melancholy."[9] Was this a wish fulfillment, as psychoanalysts tell us dreams are at their deepest level of motivation? Was it a fulfillment of a wish to be identified with the father? If so, the feelings expressed in the dream were ambivalent, obviously. Did the dream fulfill the desire of the poet to be his father, but also express his feeling that he was a much diminished version of the older man? Did it express the fear that in fulfilling his wish to be like Josef he had grown smaller, bent, and sad? Hausenstein describes the poet as "somewhat stooped." Did the horror in the dream come from self-recognition or a fantasy of self-recognition? One can only raise questions. Salomé offers no interpretation. If the poet provided one, she does not mention it. Rilke had steadfastly fought off his father's efforts to get him to take a civil service position, which he feared would reduce him to such a figure. Yet the belief that he might become this man discovered in the mirror of his dream must have remained.

Two years after the 1913 meeting which Lou describes in her *Freud*

Journal, Rilke wrote the Fourth Elegy, in which he expressed his aversion to the ordinary bourgeois whose life before his inner eye was hollow, tawdry pretense and deception, recalling Josef and Phia in his childhood, with their falsely labeled bottles of cheap wine. In the Elegy the poet asks if anyone has not sat anxiously before his own curtained heart and watched the curtain go up and then the dancer on this inner stage, only to realize in dismay that, whatever lightness and ease he brings to his performance, this dancer, under the costume and make-up, is the burgher, the commonplace, middle-class fellow who enters his house through the kitchen. The poet has had more than enough of such "half-filled masks."

> Wer sass nicht bang vor seines Herzens Vorhang?
> Der schlug sich auf: die Szenerie war Abschied.
> Leicht zu verstehen. Der bekannte Garten,
> und schwankte leise: dann erst kam der Tänzer.
> Nicht *der.* Genug! Und wenn er auch so leicht tut,
> er ist verkleidet und er wird ein Bürger
> und geht durch seine Küche in die Wohnung.

> Ich will nicht diese halbgefüllten Masken. . . .
> (*WDB,* 1:453)

After a few intervening lines the Elegy focuses upon Josef in the passage quoted earlier, where Rilke sees his father as having been "occupied with the after-taste" of his own "alien future" and as having been anxious often since his death "within my hope, in me." I have discussed the poet's feeling, expressed here, that he has internalized his father's fear for him and that it gnaws at the very center of his hopes and aspirations. What we know of Josef Rilke and the proximity of the father and the "Bürger" in the poem associate the two figures. People who are half-filled masks because they are governed by fear and timidity, such as Josef's, cannot live fully out of their own instincts and passions, must costume and mask themselves to be in conformity with the expectations of those around them. (Among such people are Herr von Tragy and the father who wrote to Rilke and Clara, demanding that they come to visit him in proper clothes—and the poet himself, insofar as he has become identified with the father who gnaws at his insides.)

This father has been introjected. He lives on in his son as a "felt presence." (In *Internalization in Psychoanalysis*, W. W. Meissner defines an "introject" as "an inner presence of an external object" and says that "relations between subject and introject may be as varied as the relations between two separate persons," though introjects may also "become phenomenologically confused with and mistaken for the sense of self in varying degrees.")[10] Unlike the military man with his dreams of glory, this bourgeois father was an antimodel, an image of what the poet feared in himself and defended himself against. But the father who became such an antimodel was also much loved and esteemed, remained long after his death an embodiment of power, love, and generosity for his son, continued to draw Rainer into identification with him and continued to be a felt presence within Rainer, because the poet wanted and needed him there.

Except for the forced service which he briefly endured during the First World War, Rilke kept clear of the military in which his father had failed to obtain a commission. He fled the bourgeois life in Prague and rejected all thoughts of a civilian career in any way resembling Josef's. The poet's inability to maintain long-term intimacy with a woman may have been partly due to Josef's loss of his wife's love and respect and his abandonment by Phia. These childhood experiences must have been traumatic. He feared that, like his father, he could not give a woman the kind of deep, sustained love many women (and men) require from lovers. In *The Notebooks* and elsewhere he lamented man's inability to reciprocate such love in women (see *The Notebooks*, 133–35). Leaving so many women after brief relationships, he may well have been motivated by the wish to avoid the pain and humiliation of being left, which his father had suffered.

IV

In the fall of 1904, although he had serious misgivings about Ellen Key's glowing essay on him, published in a Swedish periodical, he sent a copy to his father. He "was touched by" the old man's "evident pleasure at it."[1] The poet had expressed to Lou his anxiety about the essay and about Key's lectures on his life and work. "I am afraid she has ... given everything [his early work] a semblance of conclusiveness which it doesn't possess and in which people will feel cheated when they buy my books now" (*Letters* 1:165). Perhaps it was this very quality that worried him so much—Key's excessive generosity, her inflated sense of his achievement and mastery—which moved him to send the essay to his father, who was, as he wrote to Lou, "patient with me now in such a sad way" (*Letters* 1:180). Plagued by a "guilty conscience" because he was making so little progress with his work, no doubt he sent Key's essay to his father in the hope that it would reassure him, lighten his sadness, reward his patience, and thus ease the old man's infectious anxiety and his own guilt.

Expressing his doubts about her lectures and essays to Ellen Key in March 1905, Rilke urged her to speak only of his truly accomplished work, a few poems and stories. But he made an exception, saying that she could talk about his poetry and fiction without such restraint and caution in Prague, where he imagined her bringing "his long-suffering father" the news that he had finally won "recognition."[2] Although Josef Rilke could not attend Key's Prague lecture, she visited him, and his letters to his son showed that she had been an effective missionary. The poet wrote to tell her that she had achieved what he had been trying to do without any hope of success. She had convinced Josef that his son's vocation and way of life were "essential."[3] Key's effect upon his father was one of the factors, Prater says, that at this time produced "a euphoria he [Rainer] had not felt for a long time."[4]

Josef was aging. He would die the following March (1906). If only Rilke could convince his father before he died that he was on the way to becoming a grand success in his chosen profession, the happiness he could give the old man would make up for and undo the disappointment, pain, and anxiety he had caused him for so long—initially by leaving military school and rejecting a military career in which he might have rescued Josef from his own bitter failure. He had chosen a profession which the old man found, not only incomprehensible, but unreal, had cut himself off from the only kind of community and society which his father understood, and had failed to assume full responsibility for supporting himself, his wife, and his child. His dedication to poetry had left his father fearing that his only son would sink into miserable and shameful poverty, if he had not already done so.

One can see his stake in converting his father, in affording him the narcissistic delight a parent can obtain from a child's success. If only he could compensate the old man for the anxiety he had given him and replace that fear with confidence and pleasure and the self-esteem of a father who had seen his son achieve fame and praise, he could feel that he had repaid Josef's love and generosity. When his father died, Rainer could look back upon the end of his life without guilt. By relieving Josef's anxiety and by replacing it with confidence, Rilke could clear away one main source of his own self-doubt and replace it with a memory of his father that would encourage his own self-confidence in the future. If by converting Josef he could create a final image of the old man which would be largely benevolent, it would make a great difference after his father's death. I am verbalizing intuitive feelings that probably never came to reflective consciousness in the poet's mind.

As he sensed what his father's death might mean to him, he made use of Ellen Key and his growing reputation to reshape Josef's attitudes. If he succeeded in doing this, his success was due to a combination of luck, cunning intuitive foresight, and single-minded, willful creative energy.

The poet saw his father for the last time in late October 1905, when he went to Prague to give a lecture on Rodin. Josef was too weak from illness to come to the lecture. But while he was in Prague, Rainer spent much of his time with the old man. Prater notes that Josef Rilke "was understandably delighted at his son's material progress and new-found independence."[5]

Rilke's sense of liberation at the time of Josef's death is reflected in Malte's reaction to the perforation of his father's heart. Malte sees this as the destruction of the heart of the family, the cutting of his connections. His father's death gives him for the first time a firm sense of his individuality. Now his is "an individual heart" and at last it can do "its work of beginning from the beginning" (159). Years later, in 1921, Rilke developed this idea in a letter of condolence, in which he sees the loss of a father in old age as an impelling motive for gathering oneself together and relying on one's own abilities. While a father lives, the son is "modeled in relief upon him." His death is the blow that knocks us "free, alas," so that we achieve, at last, the fullness and separateness of a figure standing on its own (*Letters* 2:249).[6]

A letter written on April 6, 1906, little more than three weeks after Josef's death, leaves one in no doubt concerning its liberating effect. The poet describes "the feeling that I could do, should do something now,— something that may perhaps never come again like this" (*Letters* 1:202).

In the next two years many of the *New Poems* were written. This was a period of sustained creativity upon which Rilke was to look back with longing: "With a kind of shame I think of my best Paris time, that of the *New Poems,* when I expected nothing and no one and more and more the whole world streamed toward me merely as a task and I replied clearly and surely with pure work" (*Letters* 2:34). These poems took him well beyond the level of achievement he'd reached in earlier work. In the year and a half that followed their completion (August 1908-January 1910), he wrote much of *The Notebooks.* Never afterward was he to sustain such an outpouring of remarkable work for anywhere near the same length of time, though the month of February 1922 is more familiar to most of his readers as the period of almost miraculous creativity during which the *Duino Elegies* were completed and the *Sonnets to Orpheus* were written. The sense of liberation, of freedom, of a new beginning, and all the creative energy that came to him at the time of his father's death seem to have been reinforced by the knowledge that he had allayed his father's doubts about him, won his approval, and thus given him great pleasure and undone much of the harm he had inflicted by disappointing and worrying the old man.

These changes also helped Rilke to continue the work, which he had begun long before his father's death, of restoring and redeeming Josef's image in his own mind, creating a truly loving, generous, large-minded father. Just after Josef's death, Rilke described him as "kindness itself to me, the most loyal aid and the most touching friend."[7] Two years later the poet recalled that he had "experienced infinite bigness and generosity" through his father (*Letters* 1:329).

How useful it was to have such a father in memory, as a supportive presence in his mind, a parent with whom he could identify himself. How very different it would have been to live with the memory of a father reduced at death to bitter failure, fear, and doubt.

The work of redemption and restoration both before and after Josef's death seems to have been achieved in a number of ways. Possibly the poet's filial relationship with Rodin enabled him to associate his two fathers in such a way that, through a reverse transference, his idealization of the sculptor helped him to idealize the railway inspector. Increasingly Rilke tended to polarize the positive and negative qualities of his parents, shifting all the negative ones to his mother. As his father aged and became ill, and after his death as well, this ongoing process of polarization may have helped him to isolate Josef from the kind of hostility and revulsion which he felt toward his mother and to redeem his father in his mind. Often negative qualities are transferred from a dead parent to a living one or to a stepfather or stepmother. This defense supports the idealization of the dead parent and distances him or her from hatred, anger, and related feelings.

It is not unusual after separation or divorce for the children to attach most of the blame to one parent, sometimes the one who has left, sometimes the one who remains with them and is held responsible for all constraints and punishments, frustrations, and disappointments. This division defends the children against painful emotional conflicts. Perhaps the idealization of Josef and the concentration of negative feelings on Phia helped Rilke to defend himself against fears of engulfment, as this threat seems to have been associated far more with his mother than his father. Perhaps, also, the concentration of negative feelings on Phia helped the poet to defend himself against an oedipal attachment to her, reflected in *The Notebooks* and in his affair with Lou. Obviously, this polarization would reinforce the repression of those hostile feelings toward his father which originated in the oedipal rivalry, the focus of Simenauer's analysis of the relationship between Josef and Rainer.

Rilke defended himself against grief with a conception of the continuing existence of the dead, imperishable within the mental depths of the survivors who love them. Recalling his father, he reasons that a connection with someone else often "goes on more strongly and powerfully" in the unconscious mind. The rooting of a relationship in the unconscious results in our "possession" of the other person. And the "lasting," immutable nature of feelings, objects, and relations in those "invisible" depths makes our "possession" permanent as long as we live. (Here Freud would have agreed with the poet, to a large extent.) Rilke's reasoning on this subject takes a Kierkegaardian and paradoxical turn when he notes that acquaintance, friendship, or love, involving such possession, turns us back into ourselves, because it requires so much lonely inward activity "that it would suffice to occupy us each by himself forever" (*Letters* 1:330–31). This conception of human relationships makes more sense if we remember that the poet is thinking partly about the work of imaginative transformation he must do on everything mutable and changeable which he loves and values. The ninth Duino Elegy makes his meaning clear. In the following lines the poet reflects that ephemeral things understand he is praising them and rely upon us, the most ephemeral of all beings, for salvation, wishing that we will be impelled to transform them inwardly, invisibly, into ourselves.

> ... Und diese, von Hingang
> lebenden Dinge verstehn, dass du sie rühmst; vergänglich,
> traun sie ein Rettendes uns, den Vergänglichsten, zu.
> Wollen, wir sollen sie ganz im unsichtbarn Herzen verwandeln
> in—o unendlich—in uns! ...
> (WDB 1:475)

Rilke's letter concerning the permanence of the dead suggests an effort to achieve what the analysts would call "denial" of reality, reinforcing suppression of grief. The letter also seems to imply an assumption that a person enters into friendship or mutual love in the hope of taking the object of his feelings into himself so that he may enjoy the loving relationship in solitude or at a distance. Often this was the pattern of Rilke's life.

Did Rilke take possession of his father at last by persuading him, with Ellen Key's help, that his son's vocation was real and valuable? Writing about Josef explicitly or indirectly in short stories and poems, in *Ewald Tragy* and *The Notebooks,* and in his letters was a way of possessing and achieving mastery over him. *Ewald Tragy* shows the son assuring himself that his father loves him, even as he reassures himself that he is quite capable of separating himself from his father, objectifying and satirizing and thus distancing the older man while at the same time delineating and intimating the redeeming qualities that made Josef lovable despite his rigidity and his limitations.

Analysts might say that Rilke's theory of love and death suggests the poet preferred a relationship with an introject (the living presence of a person within the mind) to a sustained, intimate relationship with the real person. An introject may live on as long as we do, even after the real person has died. No doubt, Rilke's sense of the reality of the introjected benevolent, generous, large-minded, loving father was so powerful that, having accustomed himself to the presence of this father, he softened his grief for the real one whom he had been distancing for years. As we can see in lines of "The Book of Pilgrimage," the second part of *The Book of Hours,* written in 1901 and revised in 1905, a year before Josef's death, he had converted his father into a ghostly phantasm even before his death. On one side of an evident split in the father's image, the poet was seeing Josef as a faded old man of the distant past, withered, barely alive:

> Ist uns der Vater denn nicht das, was *war;*
> vergangne Jahre, welche fremd gedacht,
> veraltete Gebärde, tote Tracht,
> verblühte Hände und verblichnes Haar?
> Und war er selbst für seine Zeit ein Held
> er ist das Blatt, das, wenn wir wachsen, fällt.
> (*WDB* 1:68)

> Isn't the father for us what *was;*
> years gone, which seemed alien,
> obsolete gestures, dress out of fashion,
> withered hands and ashen hair?
> And if he was a hero for his time
> he is the leaf that falls when we thrive.

Another poem, "Jugend-Bildnis meines Vaters" (Portrait of My Father as a Youth), written in June 1906, is ambiguous. It expresses the poet's sense of the poignancy of his father's life, as well as Rainer's love and, perhaps, grief for that young man who had hoped for much and realized none of his hopes. But it ends with the father as a "quickly disappearing daguerreotype," his hands nearly lost to sight. Josef's eyes dream. His large mouth becomes an image of his youth. He is in full dress uniform, wearing a saber. The poet thinks of his father's hands as waiting, at rest, not impelled toward anything, perhaps suggesting a lack of motivation and direction. As they come near vanishing in the old daguerreotype, they seem to be grasping remoteness. Everything else about that young man is veiled, beyond the poet's understanding. At the end of this poem about his father's vanishing, Rilke realizes that his own hands are perishing, though more slowly than those of the youth in the photograph:

> Im Auge Traum. Die Stirn wie in Berührung
> mit etwas Fernem. Um den Mund enorm
> viel Jugend, ungelächelte Verführung,
> und vor der vollen schmückenden Verschnürung

der schlanken adeligen Uniform
der Säbelkorb und beide Hände—, die
abwarten, ruhig, zu nichts hingedrängt.
Und nun fast nicht mehr sichtbar: als ob sie
zuerst, die Fernes greifenden, verschwänden.
Und alles andre mit sich selbst verhängt
und ausgelöscht als ob wirs nicht verständen
und tief aus seiner eignen Tiefe trüb—.

Du schnell vergehendes Daguerreotyp
in meinen langsamer vergehenden Händen.
(*WDB* 1:278)

Written a few months after the father's death, this poem reflects opposing attitudes, feelings, and needs—the divided poet's ability to see his father from a distance, objectively, his sympathy and tenderness for the man, and an inclination to depersonalize and derealize him, to turn him into a "quickly disappearing daguerreotype." Yet this is countered by the last line, which suggests Rilke's sense of affinity with his father.

Prater quotes a letter describing a visit to the father's grave on All Souls Day of 1907. The inscription had "weathered into the stone," "as if it had stood in an old park undisturbed for a century."[8] The poet's feeling that his father has been dead for a century reflects the inclination to distance and derealize Josef.

The Notebooks entry in which the sight of the dead father gives Malte the feeling that he has "seen him dead several times before" reveals a struggle to suppress grief at the sight and at the memory, of that scene (*The Notebooks*, 155). It also supports the thesis that both before and after his father's death Rilke struggled to suppress all attachment by turning Josef into a thing of the past, a faded photo, furniture, someone who had been dead for a long time before his death, whose grave had been there for a century.

The poet was divided between the inclination to defend himself against his father in this way and a need to preserve him redeemed and restored as the image of paternal love and generosity. In 1923, after having completed his greatest task, the writing of the *Elegies* and the *Sonnets,* which repeatedly reaffirm the continuing presence and vitality of the dead and the past, Rilke tried once more to formulate his sense of their immediacy and influence. Recalling his fear of his father's death as a child and his fantasy that his own existence was inseparable from Josef's, he wrote to Countess Margot Sizzo, expressing his belief that death cannot end the existence within us of someone we love, as our image and conception of that person become increasingly "independent of his tangible presence" during his lifetime. The "secret influence" of someone dear to us would surely be kept safe within us. "Where can we come closer to it, where more purely celebrate it, when obey it better than when it appears linked with our own voices, as if our heart had learned a new language, a new song, a new strength" (*Letters* 2:315–16).

This comes very close to the language Freud and later analysts use to explain the way in which we successfully work through the pain experienced at death and other forms of loss. It leads one to think that Rilke had a fairly clear understanding of his introjection of his father and his identification with him as the means of overcoming the anguish and loneliness arising from the separateness, distance, and loss of his father, first during childhood, because of the older man's emotional stiffness and constraint, then at various times of physical separation when he went away to military school and when he left Prague to make a life on his own. Surely, before his father's death, he had accomplished much of what Freud and other analysts call "the work of mourning" by taking Josef into himself through introjection and by making him a part of himself through identification, two processes suggested by the language of the letter quoted above.

Anyone who has read Freud's *The Ego and the Id* can see how closely Rilke's ideas resemble the psychoanalyst's. Freud theorizes that a loved one we have lost becomes "set up inside the ego." This process makes an essential contribution to the development of character.[9] Using anthropomorphizing terms, he argues that in the process of persuading the id to give up the loved one and to accept his or her loss, the ego turns the id's love to itself by making the lost "object" a part of itself. Thus, object-directed libido becomes narcissistic libido. This change brings about the "desexualization" of the libidinal energy and its use for other aims, such as creating art. The transformation and shifting of the energy of love from object to ego involves "a kind of sublimation." Rilke's letter was written a few months before the publication of *The Ego and the Id* in April 1923, though not before the publication of "Mourning and Melancholia" (1917).[10] Had Rilke read the latter essay? Had he heard about these ideas through friends, such as Lou Andreas-Salomé, who were immersed in psychoanalytic theory, or through other analysts among his acquaintances? I know of nothing that answers these questions definitively.

More recent theory tends to confirm Freud's notions concerning the internalizing of objects that have been lost or given up, though analysts have continued to argue about the ways in which we take such objects into ourselves, the nature of the objects internalized, and the meanings of the terms—"incorporation," "introjection," and "identification." Two of the best clarifications of these phenomena and terms in recent years are Roy Schafer's *Aspects of Internalization* (1968) and W. W. Meissner's *Internalization in Psychoanalysis* (1981), cited earlier.[11]

In "Mourning and Its Relation to Manic-Depressive States," Melanie Klein observes that "the mourner obtains great relief from recalling the lost person's kindness and good qualities, and this is partly due to the reassurance he experiences from keeping his loved object for the time being as an idealized one." Klein argues that the feeling that we possess "the perfect loved object (idealized) inside," which is supported and strengthened by focusing upon the lost person's kindness and good qualities, helps us to defend ourselves against the "feeling of triumph" which may arise from the death of somebody close and one's own survival, from the hostility and murderousness which also may come near to consciousness at the death of a loved parent, and from the sense of liberation, which Rilke experienced at the time of his father's death. According to Klein, we are likely to feel that the good, kind parent whom we possess within us will defend us against the vengeful parent within, who wishes to punish us for desiring his death and for feeling triumph and liberation when he dies.

Such benevolent and malevolent introjects exist within us from a very early time, Klein believed. From infancy we reshape our parents by projecting our feelings and fantasies onto them. Meissner argues that it is these images of parents, in which object and subjective fantasy fuse, that we introject. They continue to live in us as presences, sometimes experienced as objects within the mind, sometimes closely identified with our sense of self. The death of a parent may provide such introjects with an unusually intense life. What seems especially relevant to our exploration of Rilke's response to his father's death is Klein's argument that fantasies of kind, loving, idealized parents within us help surviving children to defend themselves against hostile, even murderous emotions and a sense of triumph, as well as against guilt and the internal presence of a vengeful, punishing parent.[12]

CHAPTER 8

Rodin

I

In the summer of 1905, not having seen his old friend and "master" for more than two years, Rilke asked if he might pay Rodin a visit. The sculptor telegraphed a welcome and had his secretary write, inviting the poet to live with him at Meudon for the duration of Rilke's stay in Paris, adding that the Frenchman was looking forward to the opportunity which this visit would give them to talk. Full of excitement at this prospect, eagerly anticipating being "allowed to share all his days," the poet wrote to a friend that "the great man" was "dear as a father" (*Letters* 1:188 and 190). The relationship with this second father was no less important than the one with Salomé. During the years in which it evolved we see extraordinary changes in Rilke. He came to Paris in 1902 as a poet of obvious talent and technical skill. But, as he himself realized, most of his work, however promising, was superficial, unoriginal in feeling and thought, and facile in its music. During the next four years he developed into the author of the *New Poems* and *The Notebooks,* the first books which place him among the twentieth century's major writers. A number of factors contributed to the changes in Rilke; the relationship with the sculptor was a central shaping influence.

E. M. Butler tells us that Rilke was introduced to Rodin's sculpture as early as 1897.[1] The poet's esteem for the sculptor is reflected in his early diaries kept at Schmargendorf (1898–1900) and Worpswede (1900).[2] Clara, Rilke's wife, had studied with Rodin, and the poet's marriage probably intensified his interest in the sculptor and augmented his knowledge of the man and his work. In September 1902, having received a commission to do a monograph on the sculptor, Rilke went to France to meet him.

Rodin was one of the giants of modern art. His creative energies and the abundant productivity of his genius have been rivaled by relatively few great artists. But Rilke's idealization of the sculptor often seems to exaggerate his greatness well beyond any realistic assessment, and sometimes, in its excesses, the poet's overestimation of his "master" approaches absurdity.

One has only to read a few sentences of Rilke's letters to Rodin and his letters about the "master" to realize that his idealization of this father figure went beyond the admiration justified by the sculptor's great gifts and his accomplishments. Even before meeting Rodin in September 1902, Rilke expressed the belief that he might be the greatest of all living men: "Does anyone exist, I wonder, who is as great as he and yet is still living. . . . I have the feeling that, quite aside from his art, he is a synthesis of greatness and power, a future century, a man without contemporaries" (*Letters* 1:76). A letter to Clara, written more than three years later, shows that those years of intermittent closeness to Rodin had in no way diminished the sculptor's stature in Rilke's mind: "His example is so without equal, his greatness rises up before one like a very near tower. . . . He is everything . . . far and wide. . . . [H]e shows one everything" (September 20, 1905; *Letters* 1:192–93).

Rilke compares Rodin to "an eastern god enthroned," undisturbed by anything and anyone around him, completely self-contained and self-sufficient, the narcissist's ideal fantasy of self-realization, the antipode of the neurotic narcissist's feelings of empty and barren isolation. In the same letter Rilke says, "He moves like a star. He is beyond all measure" (*Letters* 1:191). Writing this letter, Rilke may have been thinking of the effigy of Buddha which stood on a little hill near Rodin's house in Meudon. The *New Poems* which express the poet's fascination with Buddha focus upon some of the same qualities attributed here to the eastern god and to Rodin. Rilke told the sculptor that he thought of this statue as the center of the world (*Letters* 1:194). Rodin was the center of his own world and, at times, to a large extent, of Rilke's.

In an August 1903 letter to Salomé the poet associates Rodin with the divine Creator in Genesis: "when he fashions a hand, it is alone in space, and there is nothing besides a hand; and in six days God made only a hand and poured out the waters around it and bent the heavens above it; and rested over it when all was finished, and it was a glory of a hand" (*Letters* 1:118).

These effusions concerning the sculptor's godlike nature are often joined with the poet's radically contrasted sense of himself. The "very near tower" who "shows one everything" was a strong protector as well as a needed guide, teacher, and model, who filled all of these paternal roles superbly when Josef Rilke could no longer do so. Apart from his "master," in 1902 and 1903, Rilke felt "scattered like some dead man in an old grave," as he wrote to Lou (August 10, 1903; *Letters* 1:124).

Rilke's response to Rodin as a tower of strength must be seen in relation to the illness, the fears, the near madness of those early days in Paris. Letters to Lou written that summer and fall stress Rilke's inability to work, his weariness, his anxiety, his sense that he is moving in an inescapable circle rather than advancing, that his connections with the past are disintegrating and the future is a void. His life is filled with uncertainty (November 1903; *Letters* 1:133–34).

From the first Rilke saw Rodin as a shelter from his fears and as someone who offered direction to him when he felt homeless and lost (*Letters* 1:94 and 117). If you read these letters, written in 1902 and 1903, you can see that the poet found with the sculptor, if only temporarily, a home which could fulfill his long frustrated and resisted need for one that could take the place of the parental home which he had lost when his mother left his father and he was sent to military school. (He had tried and failed to create such a home in his marriage with Clara.) Remember the longings he expressed to Paula Becker in October 1900, suggesting that seeking a home was, for him, inseparably connected with his continuing search for a mother (*Letters* 1:46). For much of his life he could not find one without the other. Curiously, for a time, the sculptor supplied both needs.

In Rodin Rilke felt he had discovered a man who had become a home and a complete world to himself. "Deep in himself he bore the darkness, shelter, and peace of a house, and he himself had become sky above it, and wood around it" (*Letters* 1:118). These images and metaphors evoke the sculptor's power as the model of the existence which Rilke wished to achieve for himself, partly through association with the "master," studying and emulating him. They also support the conclusion that Rodin was a maternal as well as a paternal figure for the poet. Writing to Clara in September 1905, after returning to Meudon to live at Rodin's, Rilke compared his reception by "the master" to "the way a beloved place receives one." He elaborates this metaphor: the sculptor becomes "a spring" that sings and mirrors, "a grove," a rose-lined "path" (*Letters* 1:191). Like the images of the sculptor as "shelter," "house," and "wood" in the letter to Lou, here the mirroring spring, the grove, and the rose-lined path of the "beloved place" associate his host with feminine and maternal qualities, and this association is reinforced as Rilke tells Clara that Rodin had "the smile of a woman."

In his next letter to Clara, Rilke asks, "[W]hat are all times of rest, all days in wood and sea, . . . and the thoughts of all this: what are they . . . against the indescribably confident repose in his holding and carrying glance . . . " (*Letters* 1:192). This "holding and carrying glance," which gave rest and health and assurance more powerfully than anything else the poet could think of, brings to mind the benevolent mother who defends the child against nocturnal fears in *The Notebooks* and the Third Elegy. It recalls the mirroring gaze of the "good enough" mother which, as D. W. Winnicott observed, confirms the child's self-love and self-esteem, supporting his sense of his own reality and value, calming fear and doubt, assuring such a sense of well-being and confidence as nothing else can give.[3] Was this "holding and carrying glance" an unconscious memory of Rilke's mother projected onto Rodin? Was it an unconscious fantasy of a benevolent mother (a wish fulfillment) projected? We can only raise these questions. But that Rodin was both mother and father to Rilke in an even more fundamental sense is made clear in an early letter from the poet to his new "master" in which he expresses gratitude for the gift of rebirth (*Letters* 1:88).

Rilke's subliminal association of Rodin with a mother has another kind of meaning. It reminds us that Phia was the original force behind René's aspiration to become an artist, as she read him poetry and encouraged him to write it.[4] His father offered René very different ideal images of male power, success, and glory. For Rilke Rodin embodied the realization of Phia's aspirations and ambitions for herself and her son, while at the same time, though he was not a victorious general, he epitomized ideals of masculine mastery, achievement, and renown. In these terms one can understand the poet's response to the sculptor as "an example given to my life, to my art" (*Letters* 1:88). Though his mother's esteem for poets and poetry ultimately had greater control over his mind and life than his father's ideal of an officer's career, his letters and poems show that the latter did have a strong influence upon the poet. While Phia dressed René as a little girl and encouraged him to play the part of a daughter, Josef drilled him like a soldier. Surely, the conflict between the parents' attempts to define their son's aspirations contributed to the confusion in René's mind about his sexual identity. In Roy Schafer's terms, the parents confronted René with "models for identification" which made "it hard for [their] son to integrate his own masculinity and femininity."[5] Rilke's discovery of a second father corresponding to the ideal notion of himself as a great artist which originated with Phia must have helped the young poet to resolve the deeply disturbing conflict between the fantasies of self-fulfillment which his mother had fostered and the sense of himself as a male rooted in childhood identification with his father.

While Josef Rilke was pressing his son to take an ordinary job, Rodin was urging the poet to immerse himself in his chosen work. Rejecting the kind of job his father had in mind as a form of death in life, he eagerly accepted the sculptor's notion that devoting himself to the labors of his vocation all day, day after day, was the way in which to free himself from a life dependent on unpredictable fits of inspiration. He had come to Rodin to ask "[H]ow must one live?" The Frenchman's answer was to urge him to immerse himself in work. The young poet, who had found that a life dependent upon infrequent inspiration was often painfully empty, began to think that "to work is to live without dying." This discovery, made during his first days with Rodin, brought with it the delighted sense of rebirth which I have mentioned (*Letters* 1:88, 82, and 84). In his book on Rodin, Rilke mentions that the sculptor had worked for a decorator and then for Carrière Belleuse at Sèvres. His beginnings as a laborer and a craftsman had disciplined him and formed his values and attitudes (*WSR*, 143).

Obviously there was a vast difference between the constant labor which the sculptor urged upon his disciple and the bourgeois job which his father offered to find him. But there may well have been an unconscious association in the poet's mind between Josef Rilke's advice and example and Rodin's. Did Rodin, as a paternal embodiment of an ideal of the self which had been fostered by Rilke's mother, provide a way of reconciling that ideal with values and attitudes concerning productive work which the father had urged upon his son?

As Rodin opposed his life of constant labor to dependence on fitful inspiration, Josef Rilke not only advocated a regular job but fought against the erratic, fitful emotional excitement which he thought Phia fueled in her son. Obviously, Rodin was a man much given to passion and impulse. But it was the other side of him, the steady worker, disciplined originally by poverty and jobs as a craftsman-laborer, which Rilke emphasized in writing about him, observing that the sculptor denied the existence of inspiration.[6] Rilke's response to his second father's opinion on this point suggests unconscious identification with attitudes of Josef which he consciously rejected. In any event, for most of the rest of his life, as various commentators have pointed out, he was not able to follow Rodin's example and advice, apart from a few periods of sustained productivity, such as the years in which he wrote most of the *New Poems* and *The Notebooks* (1906–1910). At this time Rodin's example loomed large in his mind.

In the last year of his life, Rilke wrote to a young friend that Rodin's influence had helped him to overcome superficiality in his poetry by placing him under "the obligation to work like a painter or a sculptor before nature, understanding and copying inexorably."[7] In the first part of his *Rodin,* Rilke gives high praise to the Frenchman's extraordinary powers of observation. "Keeping his eye constantly on the model and leaving the paper entirely to his experienced and rapid hand, he drew an immense number of movements which till then had been neither seen nor recorded, and it turned out they had a vitality of expression which was tremendous" (*WSR,* 114).

Following his master's example, the young poet began to observe people and things carefully. This was part of the process of learning to see which became a major theme of *The Notebooks.* The emphasis upon accurate observation of the external world, which he developed under Rodin's influence, markedly changed the nature of Rilke's poetry, as scholars have noted, with the advent of the *New Poems.* E. M. Butler argues that before he went to Paris, "the main impression produced by [Rilke's] letters, diaries and poetry is that of a mind in love with unreality and of a man evading as far as possible the insurgent claims of real life."[8] Butler says that these tendencies came from Phia. Sieber, who knew Phia, and Lou Andreas-Salomé, who met her, confirm her son's judgment that she lived amid unrealities—self-deceptions, counterfeit or inauthentic feelings and pieties, illusory perceptions of her son, affectations of religiosity, and pretensions to an aristocratic style.[9]

The crucial encouragement which Rodin gave to Rilke, in turning him outward, in making him look closely at things in the external world, and the results as we find them in the *New Poems,* bring to mind the observations of psychologists who argue that early in life the father's presence encourages the child to emerge from the narcissistic, symbiotic relationship with the mother and to come into contact with the world around him. [10] The influence of Rodin, the artist "dear as a father," may have evolved out of, built upon, drawn strength and energy from, an early, now unconscious association of the father with interest in external reality and with emergence from the highly subjective womb of infantile narcissism into the multifarious surround.

II

Contrasting himself with Rodin, Rilke wrote to Lou in August 1903, asking, "Do I lack the strength? Is my will sick?" The letter expresses his feeling that "there is nothing real about me . . . I divide again and again and flow apart" (*Letters* 1:122). He describes Rodin as a man who "has left nothing in uncertainty and has given reality to everything" (*Letters* 1:123). One can see the appeal of such a fantasy of Rodin to the young poet, plagued by a sense of his own unreality, by uncertainty, self-division, severe anxieties, and the threat of psychic disintegration in the alien chaos of Paris. To Rilke, who felt at this time that he lacked vitality, energy, direction, and even the knowledge of how to live, Rodin seemed, as he later wrote to Clara, to send a "rush of forces streaming into one" and to exemplify "an ability to live of which I had no idea" (*Letters* 1:192).

What are the origins of his idealization of the sculptor? The first section of this chapter suggests the way in which Rodin became a father for the young poet and also, subliminally, a maternal figure. He embodied unconscious projections of childhood images and fantasies of both Rilke's parents and was the object of feelings transferred from these highly subjective childhood figures in the poet's unconscious.[1]

Can we describe and define the parental figure of childhood fantasy which Rilke projected onto Rodin? In doing so, I shall avail myself of Heinz Kohut's insights. In *The Analysis of the Self* (1971) and *The Restoration of the Self* (1977), Kohut studies forms of what he calls narcissistic illness in which "the self has not been solidly established," with the consequence that "its cohesion and firmness depend on the presence of a self-object (or the development of a self-object transference)."² By "self-object" Kohut means "objects which are themselves experienced as part of the self," as the mother is in infancy. These are "archaic objects cathected with narcissistic libido . . . which are still in intimate connection with the archaic self" of infancy and early childhood. One such "archaic self-object," according to Kohut, is the highly idealized image of the parent as an omnipotent, perfect figure, which the "archaic self" is motivated to create partly by its need to preserve its own primitive narcissism and omnipotence by sharing in the idealized parent's power and perfection. The archaic self can feel all-powerful, lovable, and valuable in its fantasy of unity with this highly idealized parental figure. Hence, as Kohut argues, its idealization of the parent is narcissistic, the motivational energy comes from the infant's need for omnipotence, love, and self-esteem. According to Kohut, a child or an adult experiences another person from the perspective of narcissistic feelings and fantasies when the "expected control over such (self-object) others is . . . closer to the concept of the control which a grownup expects to have over his own body and mind than he expects to have over others."³

Kohut traces the extreme idealization of other people by adults suffering from what he calls narcissistic illness back to the beginnings of mental-emotional development in infancy. Very early in our lives, he says, "after being exposed to the disturbance of the psychological equilibrium of primary narcissism, the psyche saves a part of the lost experience of global narcissistic perfection to an archaic, rudimentary (transitional) self-object, the idealized imago." At this stage of development, "all power and bliss reside in the idealized object." Consequently, "the child feels empty and powerless when he is separated from it and he attempts, therefore, to maintain continuous union with it."⁴ Adults afflicted with narcissistic illness suffer from this infantile experience of emptiness and powerlessness in the absence of a surrogate for the "idealized parent imago." Rilke felt unreal, and he was plagued by self-doubt, uncertainty, self-division, and childhood fears in those early days in Paris.

He was drawn to Rodin by the feeling that the "master", "dear as a father," conferred reality and certainty on everything around him, sent his vitality into one like a mighty "rush of forces," held one in his "holding and carrying glance," which bestowed incomparable peace and rest, calm and shelter, and taught one, in one's helpless ignorance, how to live and how to work.

Often, according to Kohut, the unconscious fantasy underlying the relationship between the self and the idealized parental figure may be formulated as "You are perfect, but I am part of you." The adult who projects the godlike perfection of an idealized parent onto a surrogate feels that he can partake of the latter's omnipotence. Surely this was in large part the source of Rodin's effect upon Rilke when he first came to Paris.

Normally, during childhood, through timely, unexcessive disappointment and frustration, the idealization of the parent diminishes. Kohut suggests that, as this happens, the child redirects his idealizing love and esteem toward the superego. The superego thus becomes invested with this idealizing love and esteem, which help to establish its power and authority over us. "Traumatic disappointment" with parents, such as the sharp and bitter disillusionment which Rilke appears to have suffered with both his parents as a child, may undermine and disrupt the process by which the idealization of the parent imagoes is shifted to the superego.

Phia Rilke's "unreality," blind narcissism, and self-absorbed religiosity, which he repeatedly complained about in his letters; her withdrawal from her husband and son as her marriage deteriorated; her separation from them in 1884 when René was nine; her acceptance of Josef's decision to send René to military school, which seemed to him a kind of hell; his father's extreme stiffness and sterile conventionality; his crushing failure to find something better than a job as a railway official, which was such a come-down from his aspirations to a career as an army officer, suitable for a man whose family claimed noble ancestry; the parents' life of self-deception; their vulgar pretenses, which their son loathed—all these factors were, as the poet's letters reveal, sources of extremely painful disillusionment. Rilke recalled that "the worst coddling" in his infancy and early childhood made subsequent injuries and disappointments even more traumatic than they might otherwise have been (*Letters* 1:99).

Kohut observes that the child whose redirection of idealizing love and esteem to the superego has been undermined or disrupted grows into an adult who continues to "search for external ideal figures from whom he wants to obtain the approval and leadership which his insufficiently idealized superego cannot provide." Such figures may be experienced through transference as the "archaic self-objects" required for mental, emotional equilibrium.[5]

Rilke's poems and letters give the impression that Phia, lacking empathetic responsiveness, fell far short of adequate maternal mirroring, an early and necessary source of the sense of the self's reality and identity, of body-self cohesion, of self-esteem, and of the capacity for controlling anxiety. Kohut theorizes that "traumatic disappointments" in the "mirroring self-object" and the "idealized self-object" may impair essential ego functions, which develop through introjection of, and identification with, parents. These include the capacity for soothing oneself, defenses against excessive and threatening stimuli, and the ability both to control and to gratify primitive (drive) impulses, thus relieving accumulating tension and anxiety.[6]

Traumatic disillusionment, Kohut argues, frequently causes repression of the idealized parent imago into the unconscious. Or it may be split off, isolated from and disavowed by rational, realistic thinking and perception. Lacking an adequately idealized superego and crippled by the impairment of ego functions, the child remains dependent on this (often unconscious) parental presence for approval, esteem, and guidance, for confirmation of his reality, identity, and psychic coherence, and for protection against dangers and demands from within and from outside. He must seek someone in the external world to embody the "idealized self-object."

For an adult who is still "fixated" on such a figure the absence of a surrogate may create "a threat to the organization of the self," "various regressions," "fragmentation," and exposure to the terrors of childhood, among them "disintegration anxiety," the fear of annihilation, and related fears of merging and being engulfed.[7] Such anxieties and dangers abound in *The Notebooks* and in Rilke's 1903 letters appealing for help to his onetime mother surrogate, Lou Andreas-Salomé.

Kohut's relevance to my analysis of Rilke's initial response to Rodin may be summed up in a few words. An adult suffering from the kind of illness which Rilke portrayed autobiographically in Malte needs a surrogate "self-object," such as the one Rodin became for Rilke, to provide "the psychological cement that [maintains] the cohesion of the self." In this way the surrogate helps the narcissistically ill person defend himself against anxieties such as those Kohut describes, including the hypochondriacal fantasies resulting from fragmentation, in which one may feel that "various parts of his body [are] isolating themselves and [are] beginning to be experienced as strange and foreign."[8] Later in this chapter I shall explore the relationship between such frightening fantasies in Malte and Rilke's excitement on finding that Rodin could give an isolated part of a body, such as a hand, "the independence and completeness of a whole," and in so doing create a great work of art (*WSR*, 105; *Rodin*, part 1).

In *Object Love and Reality*, Arnold Modell develops another, closely related explanation of the kind of high-flying idealization we meet in Rilke's letters to and about Rodin and in his book on the sculptor. Originally, Modell says, the child invests one or both parents with omnipotence. Then he identifies with the parent(s) whom he has endowed with this quality. "The earliest core of identification that we can uncover in the analysis of adult patients is a core that is organized around such omnipotent fantasies."[9] The child creates and identifies with an omnipotent parent figure as a response to anxiety and helplessness, according to Modell. The child's sense of having made the parent's omnipotence a part of himself is magical thinking. "The essence of magical belief is that the acknowledged perceptual separation of objects is mere appearance. The magical object created by the subject becomes, in turn, part of the subject's own ego."[10]

In projecting these early parental figures upon other people, Modell notes, an adult experiences the latter as symbolic objects and thus becomes immersed in another dimension of magical thinking, identifying the symbol with the object which it represents. For Rilke, Rodin was a symbol, in this sense of the word, representing the highly idealized parental figures the poet had created as a child. Rilke unconsciously experienced Rodin as being identified with the godlike father and mother whom he symbolized.

What is the motivating need responsible for this kind of transference, according to Modell? He observes that adults who create omnipotent parent surrogates often do so because they lack the "cohesive sense of identity" which enables us to feel real and alive and well-integrated. The lack of this nucleus of the healthy adult psyche goes back to childhood failures in a person's relationships with his parents, such as those I have explored. Modell posits that a "cohesive sense of identity" is rooted in introjections of, and identifications with, "good enough" parents, those who are well integrated and intelligently empathetic in their love and in the guidance and control they provide in response to the infant's needs.

Early identifications with such parents develop a capacity for self-love and self-esteem and "facilitate" the essential functions of "ego control" that I defined while exploring Kohut's ideas. Parents whose failings are as marked and significant as those Rilke ascribes to his father and mother deprive their child of the opportunity to develop these essential capacities through identification with them. Consequently, Modell tells us, the child may "remain slavishly dependent" upon other people (as Rilke was dependent upon Lou Andreas-Salomé and Rodin) "to perform certain functions that have not been incorporated into their own egos."[11]

I have explained the way in which an adult with such needs, experiencing a child's helplessness, uncertainty, and anxiety, because of his failure to develop sufficient psychic health and strength, will project onto other adults infantile fantasies of perfect, godlike parents who have the power, wisdom, and generosity to give him everything he needs, including affection; refuge and protection from dangers; confirmation of his reality, achievements, and value; and trustworthy models for living and working.

In this kind of transference, as Modell points out, one person endeavors unconsciously to gain power over another, to bring the other individual into accord with his own needs and desires. He feels, as he does this, that he is trying to control and manipulate a parent or a parental figure. Modell compares transference in such a relationship to a child's use of "transitional objects" which symbolize its mother. His example is taken from Freud. In *Beyond the Pleasure Principle,* Freud describes a game which he watched a little boy play with a yo-yo. The boy, whose age was one and a half, would throw the reel over the edge of its cot so that it disappeared, while he held onto the string. At the disappearance of the reel, the child let out a loud sound which Freud and the little boy's mother interpreted as meaning "gone." Then the child pulled the reel back into sight and said, with apparent delight, "There."[12] Freud says the boy is mastering his anxiety over his mother's absence by proving to himself that he can bring the spool back at will. The spool is a symbolic or transitional object, and the boy's thinking in the game is magical in the sense that he feels that his mastery over the spool, which in his unconscious is identified with his mother, establishes mastery over her.

I have argued that Rilke experienced Rodin as a symbolic object, consciously seeing him as a dear father, unconsciously identifying him with both parents as idealized, omnipotent figures. The young poet called the sculptor "master." But his unconscious aim, similar to that of the boy with the spool, was to gain mastery over Rodin, to use him magically as a symbolic object in order to participate in his (illusory) omnipotence and his apparent mastery over his life and work, and thus to control his own (the poet's) anxiety and to defend himself against the threat of disintegration.

The ultimate form of such mastery over the symbolic object and the parental imagoes with which he is unconsciously identified is incorporation, total absorption. Through identification with the older man, Rilke hoped to make the sculptor a part of himself, to take Rodin's great mastery and creative power into himself, to absorb and incorporate them by means of closeness, study, and emulation. The two essays on Rodin, especially the first one, and the letters about Rilke's attempts to study him closely support this impression. The vivid, precisely detailed descriptions and all the energy of thought that went into understanding the sculptor as a man and as an artist reveal the effort to master Rodin and thus to engulf and incorporate him with the hoped-for result of becoming like him (or, in fantasy, of becoming him, yet remaining oneself), and thus overcoming all the misery and fear and illness, the sense of unreality, uncertainty, and self-division that plagued the poet at the time.

In his efforts to master the sculptor, Rilke had as his model Rodin's endeavors to obtain full and precise impressions of such subjects as Balzac and Victor Hugo. Writing about Rodin's preparations for his figure of Hugo, Rilke says the sculptor would hide himself in a window niche in a Paris Hotel to watch the French poet at his receptions, getting down on paper "hundreds upon hundreds" of Hugo's motions and facial expressions (*WSR*, 120).

III

The feeling of insecurity, self-division, and unreality which Rilke experienced during the years 1902–3 and the perception of Rodin as someone who possessed the sense of reality and psychic strength, unity, and vitality which he lacked drew the poet to the sculptor. But this contrast in Rilke's mind had negative effects, as well. The Frenchman's strengths at times intensified Rilke's already painful sense of his own psychic weakness and instability. Writing to Lou that Rodin "has left nothing in uncertainty and has given reality to everything," the young poet wondered if his own will was sick, lamenting to Lou that there was "nothing real" about him and that he was continually divided from himself (*Letters* 1:123 and 122).

He confirms Salomé's insight that Rodin was an overwhelming example. The "fearfulness" arising from this relationship seemed to focus on "the close proximity of something too hard, too stony, too big" (*Letters* 1:123). Following classical Freudian analysis, I am inclined to interpret Rilke's language here as an expression of an unconscious sense of a father's immensely superior phallus. A subsequent passage in the same letter supports this interpretation. Rilke says that his lack of the essential gifts which he attributes to Rodin impels him to try to discover "the tool of my art, the hammer, my hammer, so that it may become master" (*Letters* 1:124). In dreams, folklore, work songs, literature, and the visual arts, tools and weapons may express unconscious associations with the phallus. As Norman Holland indicates in *The Dynamics of Literary Response*, it may also become identified with the capacity for using language and various kinds of potency which follow from that. The example which Holland chooses is from *Two Gentlemen of Verona:* "That man that hath a tongue, I say, is no man/If with his tongue he cannot win a woman." Here wit consciously makes the tongue phallic.[1]

Dreams, which express through displacement and condensation unconscious connections between the phallus and weapons or tools, often reflect the tendency of young children to feel that the father's phallus is frightening in its size and power. Rilke's painful sense that his own more abstract medium did not have the vital physical presence of Rodin's sculpture and his feeling that he lacked "the tool of my art, the hammer, my hammer" suggest that in his mind his impotence as an artist was unconsciously connected with a fear of sexual and emotional impotence, which closeness to the father-master in Paris intensified.

These fantasies in the poet remind me of the *Letter to His Father* written by his contemporary and compatriot Franz Kafka, in which a son remembers his feelings as a boy when, on a swimming expedition with his father, they came out of the cabin for changing clothes. He compares his own body to a skeleton in its pitiful contrast with his father's large, strong, powerful physique and recalls his humiliating inability to learn how to swim despite his father's efforts to teach him. The father persisted and the anguished son felt increasingly desperate as he continued to fail.[2] Here we find open expression of the sense of physical impotence in relation to the father which is latent and oblique in Rilke's writings about Rodin.

Later in the letter Kafka connects his fundamental uncertainties concerning his very existence, his worth as a person, and his abilities with his doubts about his body. His need "to be provided at every instant with a new confirmation of my existence" is the craving at the core of so much of Kafka's writing, beginning with the *Conversation with a Supplicant,* in which the supplicant explains that he needs to be seen in order to feel that he exists.[3] In the letter Kafka traces the sense of being physically and psychically nothing, nonexistent, back to a terrifying experience in which his seemingly gigantic father came into his room at night when Franz was a small child, carried him out onto the balcony, and left him there, making the child feel that he counted for nothing in his father's eyes.[4]

Surely, the feelings expressed in Rilke's letter about the impossibility of making things physically, the pain in his body created by this impotence, and the sense of being up against something "too hard, too stony, too big" were closely linked with his fantasy that "there is nothing real about me," in much the same way that Kafka's feelings about his body, his sense of its skeletal insubstantiality and smallness, were connected with his fantasy of his own nothingness. Although there were large differences between the two older men and the two relationships, Rodin's negative effects upon Rilke for several years, as described in the poet's letters, are comparable to Hermann Kafka's effects upon his son.

Rilke's medium, language, seemed so much less real in its essential abstractness and in its greater distance from the world of physical objects, than Rodin's sculpture. The highly subjective nature of the young poet's early work may have exacerbated his sense, when he first came to Paris, of the unreality of his language in comparison with Rodin's *objets.* This painful sense of the contrast between the two media was connected with the poet's anguish over his comparative lack of fluency in French when he first arrived. In a letter written to Rodin shortly after his arrival, he begins by equating his French with "sickness." His words, he says, are "dead" (*Letters* 1:87). In his room he meditated on the language that he would use with Rodin, who could understand little or no German, but in the master's presence he found himself impotent in his own medium, at a loss for words. Eventually he was to master French to the extent that he could write poetry in it. And by 1905–6 he was doing Rodin's correspondence for him.

The argument of this section can be brought to a focus with the insight that Rilke's dependence on Rodin for his sense of his own reality at times intensified his anxious feeling that he was unreal. This is one unfortunate consequence of such fantasies of ontological dependence upon others.

IV

In the second part of *Rodin*, Rilke discusses the child's earliest possessions in a passage which anticipates his essay on dolls. He is attempting to clarify his special use of the word "things." He asks the reader, and perhaps himself, to summon up to mind some object from his or her childhood which, in memory, seems to have been singularly close, kind, just, necessary, not frightening, not confusing, and he wonders if we owe to just such an object any "confidence and the sense of not being alone" felt during early childhood (*WSR*, 131). Here, as in the essay on dolls, which was written years later in 1914, Rilke's thinking brings to mind Winnicott's concept of transitional objects.[1] The poet's description of the child's experience suggests that the cherished object is unconsciously identified with a benevolent, loving mother, like the one we find in the Third Elegy and *The Notebooks*, protecting the child from his own fears at night.

Winnicott observes that "transitional objects" may stand for the mother's breast, though, at the same time, the child is aware that the blanket, for example, is not the breast. The beloved blanket is pervaded with subjectivity, experienced as part of the child, yet also felt to be something else, a possession. It is never completely subject to "magical control," unlike an "internal object," such as a conscious or unconscious representation of the mother in the mind. But it is not felt to be beyond control in the way that the child comes to experience "the real mother."

If all goes well, the child's sense of control over a "transitional object" diminishes gradually, as the object gradually loses the meaning it has acquired through transference, and the aura of projected subjectivity fades. In Rilke's 1914 essay on dolls ("*Puppen*") this loss is as painful and devastating as the experience of Phia's withdrawal and desertion. In this respect the strange reflections on dolls reveal a process of development which contrasts sharply with the gentle diffusion and dispersion of the soothing, satisfying, reassuring experience of transitional objects that, according to Winnicott, ordinarily leads to mental health in children. The brilliant piece on dolls, which may have been influenced by Kleist's essay "On the Marionette Theater," is one of Rilke's writings in which we can see clearly the intersection of genius and abnormality. When the poet read the essay to Magda von Hattingberg, his "Benvenuta," she could not bear it.[2]

In *Rodin*, Rilke goes on to make another point about those things which are so meaningful to us in childhood. That early object, because it comes to represent in the child's fantasies "any and everything," helps to prepare him for "contacts with the world" (*WSR*, 131). Winnicott observes that transitional phenomena, in which subjective and objective realities fuse, reshaping each other, give the child a sense of his power and freedom to create (more precisely, to re-create) the world around him.[3] Like Winnicott, Rilke saw the cherished objects of early childhood as the prototypes of works of art. He was interested particularly in things which, like the child's dearest possessions, demand dedication, trust, and love from the artists who make them (see *WSR*, 132).

Central in his study of the sculptor is the idea that through the figures which he created Rodin assumed control and took "possession of the world" (*WSR*, 143). For Rilke, who in 1902 and 1903 felt that he lacked reality and that he might be misreading, to an alarming extent, his strange new surroundings, as did other lost people in the chaotic streets of Paris, the master's ability to possess the world through his sculpture must have seemed enviable.

As I have indicated, the terms the poet uses to describe the child's experience of his early possessions reveal that Rilke had an intuitive sense of the fact that the child unconsciously identifies these things with his mother. The curious corollary of the argument that such things are the precursors of the objects artists create is that the latter can give their maker the "confidence" and "the sense of not being alone" which originally should come from a mother. For this artist nothing else was so close, intimately known, and necessary as his own poems.

In these terms we can understand Rilke's vision of Rodin: surrounded by his own creations, enjoying their extraordinary life, which mirrored his own, and their responsiveness to him, the sculptor was constantly delighting in such kindness, devotion, and affection as transitional objects can give to a child, in whom they are unconsciously identified with a benevolent mother. With these ideas in mind we can grasp Rilke's sense of the sculptor's joy and of Rodin's belief that life was miraculous (see *WSR,* 147).

Rilke imagined that one of the most important functions of Rodin's sculpture was to act as a protection against all disturbance and danger. "His work stands like a great angel beside him and protects him . . . his great work!" (*Letters* 1:85). He lived in his sculpture as in a sheltering wood (*Letters* 1:121). In this respect one can see at least an unconscious association between the sculptor's work and a protective mother such as the one Rilke describes in *The Notebooks* passage concerning the child's nocturnal fears. To a poet plagued by the anxieties which he depicts in Malte, deeply troubled through much of his life by his mother's withdrawal, it seemed that the ability to produce works of art offered one a way of mastering the fears which threatened to tear him to pieces when he first came to Paris. Rodin epitomized this means of mastering anxiety. The Frenchman had created a whole world with his sculpture, a world in which he could be completely at home and sheltered.

Rilke's inability to produce work he could value during certain periods of his life was linked in his mind with his failure to master his worst fears (of disintegration and annihilation). If only he could write worthy poems or prose, he would not fall prey to anxiety, he would not disintegrate. He yearned for the ability to convert his fears into works of art, "real, still things that it is serenity and freedom to create and from which, when they exist, reassurance emanates [so that] nothing would have happened to me" (*Letters* 1:115). Reading the letters to Salomé written in the summer and fall of 1903, we can see that his failure at times to create such "real, still things" as Rodin was constantly producing resembled a child's inability, when frightened by his mother's absences, to demonstrate his mastery to himself with the help of such objects as the boy's spool in Freud's *Beyond the Pleasure Principle.*

The poet decided that Rodin's repudiation of his belief in inspiration ironically arose from the never diminishing strength of the divine afflatus in the sculptor, his "uninterrupted fertility" (*WSR*, 143) This argument suggests an unconscious fantasy that the benevolent maternal presence Rilke desperately needed at times was always there for the sculptor. In Rilke's fantasy Rodin had made a fertile mother an essential part of himself and had thus attained to the hermaphroditic motherhood which Rilke yearned for in *The Book of Hours*. The "master" was a man endlessly capable of maternal procreation, who was also blessed with an enduring capacity for mothering himself, for defending himself against all danger and fear and loneliness.

Rilke's conception of the artist's work (the activity) and his works (the objects) as defenses against disturbance and anxiety takes various forms. He imagines himself lifting his whole life "into a peace, a solitude, into the stillness of deep workdays" (*Letters* 1:126). In a related fantasy, creative activity becomes "the powerful flow of a stream" with a "great roar," which would not allow any of the external or internal disturbances that have plagued him to be heard or to get through. As this massive stream of creative energy, ideas, activity, and achievement would provide undeniable confirmation of his own reality, vitality, and value, which human relationships had failed to give him, he could afford to neglect the latter and leave behind the sense of his unreality and impotence, the anxieties, and the illness which his entanglements with other people often seemed to intensify. Watching Rodin, he concluded that many great artists had largely discarded their ordinary lives to live in their work (see *Letters* 1:84 and 126).

The sculptor had said to him, "[L]es amis s'empêchent. Il est mieux d'être seul" (*Letters* 1:84). This is from a letter which Rilke wrote to Clara, soon after he left her and Ruth to come to Paris. And it is clear that he understood these feelings. In his conversation with the Frenchman, the poet spoke of his sadness at separation from his daughter. But he was obviously gratified to have found a "master" who gave him the strongest possible support for choosing his work over his life as husband and father in Westerwede. And to Lou, his lifelong friend, once his lover, for years a surrogate mother, he wrote, expressing a belief which he thought Rodin's life validated, "[I]n one of my poems that is successful, there is much more reality than in any relationship or affection that I feel" (*Letters* 1:121).

Through emulation and identification, by mastering the master and making Rodin part of himself, by modeling his own life upon the sculptor's, he could free himself from the long periods when inspiration and fertility were absent, and also enable himself to produce works of art which might perform the primitive functions of transitional objects. He too might experience the joy which belonged to the sculptor but often eluded him, as it does most of us. His own work would afford him the only companionship he would need, as an infant needs and desires no one but its mother or the object (doll, bit of blanket, rocking horse) which takes her place.

Rilke's letters and various accounts of his life show that he used his work as an excuse for a solitude which could be conducive to creativity, as it was at Duino in 1912 and at Muzot in 1922, and that at times the work could provide such satisfaction and fulfillment as human relationships rarely or never gave him. But, as I have shown, his frequent self-isolation and his distancing of other people also aggravated his sense of his unreality and barrenness at times when his poetry, fiction, essays, and letters would not come and could not help him. In this respect, obviously, he differed from Rodin.

Rilke saw Rodin's sculpture, like its maker, as an ideal image of the solitary self-sufficiency which he longed to develop. A work of art, he argued, should be "untouchable, sacrosanct, separated from the influence of accident or time" (WSR, 94). I have mentioned the poet's likening of his "Maître" to an eastern god, his implicit association of the old man with the effigy of Buddha, on a hill near the Villa in Meudon, and his New Poems on the Buddha with their idealization of perfect self-containment. Rilke's desire to create objects endowed with this quality is evident in Rodin and the letters to and about the sculptor. Underlying his longing to write poems which would radiate such perfection was the fantasy that the poet, through identification with his poems, would attain to the ideal qualities of the works he created, as it seemed to him that Rodin had done. In his fantasies Rilke shared the assumptions of many great artists, who see themselves in the mirror of their works, associating themselves with the "immortality" of their creations.

The early diaries include a meditation, written before he met Rodin, in which Rilke observes that a figure by the French master stays always within an uncrossable magic circle. As with reflected images in a fountain, the spectator cannot approach nearer than a certain distance if he does not wish to lose sight of the object.[4] The metaphor of the magic circle, separating and distancing any spectator from the statue, and the notion that any attempt to come closer will only conceal the essential mystery of the object may be seen as displacements of Rilke's need to prevent anyone else from coming too close to him or seeing him too clearly.

According to Arnold Modell, the fantasy of complete self-sufficiency in isolation, reflected in Rilke's thoughts about Rodin's sculpture, may arise from a need to deny dependency upon other human beings in order to defend oneself from the fear of losing the persons on whom one feels most dependent. In Rilke the source of such fears must have been the memory or fantasy of early parental neglect and emotional withdrawal. Modell argues that this defensive fantasy of perfect self-sufficiency may also be a reaction to the intense emotions aroused and the tensions caused by contact with others. This analysis focuses upon schizoid illness and recalls Rilke's notion that "a dark, deceptive vapour" separated him from other people and his closely related image of the bird feeders in *The Notebooks*, "with a large transparent space around them, as if they were standing under a glass dome" (78).[5]

Modell observes that schizoid individuals' illusions of self-sufficiency and protective encapsulation "rest upon a belief in their own omnipotence. That is to say, they can be an omnipotent object to themselves; they can provide all the sources of gratification, create their own protective shield against the dangers of the environment. They can be a transitional object to themselves."[6] Or they may imagine that they can create the transitional objects which would assure their narcissistic self-sufficiency and omnipotence. I have traced a network of such fantasies in Rilke's thoughts about Rodin and his art and have shown that they are self-referential, that he projected onto the "master" and his sculpture a state of existence to which he wished to attain through his own creativity.

V

The relationship between Rilke and Rodin entered a new phase when, at the sculptor's invitation, the poet decided to live with him at Meudon, beginning in September 1905. From then until May 1906 he dedicated much of his time to helping his friend, writing his correspondence for him. Even when he was away from Meudon during this period, Rilke was often preoccupied with Rodin, lecturing about him and his art.

Writing to the sculptor from Prague in October 1905, Rilke cast himself in the role of an apostle preaching his Master's saving Gospel: "all who live need you, the good news of your existence is the Gospel."[1] At home in Meudon and abroad, during this period the poet showed loyalty, love, and devotion that were all any surrogate father could have dreamed of receiving from a son.

While in Prague to give his lecture, he visited his aging father for the last time. His relationships with the two fathers were never more obviously connected. The burdensome tasks which he performed for the sculptor were an indirect and magical way, through unconscious transference, of showing devotion and loyalty to Josef. His idealization of the dear father in Meudon must have helped him redeem and restore Josef's faded, frayed, and much diminished image in his own mind.

No doubt he felt that he had long neglected his sick and aging father in Prague. The tasks he performed for Rodin were probably also means of undoing or expiating this neglect. The defense of "undoing" involves a kind of magical thinking. Like many rituals of expiation, it is based on fantasies of causal connections between acts which are not causally related. In this case the task of "undoing" involved projection of a father's image onto another man and transference of feelings from the one to the other. The ultimate aims of "undoing" are to dissolve all injury done in fact or fantasy, to release one from guilt, and to allow one to believe that the person he thinks he harmed no longer blames him and will not punish him. Often, most or all of these thoughts are unconscious.[2]

The relationship between Rilke and Rodin broke apart on May 11, 1906, when the sculptor dismissed him from his correspondence-writing tasks and sent him packing "like a thieving servant," the poet's comparison in his farewell letter to the Master, written the following day (*Letters* 1:211). The heavy burden of Rilke's secretarial labors and his responsibility for constantly reminding Rodin of distasteful obligations had created tensions between the two men (see *Letters* 2:359). Rodin was in a rage because, without consulting him, Rilke had sent answers to two of the sculptor's correspondents, who had addressed letters to the poet. In one of these exchanges, Rilke had added a postscript to a letter prepared in consultation with the sculptor. His crimes were miniscule. Rodin had introduced Rilke as a friend, not as his secretary, to one of these correspondents, William Rothenstein. Deeply hurt, the poet complained in his farewell to Rodin, written the day after his dismissal, that he had been invited to Meudon out of friendship, that the sculptor's suggestion he perform some of the tasks a secretary might do, as Rodin had explained it, had been a way of providing him with some time of his own to do his writing.[3]

Probably Rilke was eager to leave Rodin when he returned to Meudon at the end of March 1906, two weeks after his father's death. On April 7 he wrote the letter to Karl von der Heydt, a friend and benefactor, from which I quoted in the preceding chapter, saying that he lacked only the liberty to be himself and was ready and eager to write, believing that he might be able to do "something that may perhaps never come again like this" (*Letters* 1:202). His lack of privacy and his tasks at Meudon were suffocating him.[4] It seems very likely that Josef's death fostered the poet's desire to get away from Rodin.

Eliza M. Butler argues persuasively that Rilke's correspondence during the months of service to Rodin reveals an increasing sense of self-sacrifice approaching martyrdom, and this may have shown itself in his demeanor, irritating the Master and finally provoking him to his outburst in May 1906.[5] He suspected that he had communicated his need for liberation to Rodin. On May 11 he wrote to Clara, saying that Rodin must have understood what he was going through (*Letters* 1:209).

When Rilke returned to Rodin after his father's death, he appears to have been moved by a curious mix of conflicting feelings. After von der Heydt, responding to his expressed needs, offered to support him for a year and let the poet live on one of his estates, he wrote to say that he could not leave the old sculptor in his sickness and weariness (*Letters* 1:204). Abandoning his second father, ill and weary as he was, so soon after Josef Rilke's death, would have intensified any guilt the poet felt about not having cared for Josef during his old age. In giving up his work for Rodin, he would also be ending this means of undoing whatever injury he had inflicted upon his father by neglecting him and by causing him such painful disappointment and anxiety for so many years.

But these motivating forces conflicted with others equally strong or stronger. Josef Rilke's death probably made Rainer feel that he no longer needed a father and no longer wanted to be any father's son. Malte's reaction to his father's death and to the perforation of his heart, taken together with the passages concerning fathers in *The Book of Hours* that I explored in the preceding chapter, supports this conclusion.

The need to resolve guilt and undo harm through the transference relationship with the sculptor may have diminished because of the poet's efforts toward the end of Josef's life to win his father's approval and to inspire his confidence and hope that his son would be a great success in his chosen profession.

The changes in Rilke during the years 1902–6 and his response to his father's aging, illness, and death suggest that Rodin's supportive, confirming, affectionate fathering had provided him with an ideal model of a father as a highly successful, gifted artist, whom he could introject and with whom he could identify himself. As a result he had gained a stronger sense of his own identity, value, and direction as an artist, as well as greater confidence in his own inner guidance. By May 1906, as I have pointed out, he had written a few of the finest of the *New Poems* and was bursting with readiness to do new work.

Considering his state of mind when he had come to Paris in 1902, we can see how much he had developed through the transference relationship with Rodin. All the inner strength and maturity he had gained through this relationship had made him ready to accept the loss of Josef, the finality of his father's separateness and absence in death. As he realized that he had reached this point, he must have understood that he was also ready to accept the separateness and the loss of the second father whom he had so desperately needed when he came to Paris. Offering insights which clarify this change in Rilke, Modell observes that the internalization of an affectionate parent can enable a person to love and be a parent to himself, and that these developments, along with the growth of a person's sense of his differentiation, can foster his ability to accept the loss of persons he loves, particularly parents.[6] Modell also remarks that where strength and health are lacking, due to childhood failure to identify with "good enough" parents, psychoanalytic therapy "can provide in part the experience of 'good enough' parental care, and an identification with the analyst can become a permanent part of the patient's ego."[7] I suggest that something like this happened in Rilke's transference with Rodin. And perhaps Josef's death enabled the poet to feel that the psychological "work" which had so badly needed doing when he first met Rodin had been accomplished through his intimate and evolving relationship with the Master.

In June 1906, a few months after his father's death, the month after his break with Rodin, Rilke wrote a poem entitled "The Departure of the Prodigal Son" ("Der Auszug des verlorenen Sohnes"). It reveals that the poet was not in a triumphant mood of expectation at the time. In the poem the speaker longs to get away from a confused existence in which what has seemed his and still sticks to him like thorns really does not belong to him. He feels incapable of understanding and incomprehensible to others. Realizing that his journey will make his existence more uncertain and precarious, he nonetheless longs for a distant land where nothing has any familiar relationship to him and to what he has known and hopes that this land will provide him with an environment which is free from emotional involvement in anything he does. This, he knows, will mean taking a great deal upon himself. Ultimately, it may mean dying alone. It may force or allow him to let go of all that he has held as possession and/or as oppressive burden. Anticipating his mental and physical journey, the speaker can only ask if it may afford him access to a new life, in which he will be able to perceive with sudden clarity and nearness, as if beginning again, in a mood of reconciliation, things to which he has been blinded by familiarity. Here is the poem in German:

Der Auszug des verlorenen Sohnes

Nun fortzugehn von alledem Verworrnen,
das unser ist und uns doch nicht gehört,
das, wie das Wasser in den alten Bornen,
uns zitternd spiegelt und das Bild zerstört;
von allem diesen, das sich wie mit Dornen
noch einmal an uns anhängt—fortzugehn
und Das und Den,
die man schon nicht mehr sah
(so täglich waren sie und so gewöhnlich),
auf einmal anzuschauen: sanft, versöhnlich
und wie an einem Anfang und von nah;
und ahnend einzusehn, wie unpersönlich,
wie über alle hin das Leid geschah,
von dem die Kindheit voll war bis zum Rand—:
Und dann doch fortzugehen, Hand aus Hand,
als ob man ein Geheiltes neu zerrisse,

und fortzugehn: wohin? Ins Ungewisse,
weit in ein unverwandtes warmes Land,
das hinter allem Handeln wie Kulisse
gleichgültig sein wird: Garten oder Wand;
und fortzugehn: warum? Aus Drang, aus Artung,
aus Ungeduld, aus dunkler Erwartung,
aus Unverständlichkeit und Unverstand:

Dies alles auf sich nehmen und vergebens
vielleicht Gehaltnes fallen lassen, um
allein zu sterben, wissend nicht warum—

Ist das der Eingang eines neuen Lebens?
(*WDB* 1:247–48)

It seems likely that "Der Auszug des verlorenen Sohnes" reflects Rilke's sense of his relationship with Rodin at the time it was written. The title connects it with his version of the Prodigal Son parable in *The Notebooks*. This connection suggests that the threat of engulfment and and the kind of impingement Rilke felt while living close to Rodin echo in his conception of the Prodigal Son's experience with his family at the end of the novel. The culminating section of *The Notebooks* precisely defines the ways in which a family can produce the blindness and confusion of which the poem speaks. The child can completely submit and become one of them, losing all sense of what spontaneous impulse, intuition, and reason tell him is true perception, authentic feeling, and honest thought. He can try to mask himself and constantly divide himself between true self and false. But this, as Malte suggests, this constant deception of family and friends may seem a form of corruption. Psychologists tell us it may also produce severe mental illness if the false self becomes compulsive, if the self-division amplifies into a pervasive structure of the psyche. Or the child can go far away, as Malte and the son in the poem do, to live as more or less a solitary.

VI

Rilke was eager to get away from Rodin in April and May of 1906. But once the break came, he tried to suppress his resentment and to protect his admiration and affection for the old man. Reading the letters he wrote at this time, one cannot help seeing that he needed to believe that the breach would be healed. He wanted to protect the image of the artist-master-father who had played such a crucial role in fostering his development as a man and as an writer. No doubt he still felt closely identified with the great sculptor.

Insofar as it had strengthened his self-esteem and his sense of his identity, purpose, and direction, the relationship with Rodin had helped to free him from infantile dependence on his father and from infantile anger toward Josef. Though at first Rodin had fulfilled a desire for a powerful father, as the relationship fostered Rilke's maturity and, thus, his independence, it enabled him to allow Josef to be himself in all his limitations, and to love him nonetheless. The poet's desire to preserve the redeemed and restored image of Josef after his death, which surfaces in numerous letters, must have impelled him to suppress negative feelings toward Rodin, as the two fathers were intimately connected in his mind.

I have quoted the letter Rilke wrote to Clara the day Rodin dismissed him (May 11, 1906), when he saw his expulsion from Meudon as an act motivated by intuitive understanding. The next day, writing to Rodin as "My Master," after complaining that he had been sent away "like a thieving servant" the poet went on to justify the old man's behavior as part of his instinctive wisdom in repelling whatever "seems harmful." The language here reflects Rilke's ambivalence. The "seems" casts doubt on the sculptor's judgment. The disciple's justification of his Master's behavior is two-edged; it is preceded by assertions of selfless devotion and self-sacrifice which make Rodin's self-protectiveness look extremely ungrateful, as the poet recalls all the time he has given up for the sculptor, while neglecting his own work.

In this farewell message he also protested that he was more loyal and devoted to Rodin than anyone else and that there was no one else his age anywhere more capable of understanding the old man. And he did his best to defend himself and the sculptor from the resentment evident in the letter with an absurd, if familiar, piece of idealization, an apotheosis of the Master in which he compares Rodin to Christ and himself to the apostles left behind on earth without their Savior (*Letters* 1:211–12).

By the following summer more realistic perceptions of Rodin had made inroads on the poet's idealization of the Master. In June 1907, writing to Clara about the lecture he had first given in the fall of 1905, he said, "I am already beginning to see too that many of its perceptions belong perhaps to the demands Rodin taught us to make, not to those which his work realizes in each case" (*Letters* 1:288).[1] He had just completed the first part of the *New Poems;* the sense of his own achievement, his mastery, must have helped him to see the old master with this new intimation of skepticism.

In September 1906 he had written to Karl von der Heydt that his second study of the sculptor would be his next project, but had been unable to bring himself to do it during the intervening time. Now, a year later, realizing that he had nothing new to say about Rodin, he decided to use the old lecture with little or no revision. He had been putting his time and energy into his *New Poems.* But he was also aware that, as he had become more detached from and critical of Rodin, a new essay on the sculptor might seem inconsistent, self-contradictory, a reflection of his confused thoughts and feelings about the old man (*Letters* 1:288).

Perhaps he also feared that a thorough clarification of his new feelings and ideas about Rodin might prove very painful, forcing him to face thoughts against which he wished to protect himself and the father-sculptor with the help of his confusion. In achieving clarity which could destroy the image of Rodin he had developed for so many years, he might undermine the strength and creativity which that image and the relationship had fostered.

The poet was in transition. Even as the extreme idealization of the paternal sculptor was deflated and a critical, independent, more realistic view of Rodin developed, Rilke defended the relationship, the attitudes, and the viewpoint that had been, or seemed, essential to his survival and his growth.

Early in November 1907 Rilke received a letter from Rodin just as he was about to give a reading of his own work in Prague. I described this occasion in an earlier chapter. His native city depressed him. He felt dismay as he realized that the dreadful old women who had wanted to devour him when he arrived had lost their appetite on hearing him read. Very likely his misery on this occasion centered on his mother, who was at the reading; all encounters with her during his adult life were very painful.

In these circumstances the first gesture of *rapprochement* from the man who had been a second father to him and whom he had also experienced as a maternal figure was especially welcome. Writing to Clara, he emphasized his own happiness on receiving the letter from Rodin (*Letters* 1:323). A week later, in Vienna, where he was arranging for the exhibition of sixty of Rodin's drawings in Hugo Heller's bookstore, Rilke got a second message from the old man. The sculptor had read an extract from part 2 of Rilke's *Rodin*, which had just been reprinted in the magazine *Kunst and Künstler*, and had found it "très belle." This new letter was full of affection. Delighted, scarcely able to believe that he could be the object of such feeling in Rodin, he read it time and again. He was particularly pleased by the Frenchman's invitation to visit when he returned to Paris (Letters 1:328).

A year and a half had passed since the break between the two men. In that time there had been an outpouring of the *New Poems*. Strengthened in his sense of his own unique genius, the poet must have greeted the old master's invitation to come to see him with the knowledge that Rodin's strength could no longer threaten to overwhelm his own sense of self and his artistic independence, that he was no longer so susceptible to manipulation or exploitation. He was not nearly so needy as he had been in 1902–3 and had left behind the helpless dependency which had made him so vulnerable to Rodin's power. These changes, which his earlier relationship with the sculptor had encouraged and which the break between them had let him confirm for himself, enabled him to respond with love and admiration, free from anxiety. His reply also reveals the feeling of equality which gave him the confidence to welcome reconciliation, trusting that he could now renew the friendship without fear of being overpowered: "I have an infinite need of you and your friendship, and I am proud that I have advanced sufficiently in my work to be able to share your glorious and simple desire for truth."[2]

VII

Rilke returned to Paris on May 1, 1908, but he put off seeing Rodin, writing to the sculptor after his arrival that he had to shut himself up with his work.[1] On August 31, having finished the second part of *New Poems* and moved into quarters in the Hôtel Biron, the Louis XIV villa which was to become the Musée Rodin, he invited his friend to come to see him.[2] Describing this visit to Clara, he foresaw that in the future he would be "as kind to him as I always was" (*Letters* 1:331).

This account of his meeting with Rodin reveals the complexity of Rilke's feelings about the sculptor at the time, his conflicting perceptions and attitudes. An emphasis upon Rodin's "dear, earnest need" of him reflects not only the desire to repay and to undo but the wish to be needed. The poet focused on the reversal of their positions, his own increasing power over the older man and the latter's loss of power over him. Later letters show a growing consciousness of these changes.

On this occasion Rilke read Rodin some remarks of Beethoven to his friend Bettina von Arnim. The composer had told von Arnim that his must be a solitary life, but he knew that in his art God was singularly close to him and that anyone who truly understood his music would become free of the wretchedness which weighed down other people (*Letters* 1:331–32). For Rilke Beethoven had become a model: the poet aspired to such superb confidence in himself and his art. The next letter to Clara shows that his sense of himself at this time, with the *New Poems* completed, was scarcely less exalted than the composer's. This letter expresses the notion that he had always been close to "the divine." He was anticipating the time when he would prepare a "potion in which all is condensed and combined, the most poisonous and most deadly," and would "take it up to God, so that he may quench his thirst and feel his splendor streaming through his veins" (September 4, 1908; *Letters* 1:336).

Never before had he been more self-confident. The idea that human genius is the source of God's vitality and splendor had evolved out of a number of sources, among them a Russian conception of the Deity, as Rilke understood it. According to Leppmann, "this God suggested rather than portrayed on icons" was "waiting to be created by the people themselves in a state of childlike naiveté (or, in moments of grace, by the poet)."[3] As Leppmann points out, *The Book of Hours,* reflects the influence of this idea. In the first part of *The Book of Hours* the speaker describes himself as helping to build God, as if the Deity were a great church.[4]

It is a commonplace of psychoanalytic theory that God is an unconscious projection of the superego, a part of the self identified with the father. Rilke too thought of God and gods as projections of parts of the psyche (see *Letters* 2:147–48). Rilke's development in the *Book of Hours* of the idea that human beings build or create God expresses a lingering reverence for the Deity, which was probably reinforced by his travels in Russia, but it also suggests a rebellion against the father's primacy and authority. In this respect it calls to mind Simenauer's explication of the son's creation of the father, Kierkegaard's argument that a truly creative individual must become his own father, and Nietzsche's belief that such an individual must become his own creator, giver of the laws by which he lives, and his own ultimate judge, as well as the German philosopher's analyses of the human creation of God and other gods.

In his September 4 letter to Clara, Rilke envisioned making God "feel his splendor streaming through his veins" by feeding Him a "potion in which all is condensed and combined, the most poisonous and most deadly" (*Letters* 1:336). Implicit here is a conception of art indebted to the influence of Baudelaire's "Une Charogne," Flaubert's "St. Julien l'Hospitalier," and Cézanne's paintings (see *The Notebooks*, 72, and *Letters* 1:314–15). But the notion that one can bring God to life and make him splendid again by quenching his thirst with deadly poison suggests an underlying thought that a person must kill the old God and the old father in order to bring new ones to life as a father to himself, recognizing and owning the divinity within him, creating his own life and character, bringing himself to new birth as the father of his work. From the classical psychoanalytic perspective such a fantasy has its roots in the oedipal son's desire to destroy and to supplant the father.

At this moment in his life the poet thought of himself as Godlike, as one "sent out . . . to be amidst the human," like Christ. As he goes about his tasks of seeing everything and rejecting nothing in the world, gathering the components of the "potion" that will make God feel splendid and vital, "the tree trunks round about stand and worship" (*Letters* 1:336).

Rodin had rented a large part of the ground floor of the Hôtel Biron. Responsible for the sculptor's discovery of the place, pleased by Rodin's immediate response to it and by the old man's decision to share it with him and other artists, Rilke rushed out and bought a wooden figure of St. Christopher. Presenting his gift, he told Rodin, "C'est Rodin portant son oeuvre, toujours plus lourd, mais qui tient le monde" (*Letters* 1:333). ("This is Rodin, bearing his work, ever heavier, but containing the world.") It scarcely needs to be said that Rilke was praising his old master as the man uniquely chosen to carry God, the Creator, here represented as the Divine Child, as well as the world.

If Rodin had nursed any sour doubts of Rilke's continuing admiration and esteem, this gift and the praise that went with it must have laid them to rest. Surely the feelings the poet expressed on this occasion were as genuine as the love and concern which he had shown for his father in the last year of Josef's life. Several times Rilke was to assure Rodin that the Master could take pleasure in his younger friend's genius and fame, as they were, in large part, due to the sculptor's example and teaching. Perhaps, these assurances were attempts to veil competitiveness and to defend himself against jealousy and resentment. But seeing them in the context of the evolving relationship, one cannot reduce the generosity, filial gratitude, and admiration expressed in the letters at this time to cant or an unconscious defense against opposing feelings (in psychoanalytic terms, "a reaction formation").

The differences between Rilke's view of women and Rodin's contributed to the poet's increasing awareness of the sculptor's failings and limitations. For Rodin, "woman is the obstruction, the snare, the trap on those paths that are most lonely and most blessed." She is *"beneath"* the spiritual. She does not want anything beyond the sensual and material satisfactions which she demands and is "like a drink which flows through him from time to time: wine" (*Letters* 1:332). Rilke came to believe that this view of women had always been an obstacle between them. The poet tried to persuade Rodin that he had a drastically limited understanding of women by talking about Marianna Alcoforado (1640–1723), a Portuguese nun whom he mentions in *The Notebooks* (134) as an example of the intensity of unrequited love, transcending its original object, transfiguring the woman who nurtures it in herself. Rilke translated eight grieving letters thought to have been written by her to the unresponsive Marquis de Chamilly. He thought of her as "that incomparable creature, in whose eight heavy letters woman's love is for the first time charted from point to point, without display, without exaggeration or mitigation, drawn as if by the hand of a sibyl" (*SP*, 318). She was one of the abandoned women, celebrated in the first Duino Elegy, "whom you found so much more loving than gratified" lovers. The poet's ideas on this subject were probably incredible to the old man. What could he think of this view of woman's love, which expressed a preference for the kind that grows into "icy magnificence" as "lamentation" in loneliness and rejection? How could he see that the love in these eight sorrowful letters soared and grew far beyond its object, the contemptible (in Rilke's eyes)

Marquis de Chamilly, and achieved beauty and majesty? (*The Notebooks*, 134; *Letters* 1:228).

Rodin's disbelief and incomprehension in their discussions of women established their separateness in Rilke's mind beyond any doubt. And then there were the consequences of Rodin's incomprehension. His egocentric oversimplification of women was already getting him into trouble and would prove disastrous, would leave this god in ruins, make him grotesque in old age, turn him into a fool. Though this had not yet happened in the fall of 1908, Rilke sensed what the future would bring. "The moment was sure to come when he would see the miscalculation in his prodigious sums" (*Letters* 1:332–33).

Writing to Clara, the prodigal disciple, now returned to his master, asserted his sense of his invulnerable independence and strength. "And I am inexorable and yield nothing of my Nun." His distinctiveness, his independence, his separate reality had at long last gotten through to the older man, who but a few years earlier had overpowered and intimidated him and, in self-absorption, had scarcely seen him except as a young artist whom he was molding, as a reflection of his own genius. Now, he thought, the sculptor had heard what he said, even if it could not change him (*Letters* 1:333). Rilke need no longer fear depersonalization or engulfment by the the old man. Hinting that Rodin was in trouble because of his blindness to the complexity of women, he regretted that his friend would not benefit from his own wiser understanding.

Reducing this old father surrogate to manageable size, he saw him as being "like a god of antiquity bound to the rites traditional in him, even to those which are not meant for us and yet were necessary for the cult of his soul in order to mold him" (*Letters* 1:332 and 333). Rodin is no longer Christ or the Buddha. He is still a god, but not one of our gods. He belongs to the past. He is not one who molds, but one who is molded by those outmoded attitudes, customs, and patterns of behavior which Rilke calls "rites traditional in him." The language of this passage and its context suggest the old man's helplessness in the snare of his blinding misconceptions.

This metamorphosis of the Master into "a god of antiquity," (an antiquated god?), not omnipotent, but "bound" to "rites . . . which are not meant for us" (because they are outdated?), brings to mind the Wagnerian perspective on the gods in their decline. It recalls as well the passage in the "Book of Pilgrimage" in which Rilke wonders if a father does not

mean "past years," "obsolete gestures," and "dead fashion," and concludes, "If he was a hero for his time,/ he is the leaf which falls when
we grow."⁵

Once frightened and intimidated by Rodin, the poet began to feel
anxiety on his behalf. He was particularly troubled by the sculptor's
relationship with an American-born marquise, later Duchesse de Choi-
seul, whom Rilke seems to identify with the vulgarity of the recordings
of music-hall performances which she played for the two of them. The
old man, who was becoming increasingly childlike, needed her to get
him down from the summits where in earlier years he had spent most
of his time (*Letters* 1:352).

It is easy to comprehend some of the motives behind the fantasy of
Rodin as a dependent child. Rilke's extreme dependency on Rodin at
first, as well as the master's real and imagined superiority, sometimes
made the young poet feel all the weaker and all the more uncertain,
insecure, and unreal. This childlike, almost infantile dependence and the
gross overestimation which accompanied it must have been humiliating
and galling in retrospect. Rilke's sense of reversal was a defense against
such painful memories.

We have looked at the letter to Lou in which he admitted being frightened by "the close proximity of something too hard, too stony, too big."
Writing to Clara just after Easter 1906, at a time when the underlying
tension between master and disciple was growing, he imagined the sculptor as a destroyer, a bird of prey. He was describing Rodin's work on a
bust of George Bernard Shaw while the playwright sat for this portrait.
Shaw was amused by the sculptor's "decapitation" of the bust with a
wire. Struck by Rodin's extraordinary swiftness as he grasped and modeled one face out of a multitude of impressions, Rilke thought of him as
having a "bird-of-prey-like clutch" (postmarked April 19, 1906; *Letters*
1:207).

"Decapitation" is humorous. Rilke shows an awareness of Shaw's
congenial sense of irony and comedy, and at first his own account is
playful. But the metaphor of Rodin's "bird-of-prey-like clutch" leaves
humor and irony behind. Considering Rilke's experience with Rodin at
this time, the old man's exploitation of his helpfulness and, perhaps, foreshadowings of the brutality with which he dismissed Rilke ("like a thieving servant"), I suspect that the letter reflects the poet's sense of the
destructiveness in this old father.

What was happening in the relationship between Rodin and Rilke, as the letters portray it, calls to mind two stories by that other native of Prague, Kafka: "The Judgment" and "The Metamorphosis." In "The Judgment," which was Kafka's first major story, the once powerful father appears to have become an old invalid, in some ways as helpless and needy as an infant, while his son, Georg, now in charge of his business, makes it prosper. Suddenly, as Georg, who is contemplating marriage, puts him to bed, the old father accuses his son of trying to cover him up, to bury him. Boasting that he could sweep Georg's bride from his side, he stands up on the bed, a giant touching the ceiling, and condemns his son to death for the sin of wishing to get rid of his father, to supplant him. "The Metamorphosis," written the following year (1914), expands upon the implications of "The Judgment" and provides a much richer, multilayered picture of the psychology of family relationships.

In "The Metamorphosis," Gregor Samsa, the son, supports his aging, decayed father, his mother, and his sister. Gregor's job engulfs him with its demands. He has no sources of pleasure, except a picture of a woman in his room and his hope that he will be able to send his violin-playing sister to a conservatory. Relief from the crushing burdens of work comes only when Gregor turns into an insect. This metamorphosis reverses the positions of father and son. Now the son, as an insect, is completely dependent upon his family and a painful burden to them. The story's interest to an interpreter of Rilke's relationship with Rodin comes from what it subtly reveals about Gregor's motivation in taking on the enormous burdens of the job which has engulfed him. (Obviously, I am thinking of the tasks which Rilke's secretarial duties for Rodin imposed upon him between September 1905 and May 1906.) Forced out of his dependent invalid state, the father in the story becomes a murderous figure for his son. One can well understand the son's need to keep the father as dependent as a child.

"The Judgment" supports this interpretation. It expresses a son's fantasy that the father is murderous and that the father's helpless, childlike dependency allows the son to prosper and to keep this father under control, and thus to remove the danger. It contemplates the possibility that these loving ministrations to a helpless, old, invalid father may hide a desire to reduce him still further, to nothing, to obliterate him, if only because he is so dangerous.

No doubt, the letters which bear witness to the old man's decay and ruin in the next few years—such as one written in November 1909 to Clara, describing Rodin as a child who must be led down from the heights, which had become precarious for him in his weakness, by a woman with vulgar tastes—those letters express genuine fear and tenderness for the sculptor as well as the poet's continuing, if unconscious, need to defend himself from the dangerous paternal figure, still very much alive in the unconscious mind, reflected in the terrifying angel of the First and Second Elegies, whom the poet wards off in the Seventh:

Wer, wenn ich shriee, hörte mich denn aus der Engel
Ordnungen? und gesetzt selbst, es nähme
einer mich plötzlich ans Herz: ich verginge von seinem
stärkeren Dasein . . .
. . . .
. . . Ein jeder Engel ist schrecklich.

Who, if I cried out, would hear me among the angels'
hierarchies? and even if one of them pressed me
suddenly against his heart: I would be consumed
in that overwhelming existence. . . .
. . . Every angel is terrifying.
(From the First Duino elegy [1912], SP, 150 and 151)

        Glaub nicht, dass ich werbe.
Engel, und würb ich dich auch! Du kommst nicht. Denn mein
Anruf ist immer voll Hinweg; wider so starke
Strömung kannst du nicht schreiten. Wie ein gestreckter
Arm ist mein Rufen. Und seine zum Greifen
oben offene Hand bleibt vor dir
offen, wie Abwehr und Warnung,
Unfasslicher, weitauf.
        Don't think that I'm wooing.
Angel, and even if I were, you would not come. For my call
is always filled with departure; against such a powerful
current you cannot move. Like an outstretched arm
is my call. And its hand held open and reaching up
to seize, remains in front of you, open

as if in defense and warning,
Ungraspable One, far above.
(From the Seventh Duino elegy [1922], *SP*, 190 and 191)

By the end of 1911 Rilke was appalled at Rodin's "simply going wrong" at the age of seventy. Unharmed by dozens of similar nemeses in the past, he had been so easily trapped by the affair with the Duchess that was "making his old age into something grotesque and ridiculous" (*Letters* 2:33). The man whom the poet had made his model, father, and master had become a ruin in the snares of his own folly. What had happened to Rodin frightened him: "What am *I* to say, with the little bit of work out of which I keep falling completely, if *he* wasn't saved?" Perhaps the fact that as a child he had been deeply affected by his father's failures and all his life had been forced to struggle with them reinforced the sense of danger he felt as he witnessed the final stages of Rodin's slippery slide. This is not to negate what I have said about the desire to cut the old man down to human size and about the way in which Rodin's decay and his need for help and support were welcome to Rilke. Opposing motives were at work in the poet.

The relationship took a turn for the worse in January 1914 when Rodin broke his promise to let Clara do a bust of him, a project which the poet had encouraged in order to help his distanced wife. At this point Rilke was reluctant to see the old man (*Letters* 2:108).

Finally, there is the retrospective view, from a much greater distance, several years after Rodin's death in 1917, when Rilke had fully come into his own with the completion of the *Elegies* and the writing of *The Sonnets to Orpheus*. In a December 1922 letter to his Polish translator, Witold Hulewicz, the poet confessed that in writing his book on Rodin (the first part of the book was twenty years behind him and the second nearly as far away) he had "lacked distance." Looking back, he thought that if he were presently doing his studies of the sculptor, his strong admiration would have to struggle against his sense of Rodin's deterioration and the disasters that had overwhelmed him. His emphasis in these comments is upon critical detachment and the difference between his youth ("my all too youthful attitude") and later age (*Letters* 2:312).

In October 1924 Rilke made a final evaluation of Rodin's influence, which shows the clarity and objectivity of distance and supremely self-confident mastery. The Frenchman's effect upon him, he said, had "outweighed" all literary influences and made them "superfluous." Contrasting Rodin with Tolstoy, who had abandoned his art, Rilke recalled that the sculptor had "assented fully and actively to the inner mission of his creative genius, the infinite divine play," so that it had "looked for a while" as if he had not only mastered his art, but, with all the insight that had come from the interplay of his shaping imagination and work with the clay, bronze, and marble, he had also taken possession of everything he had aspired to reach: "And so it may be too, not only for the artist of highest intent, but for the simple craftsman, if only he has once bitten open the kernel of his métier: the intensity arrived at within his characteristic achievement appropriates to him ... everything that is and has been which corresponds to the same degree of intensity" (Letters 2:359–60).

Was this a return to the old idealization of "the Master"? It was very high praise, but expressed in careful, measured language. The phrasing "looked for a while" tells us that the poet was not sinking back into the uncritical youthful frame of mind which he had rejected long ago. In this letter to Hermann Pongs, who was writing about him and teaching his work, he glossed over unpleasant matters. He did not even mention that Rodin had dismissed him, but explained the break by saying that he had been placed in the position of giving Rodin "irksome reminders" of tasks such as answering letters, and that his doing so had distorted their friendship. He transformed what had happened in May 1906, saying only that he had returned to Paris as master of his own life, and that his relationship with the sculptor had fallen "back into [its] earlier channel" (Letters 2:359). Was the poet rearranging his life to keep the painful twists and turns, the moments of weakness, away from curious eyes, because he thought they were comparatively insignificant in the context of the whole relationship and all it meant to him? It does not seem likely that at this time he was suppressing all memory of the actual events.

In any event, in 1924 he no longer needed to focus upon Rodin's decline and weakness. With complete confidence in his own mastery and achievement, he could rejoice in the relationship which had meant so much to him as a person and as an artist. Now his praise came not from a weak, sick man's need to idealize a new father in order to participate in his omnipotence, but from the sense that he too, like his old master, had "assented fully and actively to the inner mission of his creative genius, the infinite divine play," with awesome results.

VIII

In the winter of 1905–6 Rilke wrote "David singt vor Saul" ("David Sings before Saul"). I don't wish to reduce this poem to an allegory. It has an extraordinary life and significance as a work of literature which far exceed whatever autobiographical meaning one may find in it. But one can see how Rilke's experience with Rodin at this time consciously or unconsciously shaped the relationship of the old king and the young harper in the poem, which I reprint here before offering an interpretation:

König, hörst du, wie mein Saitenspiel
Fernen wirft, durch die wir uns bewegen:
Sterne treiben uns verwirrt entgegen,
und wir fallen endlich wie ein Regen,
und es blüht, wo dieser Regen fiel.

Mädchen blühen, die du noch erkannt,
die jetzt Frauen sind und mich verführen;
den Geruch der Jungfraun kannst du spüren,
und die Knaben stehen, angespannt
schlankt und atmend, an verschwiegnen Türen.

Dass mein Klang dir alles wiederbrächte.
Aber trunken taumelt mein Getön:
Deine Nächte, König, deine Nächte—,
und wie waren, die dein Schaffen schwächte,
o wie waren alle Leiber schön.

Dein Erinnern glaub ich zu begleiten,
weil ich ahne. Doch auf welchen Saiten
greif ich dir ihr dunkles Lustgestöhn?—

II
König, der du alles dieses hattest
und der du mit lauter Leben mich

überwältigest und überschattest:
komm aus deinem Throne und zerbrich
meine Harfe, die du so ermattest.

Sie ist wie ein abgenommner Baum
durch die Zweige, die dir Frucht getragen,
schaut jetzt eine Tiefe wie von Tagen
welche kommen—, und ich kenn sie kaum.

Lass mich nicht mehr bei der Harfe schlafen;
sieh dir diese Knabenhand da an:
glaubst du, König, dass sie die Oktaven
eines Leibes noch nicht greifen kann?

III
König, birgst du dich in Finsternissen,
und ich hab dich doch in der Gewalt.
Sieh, mein festes Lied ist nicht gerissen,
und der Raum wird um uns beide kalt.
Mein verwaistes Herz und dein verworrnes
hängen in den Wolken deines Zornes,
wütend ineinander eingebissen
und zu einem einzigen verkrallt.

Fühlst du jetzt, wie wir uns umgestalten?
König, König, das Gewicht wird Geist.
Wenn wir uns nur aneinander halten,
du am Jungen, König, ich am Alten,
sind wir fast wie ein Gestirn das kreist.

King, do you hear how my string-music casts
distances through which we're moving?
Confused stars float up to us,
and finally we fall like rain,
and flowers come up where this rain fell.

Girls blossom, whom you knew once,
who now are women tempting me;
you can scent the odor of virgins,
and the boys stand, tense,
lean and breathing, at secret doors.

That my sound could bring it all back to you!
But my music's reeling drunk;

Your nights, King, your nights—,
and how fair they were, the ones your creativity ravished.
o how beautiful were all bodies.

I believe I can accompany your remembering
as I can sense it. But on what strings
do I touch for you their dark groaning pleasure?

II
King, you who had all this
and who with loud life
overpower and overshadow me:
come down from your throne and shatter
my harp, which you're wearying so.

It's like a tree picked bare:
through the branches which bore your fruit,
a depth now looks as of days
which are coming—, and I scarcely know them.

Let me sleep no longer beside the harp;
take a look at this boy's hand:
do you think, King, that it still can't
span the octaves of a body?

III
King, you conceal yourself in darknesses,
and still I have you in my power.
Look, my strong song is not torn,
and the space around us both grows cold.
My orphaned heart and your confused one
hang in the clouds of your anger,
raging, bitten into each other,
clawed together into one.

Do you feel now, how we transform each other?
King, King, weight becomes spirit.
If only we cling to each other,
you to youth, King, I to age,
we're almost like a circling star.[1]

Reading the poem with the relationship between Rilke and Rodin in
mind, I find that its conclusion reflects the poet's feeling at this time that

he and the sculptor needed each other, that, as youth and age, they had much to give each other. It reveals the younger man's desire to cling to the older one. Yet the last part of the poem also focuses upon the anger in both of them, in powerful images, reminiscent of Dante's *Inferno:* "raging, bitten into each other/, and clawed together into one" recalls Ugolino and the Archbishop Ruggieri in cantos 32 and 33 of the *Inferno,* where Ugolino gnaws at Ruggieri's brain in hatred and they are frozen together in the ice at the bottom of Hell, so that one head seems a helmet on the other. If I am right in thinking that this poem indirectly expresses Rilke's feelings and his sense of Rodin's at the time, the anger and tension must have developed well before the break between the two men.

The line "and still I have you in my power" probably reflects Rilke's need to control this powerful and, at least in fantasy, destructive and dangerous master, which may have been part of his motivation for enduring the heavy burden of the tasks he was given to do at the time and for focusing upon the sculptor's neediness and age both then and in the fall of 1908. The story of David and Saul, as it is interpreted here, works very well as a medium in which the poet could explore these feelings obliquely, perhaps unconsciously. In reading the poem we should remember that David was appointed by God to take Saul's place, and that the king was doomed, having betrayed his God, having allowed himself to be corrupted. In so many ways the poem suggests Rilke's sense of the relationship between himself and the sculptor. Saul is remembering his pleasure with the help of David's playing. He conceals himself in darkness. David has him in his power.

"Abisag" (Abishag) precedes "David Sings before Saul" in the *New Poems.* When the two poems are read together with the poet's and the sculptor's lives in mind, the former seems to express obliquely a fantasy of Rodin. "Abisag" is based upon the story in the First Book of Kings in which a young girl is found for the old king, to sleep with him and warm him. But, as the poem emphasizes, the withering man ("den Welkenden") remains cold and impotent when the girl lies on him (*WDB,* 1:242–44).

The first part of "David Sings before Saul" is unusual in Rilke's work, which rarely has to do with explicitly sexual competitiveness between a paternal old man and a filial younger one. Here the conflict is rendered with delicacy, subtlety, and originality, and with ambivalence—the young man's desire to bring back by means of his playing those "dark moans of pleasure," as well as his delight in the realization that the girls the king once knew are the women now tempting him, while the old king has only his memories.

The second part of the poem, after affirming the king's power to "overwhelm and overshadow" the young harper with "loud life" (surely here we can see Rodin and Rilke's reaction to him), reasserts the young man's sexual power as if the older one doubts it: "take a look at this boyish hand:/ do you think, King, that it still can't/ span the octaves of a body?"[2]

As the harpist foresees the "days . . . coming" about which he knows very little, the poet senses the approach of his own new life, in which he will be able to express the new depth which he feels in himself.

But what is the feeling behind the appeal to the king to come down from his throne and shatter the harp which he has been exhausting? This exhortation calls to mind Rilke's fatiguing use of his own gifts as a writer in the service of Rodin and his role as a friend and companion, daily keeping the old man happy, giving him emotional support, a task which was wearing on the poet, as he felt the need to be alone to do his own work. During this period (September 1905 to May 1906) much of his imaginative energy went into the master's correspondence and into his supportive role.

It is a strange request, asking the king to come down off his throne and to shatter the harp. It reminds one that Rilke himself seems to have provoked the rather brutal, if temporary, sundering of the relationship by the sculptor in May 1906. Perhaps, the violence and destructiveness which the voice in the poem is appealing for reflect the poet's need to project onto Rodin the violence which he felt and his own desire to destroy the relationship. He displaces these impulses into the drama which he has taken from the Bible and projects them onto the figure in the poem who represents Rodin, defending himself from guilt. In the biblical story David was not guilty of injuring Saul, of dethroning or killing him.

The relationship between the two men and Rilke's feelings about the sculptor had gone through a complex transformation, which probably remained largely unconscious during the winter of 1905–6, and the result was not an opaque dream, but a marvelously lucid poem, in which a number of feelings were given indirect and subtle, but also primitive and powerful, expression through image and metaphor.

One can go on playing with "David Sings before Saul." Perhaps, an analyst, reading the poem, focusing on the young singer's appeal to the old King to destroy his harp, might say that there is an unconscious desire in the oedipal son to have the threatened father castrate him, so that he may not be guilty of supplanting the older man with women. But the poem as a whole is weighted against any such desire. Clearly, the playing of the harp represents the devotion of the young man's imaginative energy and all his gifts to the happiness of his old master, whose demands and needs have exhausted and withered his singing and playing. It needs to be replaced by another instrument, which, in part 2 of the poem, is the woman's body, whose octaves the young man's hands can span.

Did Rilke's feelings about his father's age, illness, and approaching death also help to mold this poem? I have argued that they probably influenced his response to the sculptor, the second father, whose power, sexual possession of many women, aging, and arousing of intense ambivalence in Rilke are reflected in the poem. The ambivalence, whose complexity shaped "David Sings before Saul," was part of a wide range of feelings originating in the relationship of father and son during the oedipal stage. Aside from this matter, one cannot help wondering if the father's aging, illness, and approaching death helped to release and strengthen the kinds of self-confidence represented in David and yet, at the same time, provided motivating energy for the harpist's sense at the end of the poem that he needs the old king and that, if only they could cling together, they might achieve the radiance, glory, and permanence of a star circling the heavens.

CHAPTER 9

Woman Within

Developments Leading to *The Sonnets to Orpheus* and the Completion of the *Duino Elegies*

I

In May 1911, more than a year after completing *The Notebooks,* Rilke wrote to his patron, Princess Marie von Thurn and Taxis-Hohenlohe, wondering why he was still unable to work, pondering "this long drought," which was "reducing my soul ... to famine" (*Letters* 2:26–27). In December of that year, having made no progress, from Duino he lamented to Salomé that he had begun to feel he was left "without a vocation, superfluous," a man without value or role, purpose or place (*Letters* 2:34). Facing the possibility that his gifts had failed him, he could think of nothing else to do.

The advent of the *Duino Elegies* in mid-January 1912 banished such thoughts, but only for a while. To Lou he wrote from Rhonda, Spain in January 1913, to say that the two Elegies which had come to him were no more than a "small ... broken off ... piece ... of what was then put in my power" (*Letters* 2:84). In October of the same year the poet's sense of his predicament could hardly have been worse. He wondered if he would ever be able to start writing again.[1]

Increasingly, he experienced the need of a companion who, from lack of love or selfless love, would feel no desire to possess him and would defend him against all threats to his solitary concentration. During the sterile periods of near despair in the years following the completion of

The Notebooks, he kept hoping for someone who would shelter him and would give him the sense of having a home in the world. He longed for a woman who could respond to the wild exaggerations which fed his art and his illness with an "ordinary and guileless" nature, someone who might calm the fears which so often distracted him and produced the defenses that left him isolated, flat, and empty (*Letters* 2:38). During the winter of 1913–14 he wrote about his search for this elusive woman in the poem "Du im Voraus / verlorne Geliebte, Nimmergekommene" ("You who never came, Beloved, lost from the beginning").

In January 1914 Magda von Hattingberg, a pianist, a divorcée without children, discovered Rilke's early *Stories of God* and wrote from Vienna to tell the author that she loved them. Delighted, he began writing her frequent, long letters, and she kept up her part of their correspondence. It was not long before he was calling her "my sister," wondering if God had sent her to him to enable him to survive. Day after day the letters to Magda poured out of him. They were detailed autobiographies of his tormented childhood, celebrations of his life and work, self-exaltations ("my art is of a splendor unrivaled even by the House of David"), avalanches of ideas and fantasies. He called his letters to her "letter-titans"; they were eruptions of fiery lava that came down on her, almost burying her. He likened himself to Stromboli. Rarely had his narcissistic grandiosity been more clearly exposed. By mid-February Magda had become not only "sister," but also "my true child" and "my true virgin mother" (*R&B:IC* 59, 88, 82, and 75).

A month after it had begun this correspondence, with all of its absurd expectations, ended, when Rilke went to Berlin to meet von Hattingberg. They traveled together to Munich, Paris, and Duino, among other places. He listened to her music, she to his readings of his work. Early in May they separated in Venice, having decided to do so while they were guests of the princess at Duino. Well before this they had both sensed that their early hopes for the relationship would be disappointed. Von Hattingberg's reaction to the poet's wish that they should remain together all their lives was expressed in a letter to her sister, Maria, which she quotes in her memoir, *Rilke and Benvenuta:* "Do I love him as a woman loves a man ... ? Do I love him so much that I want to be the mother of his children?" She realized that she did not. For her he was "the voice of God ... all that is superhumanly good, lofty and sacred, but not a human person!"[2]

As von Hattingberg got to know the poet and his later work, his poetry and prose often seemed alien and morbid to her. She also knew that he required a love which would serenely and joyfully embrace his strange and sometimes repulsive fantasies without a qualm. As she came to understand the nature of his narcissism, she grew increasingly pessimistic about the future of their relationship. She was troubled particularly by a letter in which he imagined that the woman he "left behind" would have to live, like a sailor's bride, content in her ignorance of his adventures and in her uncertainty as to whether he would ever return. And, if he did come back, she would have to be happy to accept his silence, his unwillingness, for a long while, to talk about all the strange, charged memories of what he had encountered on his travels. In this letter, sent to her before they met, he seems to be challenging her to tell him that she would be capable of superhuman self-sacrifice, that she would give him complete freedom, that her unlimited love could accept the possibility of his never returning without showing "any sign of fear, of concern, of reproach, not the slightest tear of disappointment." He imagines her waiting for him with the transparent, empty, passive selflessness of "the humble window by the stairs."

The same letter reveals the background and source, as he understood it, of this extreme narcissism, which he realized was intolerable yet hoped Benvenuta would accept with the empathetic, affirming joy her answering letters had expressed. The root of his requirements was his belief that his mother would be repelled by a child "destined to recklessly roam in and out of all sorts of creatures." But this freedom and power, he thought, was the quintessential quality of his imagination—the ability "to go into" other creatures and objects, "to tell what it was like inside" them, to be able to identify with them completely. Here he seems very close to Keats's notion of the chameleonic poet. Such an existence would be harmful to his narcissistic mother because it would mean dissolving his single-minded, symbiotic identification with her. And she sorely needed the close bond that he had been trying to escape for so long.

He suspected that she wanted him to remain "her clean little boy," a mirror image of her own purity, not strange or threatening (sexual? wild? uninhibited?) in any way. His "modern" tastes and values, his interest in many different kinds of people, creatures, objects, and places would have shocked her.[3] One can conceive the guilt he must have felt at struggling to separate himself from her so radically, at such betrayal and wounding. And he must have connected her frightening, painful early withdrawal with that struggle on his part.

The poet intimated to von Hattingberg that he could not live with a woman who would show anything like the anxiety, disappointment, and reproachfulness which Phia had expressed at the signs of his desire for autonomy. He felt vulnerable to any companion's attempts to inhibit the freedom a poet must have to wander, to love other women, and to voice disturbing new images and ideas such as those with which Baudelaire and Nietzsche had demolished and replaced stale forms of art and thought. Ironically, the self-sacrificing, unconditional love which he asked of Benvenuta resembled the self-immolating, binding devotion he felt his mother had tried to pressure out of him. To assure himself that no woman would ever threaten him again in such a way, he must reverse the relationship, though he was not conscious of wanting to do so.

Writing to Salomé on June 8, 1914, Rilke acknowledged the failure of this relationship as a flunking of "the test." Understanding the severity and persistence of his emotional "sickness," he observed that "three un-achieved months of clarity have laid something like a cold glass" over the extraordinary "flow" and "repose" and the apparent "truthfulness" opened up in his letters to Benvenuta during January and February of that year (*Letters* 2:113–14). The reality of the months they had spent together had enclosed all that like an exhibit encased in a museum, so that it had become inaccessible. Worse still, the glass barrier enclosing the pure and joyful experience of those early months had become a mir-ror, in which he saw "nothing but my old face." This image suggests that Rilke comprehended the narcissistic nature of his illness and his love. The "Narcissus" poems written in April of the preceding year support this supposition.

In the second of these two poems, Rilke has Narcissus imagine the woman who might have mirrored him lovingly and thus rescued him from his fate. But no woman does give confirmation, substance, coher-ence, and stability to his sad, sketchy sense of himself. Instead, he must study his reflection in the indifferent water, which provides nothing but a blurred, unstable image, that becomes "nothing other than the indif-ference/of stones turned over." In this loveless void the sense of self almost entirely dissolves, apart from a residue of sadness. Yet the poem ends with Narcissus wondering if his image aroused "sweet fear in her dream." Perhaps I misread this, but I find it ironic, for the woman dreaming is only imaginary, and this imaginary woman is a reminder at the end of the poem that Narcissus does not find a real one. As he thinks that he can almost feel her fear, he realizes that he is losing himself in his own gaze, dissolving. With this thought in mind, he lets his sweet fantasy of the woman's fear give him one last bit of evasive pleasure, wondering if he's "deadly." And this too might seem ironic enough in context to be amusing, if it did not seem so sad. The poem, in all its delicate loveliness of sound and image, suggests that Rilke understood the intricate deceptiveness of the illness he was describing. Here are the last four stanzas of the second "Narziss":

> Was sich dort bildet und mir sicher gleicht
> und aufwärts zittert in verweinten Zeichen,
> das mochte so in einer Frau vielleicht
> innen entstehn; es war nicht zu erreichen,
>
> wie ich danach auch drängend in sie rang.
> Jetzt liegt es offen in dem teilnahmslosen
> zerstreuten Wasser, und ich darf es lang
> anstaunen unter meinem Kranz von Rosen.
>
> Dort ist es nicht geliebt. Dort unten drin
> ist nichts, als Gleichmut überstürzter Steine,
> und ich kann sehen, wie ich traurig bin.
> War dies mein Bild in ihrem Augenscheine?
>
> Hob es sich so in ihrem Traum herbei
> zu süsser Furcht? Fast fühl ich schon die ihre.
> Denn, wie ich mich in meinem Blick verliere:
> ich könnte denken, dass ich tödlich sei.
> (WDB 2:57)

Narcissus's belief that he may be fatal leads me back to the poet's letter to Salomé on June 8, 1914. That letter comes to a final focus in a more elaborate form of the same fantasy. The poet imagines that he will be deadly to anyone, friend or lover, who ventures near enough to help him in his illness, misery, and sterility. He would imprison any such loving, caring person "in a region airless and loveless, so that his aid, unusable, would grow overripe in him and wilted and horribly atrophied" (Letters 2:112–13). One can envision the small child in the letter writer, out of sight, repressed, but very much alive in this fantasy and its underlying infantile feelings: namely the child's sense of his effect upon his mother or upon both parents (one should not forget also that this was a child whose parents largely isolated him from friends). If there were such infantile feelings underlying the fantasy in the letter, what might have been their roots? They seem to me to have grown out of the child's sense of his mother's responses and her effect on him when he attempted to give her help and support in her own emotional defectiveness and illness. And from what we know of Josef's constriction, we can see how little René might have felt about him too. Eventually, the parents who made him feel that all his efforts to help them in their worst times left him imprisoned "in a region airless and loveless," so that his generosity "wilted and atrophied," became a part of their son, René. Now, so many years later, the helpful, loving child was completely dissociated in Rilke's mind from himself and unconsciously projected onto the other people whom he longed for and kept away, though their unconscious associations with parental figures are more apparent, closer to the surface of consciousness.

Rilke's surreal image of his effect on all who might wish to love and help him was self-protective, self-destructive, and self-entrapping. (It brings to mind the image Dostoevsky gives us of the narrator at the end of Dostoevsky's *Notes from Underground.*) Yet in the depth of his private hell Rilke carried the memories of having written the first three Duino Elegies and parts of several others during the preceding two years and the sense of what the *Elegies* would be when he completed them, if only he could do so. Further behind him lay *The Book of Hours, The Notebooks, New Poems,* the friendships with Salomé and Rodin, and so much else, to strengthen his resolve to regain his full creative powers despite his crippling emotional illness.

II

Nineteen-fourteen marks a crucial turning point for Rilke. The painful conclusions about himself which he confronted more than four years after completing *The Notebooks* may have led to the writing of the poem "Wendung" (Turning), which he enclosed in his letter to Lou on June 20, 1914. "Wendung" expresses a new conception of his needs as a poet:

Denn des Anschauns, siehe, ist eine Grenze.
Und die geschautere Welt
will in der Liebe gedeihn.

Werk des Gesichts ist getan,
tue nun Herz-Werk
an den Bildern in dir, jenen gefangenen; denn du
überwältigtest sie: aber nun kennst du sie nicht.
Siehe, innerer Mann, dein inneres Mädchen,
dieses errungene aus
tausend Naturen, dieses
erst nur errungene, nie
noch geliebte Geschöpf.
(*WDB* 2:83–84)

For, see, there is a limit to looking.
And the world beheld
wishes to thrive in love.

Work of sight is done,
now do heart-work
on the images confined in you; for you
subdued them: but now you don't know them.
Look, inner man, your inner maiden,
this one wrested out of
a thousand natures, this
only appropriated, never
yet loved creature.

This is the end of the poem. It seems to reflect Rilke's grievous confrontation with his inability to love. It recalls the conclusion of an earlier poem, "Archaic Torso of Apollo," where he tells himself, "Du musst dein Leben ändern." ("You must change your life"). The change envisaged at the end of "Wendung" is evident: The poem characterizes Rilke's relationship with nature heretofore as a kind of power struggle, as conquest and appropriation. Now, if he is to become the kind of poet he wishes to be, he must become capable of feeling love for the world as he finds it within himself. As the object of his inward contemplation, it will thrive in his love. Wrested from external surroundings and imprisoned within the mind and self as images, as impressions, it can flourish in the transformations of an ardent imagination.

Poems and letters which follow "Wendung" confirm what it reveals, that Rilke came to perceive the world absorbed within him as a beloved, lovely young woman, "dein inneres Mädchen." While he continued to fall in and out of love after 1914, the sense of the beloved woman within grew increasingly important. It became a major shaping theme of his thinking about himself and about the nature of the poet in general. The notion of the woman in the poet, like many of his enduring themes, had begun to interest him relatively early. It can be found in a letter written in 1904: "It is so natural for me *to understand girls and women;* the deepest experience of the creator is feminine—: for it is experience of receiving and bearing. The poet Obstfelder once wrote, when describing the face of a strange man: 'it was' (when he began to speak) 'as if there were a woman in him—'; it seems to me that would fit every poet who begins to speak" (*Letters* 1:181). Here the woman within the poet is not the world possessed as images, but the source of his voice, his genius. In the act of creation it is a woman that speaks or writes his poems.

Rilke's sense of the woman or girl within himself originated at least partly in his having played at being the daughter his mother had lost. As an adult he felt that this sister-self still lived in him. When Maman suggests that Sophie "must certainly be dead," Malte "stubbornly" contradicts her and begs "her not to believe that" (*The Notebooks,* 100). In January 1901 Rilke expressed the feeling that his sister was still alive in one of a group of nine brief poems called "Aus einer Sturmnacht" (From a Stormy Night). He imagines that she must be growing on such stormy nights, that she must be beautiful by now. Surely, he thinks, someone is going to woo her soon:

> In solchen Nächten wächst mein Schwesterlein,
> das vor mir war und vor mir starb, ganz klein.
> Viel solche Nächte waren schon seither:
> Sie muss schon schön sein. Bald wird irgendwer sie frein.
> (*WDB* 1:220)

But, having died, one might ask, where can she live? Where has she grown beautiful? Where will someone woo her? In 1901, when he wrote this poem, the idea of his sister's continuing existence may have been simply a vague fantasy, not accompanied by any such questions. In later years he would have answered that she was alive in himself, in what he called *"the depth dimensions of . . . inner being"* (*Letters* 2:342). When he spoke of lovers, such as Magda von Hattingberg, as sisters, no doubt he experienced them as projections of the sister he had become to please his mother and with whom at times he still felt identified.

In "Wendung" the poet challenges himself to develop the ability to love, not another person, but the woman who is part of himself. Failing miserably in the relationship with Benvenuta, which had seemed to promise so much after so many other failures with women, temporarily losing the hope that his emotional impotence would ever be cured, he turned to this new commitment. His sense of the reality of his inner woman promised a resolution to a problem which had become a source of great pain. The love which he now envisioned was narcissistic, but "Wendung" reflects an essential change in his conception of narcissism, converting it from the sterile, solipsistic illness of his poems on Narcissus into a fertile, creative mode of existence.

This seems to have involved a retrieval of the early symbiotic state of partial fusion between mother and child, in which the child loves the mother as part of himself. Hence, Rilke's new commitment to loving, not another person, but the woman within, drew strength from his genius for gaining access to very early states of mind and recapturing them. There is no evidence that he was conscious of using this gift in writing "Wendung", but a number of the letters and poems which I have explored reveal that he was quite clearly aware of it at other times. In the unfinished elegy written at Schloss Berg in December 1920, he focused on this early fusion which remained available to him, saying he was "pre-world" ("Vor-Welt"). The poem suggests that he was both mother and child, both male and female, experiencing with the primal mother, Earth, the pregnant harmony ("die trächtige Eintracht") which most men (males) cannot comprehend, as well as the stillness in the universe around a growing organism (die Stille im Weltall/ . . . um ein Wachstum"). Earth has confided to him how she keeps the embryo whole and sound ("Mir hats die Erde vertraut, wie sie's treibt mit dem Keim,/ dass er heil sei" [*WDB* 2:130–31]).

"Wendung" concludes with the thought that the "inner maiden" has been "wrested out of/ a thousand natures." Ostensibly this means that the poet has taken the world within himself through thousands of perceptions. But the figure of the inner maiden here connects his internalization of the female world, as an early step in the creative process, with another important element of his experience. Just after completing the first Duino Elegy, he wrote to Annette Kolb, "What speaks to me of humanity—immensely. . . . is the phenomenon of those who have died young and, even more absolutely, purely, inexhaustibly: *the woman in love.* In these two figures humanity gets mixed into my heart" (*SP,* 318). Admiring women in love, fascinated by them, idealizing them despite or because of his inability to sustain a love for a particular woman, he identified himself with them, making them part of himself.

In *The Ego and the Id,* as we have seen, Freud offers the theory that children and, to a lesser extent, adults tend to identify with those objects of erotic love whom they are forced to give up. Such identification, closely related to introjection (consciously or subliminally experiencing an external object as having been internalized), has a primitive model in infantile fantasies of devouring or incorporating the breast or the mother. Through identification or introjection, loved ones from whom we are separated can be kept within us and become a part of us.[1]

This argument can help us to understand Rilke's identification with women in love abandoned by their lovers. So often we find him after a brief infatuation or a longer affair writing passionate letters to the women he had deserted. While defending his solitude, many of these letters seem to reaffirm his love and his sense of connection and affinity with these women. In doing so they arouse skepticism, as his recurrent emphasis upon the women whose love is unrequited seems ironic. Yet the letters and the recurrent emphasis upon the figure of the unrequited lover were authentically rooted in his own experience. With Lou Andreas-Salomé, as with his mother, it was he who felt abandoned. With his mother, as we have seen, and also with Lou, who was his most important model in adult life before Rodin, he felt himself closely identified. The bitter loss of Phia, the painful loss of Lou, no doubt intensified this sense of identification. No wonder he understood so well the women abandoned by their lovers and those whose love was not reciprocated. No wonder he felt identified with them and imagined that he had mixed them into himself. From this perspective one can see that he must have felt at least some unconscious identification with the women whom he left, whose unrequited love he was defending himself against. Very likely his feelings about some of those he left were ambivalent and confused. Probably in leaving or exiling women such as Magda von Hattingberg and Baladine Klossowska ("Merline"), who helped him during the summer and fall of 1921 prepare Muzot for the completion of the *Elegies,* he felt that he was losing them. Despite his need to get away from them, with his losses of his mother and Lou in the background, this new sense of loss and separation, however subliminal, must have reinforced both his need to take them, in their unrequited love within him and his feeling that he could identify himself with them.

The task with which he confronted himself in "Wendung" was not so dangerous, not so threatening as some of these love affairs had seemed to him. Learning to love the woman within, he would not have to fear engulfment or being smothered or devoured. Nor would he have to worry about smothering the other person's ability to love and care for him, the danger that he described in the June 1914 letter to Lou which I quoted earlier. Surely, the latter fantasy was rooted in the child's fear of destroying his mother's ability to love and help him, arising from his feeling that his mother's affection and caring were tenuous and undependable and might be repelled all too easily.

III

Rilke's outpouring of twenty-six sonnets, the first cycle of *The Sonnets to Orpheus,* in the course of a few days early in February 1922, owed a great deal to his having found a real person in whom he could embody the fantasy of the inner girl or young woman, still "almost a girl," and a vivid compelling metaphoric image for her introjection and integration with his own being:

Und fast ein Mädchen wars und ging hervor
aus diesem einigen Glück von Sang und Leier
und glänzte klar durch ihre Frühlingsschleier
und machte sich ein Bett in meinem Ohr.

Und schlief in mir. Und alles war ihr Schlaf.
Die Bäume, die ich je bewundert, diese
fühlbare Ferne, die gefühlte Wiese
und jedes Staunen, das mich selbst betraf.

Sie schlief die Welt. Singender Gott, wie hast
du sie vollendet, dass sie nicht begehrte,
erst wach zu sein? Sieh, sie erstand und schlief.

Wo ist ihr Tod? O, wirst du dies Motiv
erfinden noch, eh sich dein Lied verzehrte?—
Wo sinkt sie hin aus mir? . . . Ein Mädchen fast. . . .
(Sonnet I.2; *WDB* 1:487–88)
And it was almost a girl and emerged
out of this united happiness of song and lyre
and shone brightly through her spring veils
and made herself a bed in my ear.

And slept in me. And her sleep was everything:
the trees that filled me with wonder, these
palpable distances,the felt green field,
each moment of astonishment that surprised me.

She slept the world. Singing god, how did you
perfect her so that she had no desire
to wake some time? See: she arose and slept.

Where is her death? Oh, will you conceive
this theme before your song expends itself?—
Where does she fade from me? . . . A girl almost. . . .

In evoking the figure of the girl, Rilke was probably thinking of Vera
Knoop, to whom he dedicated the *Sonnets.* A year later (April 12, 1923), he
wrote Countess Margot Sizzo, saying that he had only gradually understood the relation of the *Sonnets* to Vera, whom he had met only a few
times during her childhood, when she was a friend of his daughter.[1] At the
beginning of January 1922, Rilke received from Vera's mother an account
of her daughter's illness and death at nineteen. Frau Knoop had written to
him in November 1921 to congratulate him on Ruth's engagement. Answering this old friend, he complained that the announcement of the engagement had revealed to the world the place where he was located at a
time when he desperately needed solitude. Of course, he hoped and expected that Ruth would be a good wife. But the letter reveals that he was
not much interested in his daughter's marriage. What concerned him, he
wrote to Frau Knoop, was guarding his seclusion, in the hope that, after
years of frustration, he would at last become fully creative again. The contrast between his attitude toward his daughter and the intense interest he
expressed in Vera is striking. Closing his letter, he asked the bereaved
mother to tell him about the dead girl so that he might gain a vivid sense of
the end of her life. Frau Knoop seemed to understand that he wanted to

hear about her daughter's reaction to her mortal illness and the end of her life. His response to her account, which he received a month before he began the *Sonnets*, gives one a clear grasp of the girl's new meaning for him and helps us to see why and how his impressions of her and his feelings about her inspired and, to some extent, shaped these poems.

Frau Knoop's letter had brought back Vera's "dark, strangely concentrated charm" so vividly that he felt it would overwhelm him if he closed his eyes to concentrate upon the girl. He imagined that the "excess of light" in Vera's heart had come from the swiftness with which her life consumed itself in her suffering, when she was faced with the imminence of death (*Letters* 2:283–84). From her mother's description, he gathered that her illness and her suffering had brought openness to, and unity with, everything around her, reinforced by a joyous affirmation of life.

A year later, in April 1923, he remembered Vera's dancing as a child; her body in motion had seemed naturally gifted with art and the power of metamorphosis. Attacked by the glandular disease that later killed her, she had grown heavy, renounced dancing, and devoted herself to music, then drawing. In these forms, the poet fantasized, the dancing in her had expressed itself indirectly, and with increasing subtlety (see *SO*, 160).

The poet's sense of his relation to Vera had another dimension. His transformation of the perishing world in the *Sonnets*, and in the late Elegies written largely or entirely during February 1922, had been fostered by his sense of intimate connection with this dead girl, who, because of her "incompletion," held "open the gate of the grave" to him (*Letters* 2:376). She had died so young, comparatively innocent, never having lost the extraordinary intensity of youth, which approaching death had made all the more vivid. It was because, though dead, she was still very much alive for him that she kept open the ordinarily impenetrable barrier between the living and the dead, which had also, according to legend, given way to Orpheus.

Frau Knoop's account of the end of Vera's life enriched and clarified his conception of death as a kind of plenitude. Even her suffering was, for him, an essential part of that fullness: "something like a privilege is involved when human beings are not spared such monstrous torment, as if this ruthlessness were the expression of a kind of initiation, a sign of election to the inordinate—as though this desperate suffering could happen only to a being from whom there were to be no secrets."[2] Through his connection with Vera, he felt, many dimensions of existence related to or shaped or touched by death were illuminated for him, opened to him. The proof of this came from the multifarious ways in which he evoked the presence of death and the enduring life of the dead and the past in the *Sonnets.*

We can think of Orpheus's descent into the world of the dead as a metaphor for the closeness one can feel to an intimate who has died. (In Rilke, self-aware imaginative genius created a sense of intimacy with Vera out of a few meetings which took place years before he heard the news that she had died, and out of a grieving mother's descriptions of her daughter, her dancing, music, art, illness, and death. Only the *Sonnets* can answer the skeptical response that this sense of connection was an illusion.) One may feel that so much of oneself is still united with a dead person that one exists largely in the world of the dead. The man who descends into Hades in "Orpheus, Eurydice, Hermes" (1904) has a different reaction to death—a desire to overcome it, to bring his wife back. But the Orpheus of the *Sonnets* bodies forth Rilke's belief that his poetic genius was very much in touch with the dead and existed in a dimension of experience in which their presence took on all kinds of vital meaning in his feelings and thoughts and in his poems, as he tells us in Sonnet I.9:

> Nur wer die Leier schon hob
> auch unter Schatten,
> darf das unendliche Lob
> ahnend erstatten.
>
> Nur wer mit Toten vom Mohn
> ass, von dem ihren,
> wird nicht den leisesten Ton
> wieder verlieren.
> . . . .
> Erst in dem Doppelbereich
> werden die Stimmen
> ewig und mild.
> (*WDB* 1:492)
>
> Only he who has raised the lyre
> among shades too
> may, fathoming, restore
> the endless praise.

Only he who has eaten
with the dead their poppy,
will not lose again
the softest note.

Only in the double sphere
do voices grow
eternal and gentle.

The "double sphere" is the world in which the poet exists in the presence
of the living and the dead, responsive to and connected with both. Insofar
as the *Sonnets* show that Rilke did realize such an existence, he fulfilled
in his response to Vera's death the exhortation which he voices in Sonnet
II.13, "Sei immer tot in Eurydike" ("Be forever dead in Eurydice").

Sonnet I.2 ("And it was almost a girl ... ") seems to refer to Vera
Knoop, though she is not named. The girl has made herself a bed in the
poet's ear and slept in him. Her sleep, her death, was not a falling away,
but a rising into the life of the poet's songs ("she arose and slept").
Through his association with Orpheus in these sonnets Vera is implicitly
associated with Eurydice, who inspired and was reborn (embodied anew)
in Orpheus's songs and thus found a new life in the hearing of the creatures that listened to him, where he built temples to receive his music:
"da schufst du ihnen Tempel im Gehör" ("you created temples for them
in their hearing"). This is the last line of Sonnet I.1, anticipating the
beginning of the second Sonnet, where Rilke celebrates his creation with
his songs of the girl who made herself at home in his hearing (his creative
imagination), sleeping and waking, alive in death.

In Sonnet II.28, dedicated to Vera in Rilke's note, the girl's dancing
is said to have surpassed nature, just as nature transcended herself when
Orpheus's singing moved her to "complete hearing" ("völlig hörend").
Rilke implicitly associates Vera, the dancer and musician, with poetic
genius because she seemed to hear the ordinarily unheard music within
the hidden, innermost core of the psyche. "Du wusstest noch die Stelle,
wo die Leier/ sich tönend hob—; die unerhörte Mitte" ("Still you were
aware of the place where the lyre rose/ resonant: the unheard center").

The innermost music in the mysterious center of the psyche, which
Vera heard, came from the lyre of Orpheus, who, as the archetype of
poetic genius, sings once more when he is discovered there: "Ein für alle
Male/ ists Orpheus, wenn es singt" ("Everytime there's singing/ it's Or-

pheus" [*WDB* 1:489]). The sonnet tells us that Vera has been moved by Orpheus's music "von damals" ("from that time"). Ostensibly "damals" refers to the fabulous past in which the legendary Orpheus sang. But here it also suggests the time of infancy or early childhood, when, in the framework of Rilke's thinking, "the unheard center" takes form, before it is repressed or forgotten in the adult's unconscious mind. In *The Notebooks, Letters to a Young Poet*, the unfinished elegy of 1920, and other writings, Rilke makes it clear that the artist must return to that age of innocence and purity of impulse, buried within him, when the Angel, the vital form of his genius, first visited him.[3]

Drawing some of his inspiration and some of his ideas, as a number of critics have noticed, from Paul Valéry's dialogue "L'âme et la danse," at the beginning of Sonnet II.28 Rilke sees Vera dancing as an exemplary image of artistic metamorphosis or transformation. Though she is scarcely more than a child, he calls upon her to perfect the configurations of her art into "the clear constellation of one of those dances/ in which we briefly surpass nature" in her dull ordering of things.

> O komm und geh. Du, fast noch Kind, ergänze
> für einen Augenblick die Tanzfigur
> zum reinen Sternbild eines jener Tänze,
> darin wir die dumpf ordnende Natur
> vergänglich übertreffen . . .
> (*WDB* 1:525–26)

Meditating upon Vera's dancing, he feels drawn into her "flawless celebration" and imagines her hoping that he would be:

> Für sie versuchtest du die schönen Schritte
> und hofftest, einmal zu der heilen Feier
> des Freundes Gang und Antlitz hinzudrehn.
> (*WDB* 1:526)

Sonnet I.2 metaphorically suggests an act of introjection, incorporating someone who has been lost, like Eurydice, through death. Vera becomes Rilke's inner girl or woman. A dancer, musician, and artist, she is inextricably mingled with the poet in his creativity. In her sleep of death, she also brings the world into him, for this sleep seems to absorb everything around her and to fuse her with it: "Und alles war ihr Schlaf," "Sie schlief die Welt" (*WDB* 1:487 and 488). Rilke's letter to Frau Knoop emphasizes his sense of Vera's openness to, and unity with, the world (*Letters* 2:284). He thought of her as one of those rare human beings who feel themselves to be part of nature before they die, as Malte imagines Bettina von Arnim felt, as animals and small children do, according to the Eighth Elegy; as Rilke did in the mystical dissolution of boundaries between himself and the universe described in his 1913 prose fragment "An Experience."

In the Seventh Elegy, written a few days after Sonnet I.2 (February 7, 1922), the poet thinks of himself wooing a "silent", "still invisible" "friend," in whom a gradually awakened emotional response becomes a warm companion to his own ventured feeling:

> würbest du wohl, nicht minder—, dass, noch unsichtbar,
> dich die Freundin erführ, die stille, in der eine Antwort
> langsam erwacht und über dem Hören sich anwärmt,—
> deinem erkühnten Gefühl die erglühte Gefühlin.
> (*WDB* 1:465)

In his notes for the Elegy, Stephen Mitchell connects this silent, still invisible friend with the "inner woman" (or girl) whom the poet urges his inner man to see in "Wendung" (*SP*, 327). Mitchell makes the same connection with Sonnet I.2 (*SO*, 163). The immediate proximity in time of the *Sonnets*, with their inner "Mädchen," and the Seventh Elegy supports his interpretation of the silent friend in that poem. So does Rilke's emphasis in both the Seventh and the Ninth Elegies (most of the latter was written on February 9, 1922) upon the inner, invisible reality which must replace the perishing external world. In the Ninth he conceives of Earth as a beloved or dear one ("du liebe") who wishes to arise invisible and transformed within us and seems to command the poet to enable her to do so.

The Seventh Elegy associates the poet's wooing and the responsive awakening of the inner woman with his ability to sing with the purity of a bird's cry ("zwar schrieest du rein wie der Vogel" [*WDB* 1:465]). In a February 1914 letter to Lou Andreas-Salomé, Rilke says that a bird's song can fleetingly transform "the world into inner space" because we hear in the song the bird's innocent fusion of her inner life with the perceived life of the world around her (*SP*, 327). Sonnets I.2 and II.28 and the letters about Vera reveal that the fantasy of this girl, who had moved him so deeply, living within him, as a part of him, now that she was dead, helped Rilke to attain to this sense of unity in his own singing.

As Vera enjoyed the experience of being one with all nature while she was still alive, her death, which dissolved all vestiges of the separation of the conscious mind from nature was a perfection of the sleep which Rilke describes in Sonnet II, 14 as "intimate sleep" ("innige Schlafen") with things at a depth shared in common ("gemeinsamen Tiefe" [WDB 1:516]). The conceit in Sonnet I.2 that the girl made her bed in his ear and slept in him suggests that his memory of Vera and her mother's moving account of her dancing, her music and art, her illness and death, brought him closer to the intimate depth of awareness which he evokes in this Sonnet. Sonnet II.14, like Rilke's conception of Vera, calls to mind one of the *New Poems*, "Der Tod des Dichters" (Death of the Poet), written in Paris in 1906:

> Die, so ihn leben sahen, wussten nicht,
> wie sehr er Eines war mit allem diesen;
> denn Dieses: diese Tiefen, diese Wiesen
> und diese Wasser *waren* sein Gesicht.
> (*WDB* 1:252)
> Those who saw him alive did not know
> how much he was one with all this:
> For this: these gorges, these meadows
> and these waters *were* his face.

The poet's death completes or perfects the oneness with nature which he has enjoyed while alive.

Vera's presence can be felt in a number of related sonnets, where flowers become images of what is "earthly" and of openness, inclusiveness, or receptivity. Sonnet II.14 begins with a line in which flowers are described as "true to the earthly" ("Siehe die Blumen, diese dem Irdischen treuen"). In Sonnet I.25 Rilke compares Vera (his dedicatory note to the poem identifies her as the person to whom he speaks) to a flower he knows, though he does not know its name: "*Dich,* die ich kannte/ wie eine Blume, von der ich den Namen nicht weiss." In the last stanza of this Sonnet, he reflects that during her illness, when she felt the approach of death, her blood nonetheless thrust into its natural springtime and shone with an earthly gleam, like the flowers of Sonnet II.14.

In Sonnet II.5 an anemone becomes an image of the extraordinary openness, the "limitless receptivity" ("unendlichen Empfangs"), that the poet found in Vera as well:

BLUMENMUSKEL, der der Anemone
Wiesenmorgen nach und nach erschliesst,
bis in ihren Schooss das polyphone
Licht der lauten Himmel sich ergiesst,

in den stillen Blütenstern gespannter
Muskel der unendlichen Empfangs . . . .
(*WDB* 1:509)
Blossom muscle which gradually reveals
the anemone's meadow morning,
until the polyphonic light of the resonant
skies pours into her womb,

muscle of limitless receptivity,
expanded in the quiet flower-star . . . .

This anemone calls to mind Vera, as Rilke conceived of her, with her openness to everything around her and her experience of joyous harmony and union with the world (see *Letters* 2:284). The poem reverses the poet's original reaction to an anemone in a Roman garden, described in a June 1914 letter to Salomé. The flower in the poem is stretched so wide open it has trouble closing to rest at night. The anemone in the Roman garden could not close at all. Seeming to be "frantically torn open," it could not stop taking in the excessive night, while other flowers around it had folded their petals to rest, filled with the bright day's "abundance." The poet saw the flower which could not close as an image of his helpless absorption in external distractions: "if there is a noise, I give myself up and *am* that noise."[4] This recalls the opening pages of the *The Notebooks*, where the noises of the city create pandemonium in Malte's room all night, as well as Malte's tendency to become identified with other people he sees, his fear of engulfment and impingement or invasion.

If we come back to Sonnet II.5, we cannot miss the difference in the poet's response to the anemone. Rilke can enter fully, without anxiety, into the image of the flower's openness. This is not to say that he had become a sadhu in February 1922. The Sonnet ends with the question "Aber *wann*, in welchem aller Leben,/ sind wir endlich offen und Empfänger?" ("But *when,* in which of all [our] lives,/ are we to be finally open and receptive?"). And the Eighth Elegy, written earlier the same month, ends with the sense of human beings as always in the process of departing, bidding farewell ("so leben wir und nehmen immer Abschied"), homeless on earth, displaced out of "das Offne" ("the open")—out of the existence free from the constraints of time, the haunting of death, the sense of spatial limitation, the opposition between self and other and self and world, the feeling that someone is watching and judging us—that life enjoyed by animals and small children, free from all these crippling wounds in adult human consciousness. The anemone Sonnet, like the Eighth Elegy, reflects the fact that the poet had clarified and mastered his conception of "the open," so that he could evoke it in compelling language and imagery, even if he realized that it was not a permanent possession and that human, all too human as he was, he must slip back into a sense of deprivation and transience.

Vera became an embodiment of Rilke's long-held belief that women have a much stronger awareness than men of the natural processes and cycles, such as those of birth and death, which profoundly influence and connect the existence of all living things: "Women, in whom life lingers and dwells more immediately, more fruitfully and more confidently, must surely have become fundamentally riper people, more human ... than easygoing man, who is not pulled down below the surface of life by the weight of any fruit of his body, and who ... undervalues what he thinks he loves" (*LYP,* 58).

The characterization of Eurydice in "Orpheus, Eurydice, Hermes" (1904) is closely related to the notion in *The Notebooks* that women have a subliminal awareness of the death growing in them (meaning, I suspect, the mental and physical processes of maturing and aging) similar to their consciousness of a fetus ripening within. In *The Notebooks* and in Rilke's letters, this blissful awareness is implicitly contrasted with the fear, loathing, and denial of death which are impoverishing and self-destructive.

Unlike the man in "Orpheus, Eurydice, Hermes," the woman (except in its title the poem never refers to them by name) is not anxious or impatient. Absorbed in herself, she is scarcely aware of the man nervously pacing ahead of her toward the exit from the realm of the dead. The man, in contrast, is divided within himself. His sight races ahead, implicitly seeking hints of light and life. His hearing lingers behind, listening for her footsteps, uncertain that he hears them, worried that she is not following him, eager to look back, restraining himself in the realization that doing so would ruin "this whole undertaking" ("dieses ganzen Werkes") which he has so nearly brought to completion, concerned in typical male fashion with the struggle toward achievement and the possibility of failure.

The woman is far removed from this kind of consciousness. Her inward absorption is compared to the mental state of a woman in late pregnancy. Death fills her as a fruit is filled with its own dark, mysterious sweetness. Death is plenitude, ripeness, and fulfillment. It frees the woman from all desire, all craving, from the tensions of marriage and the sexual life: "ihr Geschlecht war zu/ wie eine junge Blume gegen Abend" ("her sex was closed/like a young flower toward evening"). She is no longer the man's property. She no longer exists through her relationship with him, no longer thinks of herself as the beauty in his songs. When the god (Hermes) tells her that the man has turned around in his impatience and anxiety to see if she is there, she asks, "Who?" As Orpheus stands far off at the bright exit into the world of the living, she does not recognize him.

Rilke compares Eurydice in death to long hair loosened. He descibes her, in a complex metaphor, as having been given away, like rain that has fallen. She has been distributed like a plentiful supply.

Sie war schon aufgelöst wie langes Haar
und hingegeben wie gefallner Regen
und ausgeteilt wie hundertfacher Vorrat.
(*WDB* 1:301)

Though Rilke characterizes her new state of existence as "a new virginity" ("einem neuen Mädchentum"), these are images of fullness and fertility as well as freedom and beauty, which suggest her becoming one with nature. Finally, the poet associates her with roots: "Sie war schon Wurzel." This anticipates "Gegen-Strophen" ("Anti-Strophes"), begun in the summer of 1912 and completed in February 1922, originally meant to be the Fifth Elegy. In "Gegen-Strophen," Rilke addresses women as Eurydice's sisters, describing them as "Blumen des tieferen Erdreichs,/ von allen Wurzeln geliebte," ("Flowers of the deeper soil/loved by all roots," [*SP*, 222 and 223]).

In these poems, as in *The Notebooks,* the *Letters to a Young Poet,* and his writings about Vera, Rilke imagines that women tend to have a different, more profound, less limited and less defensive understanding of the relationship between life and death. *The Sonnets to Orpheus* develop and clarify insights toward which Rilke was groping in "Orpheus, Eurydice, Hermes" when he described death as a sweet, mysterious ripeness and fullness in Eurydice. His conception of Vera's response to fatal illness and the approach of death in Sonnet I.25 is far more accessible:

Tänzerin erst, die plötzlich, den Körper voll Zögern,
anhielt, als göss man ihr Jungsein in Erz;
trauernd und lauschend—. Da, von den hohen Vermögern
fiel ihr Musik in das veränderte Herz.

Nah war die Krankheit. Schon von den Schatten bemächtigt,
drängte verdunkelt das Blut, doch, wie flüchtig verdächtigt,
trieb es in seinen natürlichen Frühling hervor.

Wieder und wieder, von Dunkel und Sturz unterbrochen,
glänzte es irdisch. Bis es nach schrecklichem Pochen
trat in das trostlos offene Tor.
(*WDB* 1:503)

Dancer, who suddenly stopped, your body full of hesitation,
as if your young being had been cast in bronze;
sorrowing and listening—. Then, from the high powers
music descended into your changed heart.

Illness was near. Already held by the shadows,
darkened, your blood hurried, but, as if momentarily doubtful,
it put forth into its natural springtime.

Time and again, disrupted by darkness and collapse,
it shone with an earthly radiance. Until after a frightful knocking
it entered the comfortlessly open door.

The conceit of the young girl who has died making her bed in his ear and Vera's presence in a number of the other Sonnets reflect the poet's sense of having attained to gifts and strengths he had longed for and envied in some of the women about whom he had written, such as Bettina von Arnim, the other unrequited lovers, and Lou Andreas-Salomé.

His notion of taking Vera within him helped to make possible the joyful belief that these longed-for virtues were blossoming in him and that he had gained access to the kinds of power and richness which, until this triumphant moment in his life, he had defined largely through his meditations on women.

IV

The conceit of the girl making herself a bed in the poet's ear and sleeping in him suggests a retrieval in disguise, through displacement, of the partial fusion between mother and son, the original symbiosis, along with its conditioned omnipotence, its large degree of freedom from negation and limitation, from the sickness of adult alienation, and from the fear of death and the burden of time. And in many ways *The Sonnets to Orpheus* are a triumphant expression of the poet's sense of the fullness of this retrieval.

The poet's image of introjecting Vera also recalls the games in which Malte became Sophie to please his mother. The fantasy that the girl made herself a bed in his ear and slept in him, if it satisfied a still-living but unconscious need in Rilke to become a girl in order to gain his mother's love, must have been such a thick disguise for this self-transformation that it defended him against the shame and anger associated with those early games in which he assured his mother that the "naughty" little boy was no longer there. The idea that Vera was alive within him is Rilke's most compelling variation on the fantasy of a hermaphroditic nature which he expressed in *The Book of Hours*. There, as we have seen, he connected the longing for completeness, mastery, and fertility as a poet with the fantasy of being made a hermaphrodite and with the wish that he might be become capable of motherhood ("Mutterschaft").[1]

Malte's mother's younger sister, Abelone, who is his first love after Maman's death, seems to mirror him. Rilke gives her hermaphroditic qualities. Comparing her singing with that of the angels, imagining that it raises him into heaven, Malte hears her voice as radiantly masculine (see *The Notebooks*, 125). Later in the novel we are told that Abelone gave Malte Bettina von Arnim's correspondence with Goethe to read. Associating this young woman, a friend of Goethe and Beethoven, with Abelone, crediting her with extraordinary gifts of imaginative, creative perception, Malte imagines that Bettina's love, which did not receive an adequate response from Goethe, did not need one: "it contains both call-note and answer in itself; it is its own fulfillment" (206). Such love, not contained or limited by a responsive lover, can ignite and shape the visionary transformations which Rilke defined in the Ninth Elegy as the purpose of his existence. Speaking to Bettina in his thoughts, Malte asks, "And isn't the whole world yours? For how often you set it on fire with your love and saw it blaze and burn up and secretly replaced it with another world while everyone slept" (206).

Rilke's longing for a hermaphroditic nature also expresses a desire for a self-sufficiency in which his love would be focused within himself; the man and the woman in him would love each other rather than somebody else. For the poet this would not be merely a regression to the primitive narcissistic symbiosis between the infant and the idealized mother with her illusory omnipotence. As Rilke moved through Abelone and Bettina and his conception of the inner woman or girl in "Wendung," to the silent friend of the Seventh Elegy and the metaphor of introjection in Sonnet I.2, he seems to have made progress toward the attainment of a truly hermaphroditic self-sufficiency and wholeness. Time and again he reintegrated a mothering female, in numerous transformations, with his sense of himself. And thus he became, in his experience of himself and in his writings, male and female; the unicorn and the inner woman who is his mirror in *The Notebooks* and in Sonnet II.4; female world within and contemplating poet; brother and sister; parent and child. He would be mother and father to himself and to the poems which reflected his face and love back to him, as the world does to the Angels in the Second Elegy:

> *Spiegel:* die die enströmte eigene Schönheit
> wiederschöpfen zurück in das eigene Antlitz.
> (*WDB* 1:445)
> *mirrors:* which draw back into their own face
> the beauty which has streamed from it.

In these lines the locus of the mirror is ambiguous. The world in the Angels' eyes reflects their beauty. They, in their perceptions, re-create it in their own image, so that they and the world mirror each other. In this respect they represent Rilke's conception of creative genius as consisting in the transformation of the world into "the invisible," and thus into the form given it by the artist's hidden inner life. Thinking of the Spanish landscape at Toledo, he wrote that its towers, hills, and bridges seemed already transfigured with the visionary "intensity of the inner equivalents through which one might be able to represent" them. One way of understanding his perceptions of Toledo was to imagine a blind angel encompassing that landscape and all space, contemplating them within himself. Seeing things "in the angel," as he was able to do at Toledo, where each object seemed a fusion of "external world and vision," was his self-appointed "task" (*Letters* 2:146).

Rilke's conception of hermaphroditic motherhood in *The Book of Hours* may have been influenced by traditional Greek and Asian myths. In Plato's "Symposium," Aristophanes imagines that some of the first human creatures were hermaphrodites and that the gods sliced them in two, creating male and female halves which ever since then have sought each other to regain their original wholeness. In *Life against Death*, Norman O. Brown, before naming Rilke as an example of "the reunification of the sexes in the self," quotes a text from the *Tao Te Ching*, which teaches that the man who integrates female elements into his psychic functioning and sense of self can return to the original wholeness of infancy and, in doing so, receive "all things under heaven":

> He who knows the male, yet cleaves to what is female
> Becomes like a ravine, receiving all things under heaven
> . . . .
> This is returning to the state of infancy.[2]

In a traditional psychoanalytic reading, Rilke's fantasy of himself as a hermaphrodite might be interpreted as a disguised expression of a repressed childhood desire to be made a woman by his father (represented, through displacement, by the Lord in *The Book of Hours*, to whom the poet appeals to grant him such a nature) so that his father can make love to him. In his essay "Some Pathological Consequences of the Anatomical Distinction between the Sexes" (1925), Freud observes, "A boy also wants to take his *mother's* place as the love-object of his *father*—a fact which we describe as the feminine attitude."[3] From this viewpoint, an adult's desire to be made a hermaphrodite might well involve a regression to such boyhood longings. I have explored Rilke's need of his father's love, but have nowhere discovered in his writings any consciousness of harboring a child's desire to have his father make love to him.

In *Three Contributions to the Theory of Sexuality* Freud stresses the bisexuality of children, but he does not argue that the survival or return of the child's bisexuality in an adult may bring a richer integration, self-sufficiency, and wholeness. In his essay "Dostoevsky and Parricide," he sees Dostoevsky's "bisexual predisposition" as "one of the predispositions or reinforcements of neurosis." He also argues that it was responsible for Dostoevsky's "remarkable understanding of situations [in his novels] which are only explicable by repressed homosexuality." But the novelist's artistic gift is "unanalyzable."[4]

Rilke's long-enduring and evolving conception of the poet as hermaphrodite may be better understood with help from Freud's comments on "the ego-ideal" in his essay "On Narcissism: An Introduction" (1914). In this essay Freud conceives of the ego-ideal as drawing to itself the narcissism which the child enjoys and the adult must give up. The child creates this ideal as a substitute for the "narcissistic perfection" of his early childhood, "when he was his own ideal." Although "libido" is withdrawn from the self as one grows up and transferred to the ideal one has created for oneself, its attainment promises a recovery of something like the much-missed narcissistic gratification of early childhood. Part of the self-esteem one feels in the fulfillment of one's ego-ideal comes from its confirmation, however limited and unconscious, of the infantile fantasies and feelings of omnipotence which often remain dormant within us.[5]

In a strict central European family of the late nineteenth century, hermaphroditism would have seemed obnoxious and far removed from any conception of an ideal self or object. But in his upbringing, in his psychology, and in his genius, Rilke was radically original. He may have been aware of the ancient legends and teachings which I have mentioned. He must have known that prophetic and magical powers were sometimes associated with bisexuality, as in the myth of Tiresias. And this ego-ideal may have been shaped in his childhood by his feeling that his mother, despite her flaws and weaknesses, was the stronger, more vital, and more creative parent. So much of his life reflects this feeling. Obviously, as I have suggested, his mother's clearly expressed attitude that a male child was undesirable, her longing to have him become a girl, helped to engender and to nurture the hermaphroditic ideal which we find in his work.

In contrast to the hermaphroditic figures of Rilke's fiction and poems, the ordinary male, as Rilke conceives of him, especially in those passages of *The Notebooks* where the male is accused of lacking the capacity for love (a foreshadowing of the 1914 letters which Rilke writes about his own incapacity), seems a poor, limited, crippled specimen of humanity.

Considering the still-invisible, silent friend in the Seventh Elegy, whose response gradually awakens and grows warm, as she hears the poet's wooing, and Vera as she appears in Sonnet I.2, we realize that Rilke discovered a complex version of fruitful, creative narcissism which invites comparison with other writers' versions of that state of mind, as, for example, the image of the poet turning over upon himself and sinking his tongue into his own chest in the fifth section of Whitman's "Song of Myself." Whitman images self-love as a physical act, highly original in its nature, a mating of soul and self (the "you" in the poem is the soul), a penetration of the one by the other which suggests both a kiss and genital sex, whose location is ambiguously chest and hips, heart and genitals. The "you" of this section, after parting his shirt, plunges his tongue to the poet's heart, but his head is "athwart my hips," and he feels the poet's beard while holding his feet. The suggestiveness of the sexual act in Whitman's poem has no counterpart in the Seventh Elegy. But, unlike Whitman, Rilke makes one feel the distinctive personal presence of an invisible, silent, but ardent friend within the poet.

I have contrasted creative narcissism with the narcissism of mental and emotional illness. I should point out that Freud himself connects narcissistic libido with sublimation and thus with creativity. In *The Ego and the Id,* he theorizes that by taking a beloved object into ourselves through identification or introjection and by thus making the object part of us, we draw to ourselves the love (Eros or libido) originally directed toward the object. Some of this new narcissistic libido becomes the energy for sublimation and thus for creative work. "Indeed, the question arises, and deserves careful consideration, whether all sublimation does not take place through the mediation of the ego, which begins by changing sexual object-libido into narcissistic libido and then, perhaps, goes on to give it another aim."[6]

So many women whom Rilke loved and from whom he was separated, and finally the girl Vera, whom he found lovely and deeply moving, were taken into himself. Finding them in himself, he drew the love he felt for them to himself. His way of transforming object love into narcissistic love was surely a source of creative energy at the time when the *Sonnets* were written and the *Elegies* completed.

There is an evident affinity between Freud's speculations concerning narcissistic libido and sublimation in *The Ego and the Id* and Rilke's evolving concept of transformation in *The Notebooks,* "Wendung," and the Seventh and Ninth Elegies. For Rilke, the poet's task was to take beloved objects into himself and transform them into elements of the "invisible," the inner life, where, as parts of himself, they might be transfigured through his love. Out of this process would come the substance and energy of his creative work, as they were reborn in his poems. In the Ninth Elegy, Rilke imagines that the Earth dreams of becoming part of that invisible life within human beings, in order that she and many a perishing thing worth saving may be transformed there, in the alembics fired by intense feeling, into something that will endure. The Elegy implies that at the end of this process poems or other works of art will offer new existence in new forms to the earth and the ephemeral objects and events which the poet has taken into the refuge of his unconscious mental and emotional life. And he promises that he will continue to respond to her mandate, assuring his beloved Earth that her spring seasons have won him, acknowledging that death is the sacred means by which she inspires poets to do the invisible work of transformation. These insights lead to the conclusion of the Elegy, in which he celebrates the "immeasurable life" welling up within him:

> ... Ist nicht die heimliche List
> dieser verschwiegenen Erde, wenn sie die Liebenden drängt,
> dass sich in ihrem Gefühl jedes und jedes entzückt?
> . . . .
> Erde, ist es nicht dies, was du willst: *unsichtbar*
> in uns erstehn?—Ist es dein Traum nicht,
> einmal unsichtbar zu sein?—Erde! unsichtbar!
> Was, wenn Verwandlung nicht, ist dein drängender Auftrag?
> Erde, du liebe, ich will. Oh glaub, es bedürfte
> nicht deiner Frühlinge mehr, mich dir zu gewinnen—, *einer,*
> ach, ein einziger ist schon dem Blute zu viel.
> Namenlos bin ich zu dir entschlossen, von weit her.
> Immer warst du im Recht, und dein heiliger Einfall
> ist der vertrauliche Tod.

Siehe, ich lebe. Woraus? Weder Kindheit noch Zukunft
werden weniger. .... Überzähliges Dasein
entspringt mir im Herzen.
(*WDB* 1:474 and 476)

V

In chapter 3 I discussed Rilke's emphasis upon solitude and his endeavor
to develop the capacity to be alone. The silent inner friend of the Seventh
Elegy and the girl who made her bed in the poet's ear and slept within
him in Sonnet I.2 suggest the resolution of this struggle. For most of his
life, being alone was as painful as it was necessary. This dilemma was the
subject of the letter he wrote to Lou Andreas-Salomé from Duino in
December 1911, a few weeks before the First Elegy came to him. He
lamented the state of mind that made him long for people, and the conflict, confusion, and guilt which accompanied this longing. Preoccupied
with the fantasy that he could find someone to shelter his solitude, he
had made no progress with his work (see *Letters* 2:34).

Often Rilke felt that he could not work unless he was alone. Responding to Karl von der Heydt's offer of a refuge in April 1906, when he
needed to escape Rodin, he said that even the most generous and hos-
pitable friends could not give him the "limitless solitude" which made it
possible to experience each day as if it were a lifetime. Completely alone,
one cannot see to the end of the spacious cosmos in which one is at
home "with-everything," surrounded by "the innumerable." Only in
solitude could he come to an understanding of his experience and give
it an intelligible shape (*Letters* 1:203). Two years after the arrival of the
first elegies at Duino, he returned to this subject with renewed emphasis,
calling his solitude "inexhaustible, greater, more spontaneously blissful"
than anything else he could think of, claiming that it had given him "all
that was greatest, all that was always *too great*"—meaning, I suspect,
that the experience of giving birth to his Elegies and other major poems
had been almost insupportable (*Letters* 2:106–7).

Perhaps it was only in Muzot, at the time when he completed the
Elegies and wrote the *Sonnets,* that he became at last truly comfortable
with, and at home in, extreme seclusion. And it may be that his magical
internalization of Vera, his vivid, completely convincing sense of the girl

or woman within, his union with his own Eurydice, enabled him to enjoy a sense of companionship even in such a solitary existence, relieved only by a delightfully unobtrusive housekeeper. We can understand just how complete and unremitting Rilke's isolation was at Muzot from an objective viewpoint if we read Paul Valéry's impressions of the place in his 1926 essay *Reconnaissance à Rilke:*

A very small castle terribly alone in a vast, rather sad mountainous place; rooms antique and pensive, sombre furniture, constricted days, that oppressed my heart. My imagination could only hear in your interior the endless monologue of a completely isolated conscience, which nothing distracted from itself and from its sense of itself as a unique being.[1]

D. W. Winnicott sees the capacity to be alone as "one of the most important signs of maturity in emotional development."[2] For Winnicott such maturity means freedom from the kinds of anxieties which beset Malte in his isolation. It entails a high degree of integration and a well developed capacity for differentiation. It means also that one can achieve a sense of personal unity which makes it possible to say to oneself "I AM, I am alive, I am myself." It enables one to be at ease with "creative apperception," the fertile interaction between "subjectivity and objective observation," the mental interplay of private "inner reality" and what we experience as "the shared reality" of an external world. Winnicott contrasts a life of intelligent imaginative perception with one dominated by a constant compulsion to conform and adaptation to real or fantasied demands from the environment. Such an existence, controlled by the need to comply and fit in, is accompanied by "a sense of futility."[3]

The opposition between creative thinking and compliance was an essential criterion of health for Rilke. In the Prodigal Son episode of *The Notebooks* the need to be alone is a response to the threat that the son, having returned home, will be forced into compliance with family pressures to become all too much like them. In Malte, the compulsion to isolate himself, arising from closely related fears of other people, is intensified by an emotional illness which makes the solitude he needs painful and frightening. In such emotional illness, the capacity to be alone, as Winnicott conceives it, is likely to be weak or absent.

Compulsively seeking company during the long period of sterility between the completion of *The Notebooks* in 1910 and the arrival of the *Elegies* in 1912, Rilke felt that he was often converted into a walking, talking facsimile of the people around him. Emerging from his room in a state of mental chaos, he would find himself "expressing well-formed things" with a facility and poise that made him a mirror image of the person to whom he was talking. Or he would become the person others took him for, "without being too particular about my really existing" (*Letters* 2:37). His friends and acquaintances could bring him out of his "lifelessness" superficially and without awakening any resurgence of emotional vitality and strength. As his talk and behavior were drawn into identification with theirs or into conformity with their expectations, he often felt he was no longer himself at all.

He was still far from developing "the capacity to be alone" and the emotional health and maturity which make it possible. Winnicott's analysis of the origins of this capacity is particularly pertinent to a discussion of the changes which made possible Rilke's period of greatest creativity at Muzot.

Winnicott observes that the capacity to be alone originates in the infant's assurance of his mother's dependability. A supportive mother, empathetically oriented to her child's needs through her identification with him, making few demands on him, expecting little from him, creates in him a sense of a "protective environment." And it is this sense of a reliable, continuing, supportive, protective environment which makes possible the beginnings of the feeling "I am."[4]

The presence of such a mother defends the infant against impingements which might disrupt his sense of his continuity of being. Her protective presence makes it possible for him to relax, to become unintegrated and undifferentiated, to enjoy the spontaneous flow and play of his thoughts and feelings, to exist without anxiety about the external world or anxiety arising from a lack of conscious purpose or direction. In this way he develops the ability to be alone in her presence. In this largely unintegrated, undifferentiated state of mind, he is likely to be open and receptive to the energies and impulses arising from the unconscious (Winnicott uses the term "id"), which gradually afford him the confident feeling of his own reality and vitality. Introjection of a supportive, empathetically oriented mother makes this kind of receptivity possible later in life, with the result that an individual may continue to be gifted with a strong sense of his distinctive, personal reality in the absence of parents and surrogates. In more general terms, he has internalized the "protective environment" of infancy.[5]

In December 1913, writing to Princess Marie, Rilke asked her not to come to see him in Paris. Being "in a cocoon," he had to keep himself solitary. She had already seen how repulsive he could be in his caterpillar phase; he urged her to wait until the new butterfly emerged. Then again, changing his metaphor, he was a bird "all molted and shabby" (*Letters* 2:100). He needed to be alone in order to molt, to fall apart in order to come together again as a writing poet. Like Malte, he believed that he had to go through a kind of mental disintegration as a preparatory stage for the emergence of his unique gifts of seeing and saying. We saw how dangerous and frightening this experience was when he first came to Paris.

At such a time he had to be alone, because, in the radically undifferentiated and unintegrated state which he needed to rediscover his genius, he felt extremely vulnerable to the impingements of other people upon his internal freedom, his unique sense of himself, and his emerging work. At such times the capacity to be alone, as Winnicott defines it, was essential to him, because it meant that he could feel sheltered and protected as he came apart, lost himself, and dissolved into the undifferentiated state which he celebrates and praises as "das Offne" ("the open") in the eighth Duino Elegy, in "An Experience" (the prose fragment of 1913 describing a mystical event), and in a number of the *Sonnets to Orpheus.*

When a child feels that he can be alone in himself because someone else is there who asks "nothing but to be there functioning and protecting at the border of the invisible" (Rilke's fantasy of the perfect companion, who resembles the mother calming the terrified child at night in *The Notebooks*), then, as Winnicott says, the child "is able to become unintegrated, to flounder, to be in a state in which there is no orientation, . . . to exist for a time without being either a reactor to an external impingement or an active person with a direction of interest or movement" (to Princess Marie, December 27, 1913; *Letters* 2:102).[6] Only the individual who has developed the capacity to be alone in this way, by internalizing or creating such a "protective environment," "is constantly able to rediscover the personal impulse," or, as we might say, with Rilke in mind, the source, voice, and vision of his own unique and original genius.[7]

Drawing upon the work of Melanie Klein, Winnicott argues that the capacity to be alone "depends on the existence of a good object in the psychic reality of the individual." Confident relationships with such mental objects can make it possible to be solitary at times and still enjoy what he calls "a sufficiency of living."[8]

Do I distort the meaning of this theory if I suggest that Rilke's inner woman or girl was such an internal good object, transformed through displacement and condensation and brought into consciousness? How strange it is that Vera, a young woman, "almost a girl," assumed the place of the maternal surrogate in his imagination and in his poems at the moment when his creative genius was most fully and richly released! As I suggested earlier in this chapter, the choice of Vera may have been motivated partly by the thickness of the disguise. Surely, she could never have been threatening to him as Phia and Lou had been, even if she had been alive. His introjection of Vera, imaged in Sonnet I.2, reminds me, in this respect, of his gravitation to Clara as he moved away from Lou in 1900 and 1901, and of the many young women and girls, such as Marthe Hennebert in Paris, whom he turned to for love and companionship. Marthe was seventeen or eighteen when he met her in 1911; he was thirty-five.[9] According to the princess Marie, "This very young girl meant more to him than any other woman. He was always dreaming about Marthe."[10] I shall have more to say about the young women and girls with whom Rilke fell in love in the last part of this chapter.

In sum, Rilke found a way to create in the *Sonnets* a thickly disguised substitute for the supportive mother whom he had been seeking most of his life; and now, in 1922, she was not a separate individual, such as Salomé, whom he could lose, for he imagined her existing within himself. This figure in the *Sonnets* reflects and, perhaps, reinforced his attainment of the capacity to be alone and all the ease of creativity which flowed from this attainment. He had been struggling toward it from the time that he had written about Abelone and Bettina in *The Notebooks* and more obviously from the time that the idea of the inner woman or girl had become a major focus of his thought, reflected in the crucial poem of self-confrontation, "Wendung." No doubt, by giving conscious form to these changes, the writing of the *Sonnets* helped to bring to completion and to clear definition a psychic transformation which had been in the process of taking place over many years.

VI

Vera Knoop's importance for Rilke while he was writing the *Sonnets* can be understood more fully if we look back through the "inneres

Mädchen" of "Wendung" to the little girl which Malte became for Maman and realize that this girl was alive in and for Rilke all his life, that he expressed his sense of her in his work and found a splendid embodiment for her in Vera, whose death made it possible for him to fuse her with his sense of the girl in himself and thus to give that vague being a more definite form.

A chapter in Winnicott's study of the psychology of creativity, *Playing and Reality,* adds a fascinating dimension to this aspect of Rilke's psychic life. Winnicott describes a therapy session in which he realized that a middle-aged, married, male patient with a family, who was talking about penis envy, sounded like a girl. Winnicott told the patient, "I know perfectly well that you are a man but I am listening to a girl." He assures us that this had nothing to do with homosexuality.[1]

The patient's reaction was "intellectual acceptance ... and relief." When he said, "If I were to tell someone about this girl I would be called mad," the analyst made another surprising self-discovery. Since, without prompting by the patient, he had heard a "girl talking," when in reality the person on his couch was a man, Winnicott suggested that *he* must be the "mad" one. This interpretation reassured the patient that he was not insane, though he was experiencing himself as a man and a girl at the same time. Releasing the patient from the spectre of insanity by telling him that this strange perception of him had come spontaneously into his analyst's mind as well, Winnicott enabled him to confront the split between the man and the girl (not woman) in himself. This unpremeditated therapeutic maneuver also put Winnicott in the position of the man's mother early in his childhood. Having wanted a daughter, she saw her baby as a girl and only later thought of him as male. Winnicott was able to bring "into the present" the mother's radical misperception and thus to help the patient locate the "madness" in his mother rather than himself.[2]

This account has obvious relevance to Rilke's inner life and work. The origin of the patient's self-division in his mother's experience of her little boy as a girl calls to mind the role that Rilke played for Phia, though there are evident differences between the two cases. Winnicott does not say that his patient colluded with his mother's "madness" by consciously playing the role of a girl for her. And his account does not suggest that the patient, defensively dissociating himself from the girl in him, was anywhere nearly so conscious of the sexual ambiguity in himself as Rilke seems to have been or that he felt anything like the poet's fascination with his own departure from the norm.

As I have noted, *The Notebooks* and, more explicitly, Rilke's letters suggest that his having been induced to be a girl for his mother was a source of shame and anger and of the confusion about his identity which was an important element of his emotional illness and misery. I have also discussed Rilke's interest in fusing the man and the girl in himself. In Sonnet I.2 he finds ways of bringing them into a vital, creative, and harmonious relationship. Winnicott tells us that in his patient the defensive dissociation between his two different experiences of himself was abandoned as he accepted his bisexuality and achieved a new sense of psychic unity. For the patient apparently this was a crucial step in the direction of health. For the poet a comparable resolution of long-standing confusion was an essential element in the rich integration, the openness, and the fluidity which made possible the *Sonnets,* the completion of the *Elegies,* and the other splendid poems written in February 1922 and subsequently. One can see that, more than ever before, Rilke was successful in finding ways in which to enjoy, and to make imaginative use, of his bisexuality during the period of his greatest creativity and that his poetry at this time expresses the resolution of the uncertainty, doubt, and confusion which we have found earlier in his life (most notably in his inability to remain with any woman) and in his poetry, fiction, and letters.

Winnicott observes that often the split-off female in an individual like his patient does not grow and age along with the man.[3] When middle-aged men who have such a female within them seek girls or women much younger than themselves as sexual partners or objects of their love, they are looking for someone who can embody the split-off girl within, someone onto whom they can project her. Perhaps this helps to explain Rilke's choice of Vera, a girl who died at nineteen, as his muse for the *Sonnets* and his conceit of her making herself a bed in his ear and living in him. Reading his letters and the biographies, one finds that as a middle-aged man he was often taken with much younger women. Earlier I mentioned Marthe Hennebert. In 1914, at thirty-eight, Rilke had a passionate affair with Lulu Albert-Lazard, who was twenty-three when he met her. Elya Maria Nevar (her real name was Else Hotop) was in her early twenties when Rilke, in his forties, had his affair with her soon after the First World War. In September 1926 there was Nimet Eloui, an Egyptian divorcée of twenty-three. It was for her that Rilke picked the roses which pricked his hand, leading to an infection which gave birth to the myth that he died for the love of a beautiful young woman.[4]

In his comments on men who seek much younger women as embodiments or projections of their split-off inner girl, Winnicott observes that they tend to move quickly from one girl to another. Often such a man feels "more identified with the girl than with himself." This enables him to empathize with her and thus to intensify and to satisfy her sexual desires. But in his identification with her, he is largely unable to gratify the male in himself.[5] This frequent lack of satisfaction helps to explain the man's need to move on from one girl to another. Repeated lack of satisfaction in such experiences contributes to a sense of futility and may inhibit the man's ability to give himself in love. The tendency to move rather quickly from one young woman to another, which we find in Rilke, may also follow from the fact that the girls or young women such a man is attracted to must never become so real or individually distinctive in his mind that they can get in the way of the man's need to use them as embodiments of the girl in himself. With Vera, at last, Rilke found a girl who could never obstruct him in his fulfillment of this need.

Notes

Chapter 1, Part I

1. Harold J. Vetter, Introduction, *Language Behavior in Schizophrenia*, ed. and comp. Vetter (Springfield, Ill.: Charles C. Thomas, 1968), 3.

2. Rainer Maria Rilke, *The Notebooks of Malte Laurids Brigge*, trans. Stephen Mitchell (New York: Random House, 1982), 52. Hereafter page numbers for this translation of *The Notebooks* will be indicated in the text in parentheses.

3. *Letters of Rainer Maria Rilke, 1892–1926*, trans. Jane Bannard Greene and M. D. Herter Norton, 2 vols. (New York: Norton, 1945, 1947, and 1948; Norton Library, 1969), 2:147 and 1:115. Hereafter page numbers will be indicated in the text in parentheses with the designation *Letters* 1 or *Letters* 2.

4. John Dryden, "Absalom and Achitophel," l. 163 ("Great Wits are sure to madness near allied"), and William Butler Yeats, "Mad as the Mist and Snow," section 18 of "Words for Music Perhaps."

5. See chapter 2, part 4. Anton Ehrenzweig, *The Hidden Order of Art: A Study in the Psychology of the Artistic Imagination* (Berkeley: University of California Press, 1967), 117–18.

6. Rilke, *Where Silence Reigns: Selected Prose*, trans. G. Craig Houston (New York: New Directions, 1960; New Directions Paperbook, 1978), 104. Hereafter page numbers will be indicated in the text in parentheses with the designation *WSR*.

7. See Robert L. Delevoy, *Dimensions of the 20th Century: 1900–1945*, trans. Stuart Gilbert (Geneva: Éditions d'Art, Skira, 1965; distributed by World Publishing Company), 71–76.

8. Harold F. Searles, *The Nonhuman Environment in Normal Development and in Schizophrenia* (New York: International Universities Press, 1960), 30. Searles is quoting from C. Savage, "Variations in ego feeling induced by d-lysergic acid diethylamide (LSD-25)," *The Psychoanalytic Review* 42 (1955): 8–13.

9. Harold F. Searles, *Collected Papers on Schizophrenia and Related Subjects* (New York: International Universities Press, 1965), 467.

10. D. W. Winnicott, *The Maturational Processes and the Facilitating Environment* (London: Hogarth Press and the Institute of Psychoanalysis, 1965), 185.

11. See chapters 5 and 8 and the works of Searles, Kohut, Laing, Winnicott, and Modell listed in these notes and in my Select Bibliography.

12. Winnicott, *The Maturational Processes,* 29.

13. Ibid., 33.

14. J. F. Hendry, *The Sacred Threshold: A Life of Rainer Maria Rilke* (Manchester, England: Carcanet New Press, 1983); Hans Egon Holthusen, *Portrait of Rilke,* trans. W. H. Hargreaves (1958; trans.: New York: Herder and Herder, 1971); Wolfgang Leppmann, *Rilke: A Life,* trans. Russell M. Stockman (New York: Fromm International, 1984); Donald Prater, *A Ringing Glass: The Life of Rainer Maria Rilke* (Oxford: Clarendon Press, 1986).

Among other works of scholarship and commentary, *published since 1953,* which have been helpful are the following: Beda Allemann, *Zeit und Figur beim späten Rilke* (Pfullingen: Verlag Günther Neske, 1961); Rudolph Binion, *Frau Lou: Nietzsche's Wayward Disciple* (Princeton: Princeton University Press, 1968): Geoffrey H. Hartman, *The Unmediated Vision, An Interpretation of Wordsworth, Hopkins, Rilke, and Valéry* (1954; rpt. New York: Harcourt, Brace and World, Harbinger Books, 1966); Robert Hass, "Looking for Rilke," in *Twentieth Century Pleasures, Prose on Poetry* (New York: Ecco Press, 1984), 226–28; Erich Heller, "Rilke and Nietzsche, with a Discourse on Thought, Belief and Poetry," in *The Disinherited Mind, Essays in Modern German Literature and Thought,* expanded ed. (New York: Harcourt Brace Jovanovich, 1975), 123–77; H. F. Peters, *Rainer Maria Rilke: Masks and the Man* (1960; rpt. New York: McGraw-Hill, 1963); James Rolleston, *Rilke in Transition: An Exploration of His Earliest Poetry* (New Haven: Yale University Press, 1970); Elizabeth Sewell, *The Orphic Voice: Poetry and Natural History* (1960: rpt. Harper and Row, Harper Torchbooks, 1971); Priscilla Washburn Shaw, *Rilke, Valéry and Yeats: The Domain of the Self* (New Brunswick, N. J.: Rutgers University Press, 1964); Walter H. Sokel, "The Devolution of the Self in *The Notebooks of Malte Laurids Brigge,*" in *Rilke, the Alchemy of Alienation,* ed. Frank Baron, Ernst S. Dick, Warren R. Maurer (Lawrence: Regents Press of Kansas, 1980); Frank Wood, *Rainer Maria Rilke: The Ring of Forms* (1958; rpt. New York: Octagon Books, 1970).

15. Lou Andreas-Salomé, *Rainer Maria Rilke* (Leipzig: Insel, 1929); *The Freud Journal of Lou Andreas-Salomé,* trans. Stanley Leavy (New York: Basic Books, 1965); *Lebensrückblick: Grundrisse einiger Lebenserinnerungen,* ed. Ernst Pfeiffer, rev. ed. (Frankfurt: Insel, 1977).

Chapter 1, Part II

1. Andreas Huyssen, "Paris/Childhood: The Fragmented Body in Rilke's *Notebooks of Malte Laurids Brigge,*" in *Modernity and the Text: Revisions of*

German Modernism, ed. David Bathrick and Andreas Huyssen (New York: Columbia University Press, 1989), 116.

2. Ibid., 115.

3. Jacob Steiner, *Rilkes Duineser Elegien,* 2nd ed. (Bern and Munich: Francke, 1969), 10.

4. Ibid., 8.

5. Kathleen L. Komar, *Transcending Angels: Rainer Maria Rilke's Duino Elegies* (Lincoln, Nebr., and London: University of Nebraska Press, 1987), 79.

6. Richard Exner and Ingrid Stipa, "Das Phänomen der Androgynie des Schaffenprozesses im späten Rilke: Das Beispiel. "Solang du Selbstgeworfnes fängst . . . ," in *Rainer Maria Rilke,* Wege der Forschung, vol. 638, ed. Rüdiger Görner (Darmstadt: Wissenschaftliche Buchgesellschaft, 1987), 361. Exner and Stipa are referring to Simenauer's essay "Rainer Maria Rilke in psychoanalytischer Sicht," *Psyche* 30 (1976); 1102.

7. Sonnet I.3 may be found in Rainer Maria Rilke, *Werke in drei Bänden,* hereafter designated as *WDB,* ed. Ernst Zinn, 3 vols. (Frankfurt: Insel, 1966), 1:488. "Solang du Selbstgeworfnes fängst, ist alles," may be found in *WDB* 2:132.

8. Exner and Stipa, 372.

9. Anthony Stephens, *Rainer Maria Rilke's "Gedichte an die Nacht"* (Cambridge: Cambridge University Press, 1972), 193 and 231.

10. Ibid., 193.

11. Ibid., 241.

12. Ibid., 116–28.

13. Quoted by Stephens, 226, from Rainer Maria Rilke, *Sämtliche Werke,* ed. Ernst Zinn, 6 vols. (Wiesbaden and Frankfurt: Insel, 1955–66), 5:360.

14. Brigitte L. Bradley, *"Die Aufzeichnungen des Malte Laurids Brigge:* Thematisierte Krise des literarischen Selbstverständnisses," in *Zu Rilke's Malte Laurids Brigge* (Bern and Munich: Francke, 1980), 52.

15. Quoted from *Sämtliche Werke,* 5:363, by Bradley, 46.

16. Bradley, 46.

17. Ibid., 53.

18. Ibid., 54.

19. Ibid., 55.

20. *WDB* 1:519–20.

21. Egon Schwarz, *Das verschluckte Schluchzen: Poesie und Politik bei Rainer Maria Rilke* (Frankfurt: Athenäum, 1972).

Chapter 2, Part I

1. See Hendry, 43.

2. See chapter 6, part 1, and Prater, 76–77 and 79.

3. Shaw, 16–17.

4. *WDB* 2:12.

5. Rilke, *Where Silence Reigns,* 36.

6. Quoted from René Spitz, *No and Yes: On the Genesis of Human Communication* (New York: International Universities Press), 127–28, by Searles, *Collected Papers on Schizophrenia,* 645.

7. See D. W. Winnicott, *Playing and Reality* (1971; rpt. New York: Tavistock Publications, Social Science Paperbacks, 1982), 111–18.

8. Searles, *Collected Papers on Schizophrenia,* 646. Searles quotes Phyllis Greenacre's essay "Early Physical Determinants in the Development of the Sense of Identity," *Journal of the American Psychoanalytic Association* 6 (1958): 612–27.

9. Searles, *Collected Papers on Schizophrenia,* 647.

10. Jacques Lacan, "The mirror stage as formative of the function of the I as revealed in psychoanalytic experience," in *Écrits: A Selection,* trans. Alan Sheridan (London and New York: Tavistock and Norton, 1977), 4.

Chapter 2, Part II

1. Searles, *The Nonhuman Environment,* 363.

2. Ibid., 363 and 365.

3. Renée (last name unknown), *Autobiography of a Schizophrenic Girl,* with analytic interpretation by Marguerite Sechehaye, trans. Grace Rubin-Rabson (1951; rpt. New York, New American Library, Signet Books, 1970), 37.

4. Searles, *Collected Papers on Schizophrenia,* 467.

Chapter 2, Part III

1. Searles, *Collected Papers on Schizophrenia,* chapter 16.

Chapter 2, Part IV

1. Rilke, *Letters to a Young Poet,* trans. M. D. Herter Norton, rev. ed. (New York: Norton, Norton Library, 1963), 68–69. Hereafter page numbers will appear in parentheses in the text with the designation *LYP.*

2. Rilke, *Letters to Merline, 1919–1922,* intro. J. B. Leishman and trans. Violet M. MacDonald (London: Methuen, 1951), 48–49.

3. *Rilke and Benvenuta: An Intimate Correspondence,* ed. Magda von Hattingberg, trans. Joel Agee (New York: Fromm International, 1987), 109. Hereafter page numbers will be cited in the text with the designation *R&B:IC.*

4. Angela Livingstone, *Salomé: Her Life and Work* (Mt. Kisco, N. Y.: Moyer Bell, 1984), 108. She is quoting and translating from Salomé, *Rainer Maria Rilke,* 19.

5. See *Letters* 1:41, and Binion's analysis of the varying accounts of the meeting with Tolstoy in *Frau Lou: Nietzsche's Wayward Disciple,* 266–271. He quotes Maurice Betz's recollection that, twenty-five years after the meeting with Tol-

stoy, he heard Rilke give two different accounts of it. Betz, *Rilke vivant: Souvenirs, lettres, entretiens* (Paris: Émile-Paul Frères, 1937), 154.

6. *A Glossary of Psychoanalytic Terms and Concepts*, ed. Burness E. Moore and Bernard D. Fine (New York: American Psychoanalytic Association, 1967), 86.

7. Rilke, *Letters on Cézanne*, ed. Clara Rilke, trans. Joel Agee (New York: Fromm International, 1985), 4–5.

8. See E. M. Butler, *Rainer Maria Rilke* (New York: MacMillan, 1941), 204–11. And see Erich Simenauer, *Rainer Maria Rilke: Legende und Mythos* (Bern: Paul Haupt, 1953), 462. He discusses the relevance of the scapegoat metaphor but argues that concepts of the double and the alter ego more nearly describe Malte's relation to Rilke because of the close resemblance between the two men and because of Rilke's sense that Malte was often with him in various parts of Europe.

9. Sigmund Freud, "Dostoevsky and Parricide," in *The Standard Edition of the Complete Psychological Works of Sigmund Freud*, ed. James Strachey, 24 vols. (London: Hogarth Press, 1953–1974), vol. 21 (1961), 177–94.

10. Ehrenzweig, 117.

11. Ibid., 118.

12. Ibid., 124 and 125.

13. Ibid., 124.

Chapter 3, Part I

1. Sokel, 183–84.

2. R. D. Laing, *The Divided Self: An Existential Study in Sanity and Madness* (New York: Viking Penguin, Pelican Books, 1965), 45.

3. Friedrich Nietzsche, *Beyond Good and Evil*, in *Basic Writings of Nietzsche*, trans. and ed. Walter Kaufmann (New York: Random House, Modern Library, 1968), 241.

4. J. R. von Salis, *Rainer Maria Rilke: The Years in Switzerland*, trans. N. K. Cruickshank (Berkeley: University of California Press, 1964), 138. See Heller's chapter on Rilke and Nietzsche in *The Disinherited Mind*, 123–177.

Chapter 3, Part II

1. Nietzsche, *Basic Writings*, 419.

2. Søren Kierkegaard, *Concluding Unscientific Postscript*, trans. David F. Swenson and Walter Lowrie (1941; rpt. Princeton: Princeton University Press, 1968), 67–74.

3. Winnicott, *The Maturational Processes*, 185.

4. Leppmann, 303. He is quoting from Wilhelm Hausenstein, *Liebe zu München*, 2nd ed. (Munich, 1958), 249–50.

5. See Laing, chapters 4 and 5.

6. Winnicott, *The Maturational Processes*, 15–16.

7. Laing, 98.

8. Leppmann, 13.

9. Rilke, *Ewald Tragy*, trans. Lola Gruenthal (New York: Twayne, 1958), 20. Hereafter page numbers will be cited in the text with the designation *ET*.

10. See Laing, 80–85.

11. See Leppmann, 4–7 and Prater, 3–4.

12. Carl Sieber, *René Rilke: Die Jugend Rainer Maria Rilkes* (Leipzig: Insel, 1932), 47. Leppmann, 13.

13. Leppmann, 13.

14. Winnicott, *The Maturational Processes*, 187.

15. Ibid., 187.

Chapter 3, Part III

1. Laing, 44.

2. Rilke, *Letters to a Young Poet*, 45–46.

3. Rilke, *Werke in drei Bänden* 1:260, 262, 265, 266, 268, 283, 286, 308.

4. Rilke, *Letters to Merline*, 63 and 58.

5. Nancy J. Chodorow and Susan Contratto, "The Fantasy of the Perfect Mother," in Nancy J. Chodorow, *Feminism and Psychoanalytic Theory* (New Haven: Yale University Press, 1989), 79–96.

6. Hass, 231.

Chapter 4, Part I

1. Letter to Clara, dated November 2, 1907. See Simenauer, 236–37, and Hendry, 13.

2. Prater, 14.

3. Betz, 130.

4. Sieber, 45–46.

5. Ibid., 70.

6. Magda von Hattingberg, *Rilke and Benvenuta*, Trans. Cyrus Brooks (New York: Norton, 1949), 8.

7. Ibid., 8.

Chapter 4, Part II

1. Heinz Kohut, *The Restoration of the Self* (New York: International Universities Press, 1977), 159–61.

2. Ibid., 105.

3. Searles, *Collected Papers on Schizophrenia*, 41.

4. Rilke, *Ewald Tragy*, 20.
5. Leppmann, 7.

Chapter 4, Part III

1. Sigmund Freud, "Family Romances" (1909), trans. James Strachey, in *The Sexual Enlightenment of Children*, ed. Philip Rieff (New York: Crowell-Collier, Collier Books, 1963), 43–45 (*Standard Edition*, vol. 9). See Simenauer's chapter "Der Familienroman," 381–414.
2. Simenauer, 257.
3. Ibid., 241.
4. Ibid., 240–41.
5. Ibid., 248. Butler, 130.
6. Leppmann, 101.
7. Simenauer, 308–09.
8. Searles, *Collected Papers on Schizophrenia*, 231.
9. Ibid., 233–34.
10. Moore and Fine, 89.

Chapter 4, Part IV

1. Searles, *Collected Papers on Schizophrenia*, 42.
2. Sieber, 74.
3. Butler, 13.
4. Kohut, *The Restoration of the Self*, 89.

Chapter 5, Part I

1. Rilke, *Ewald Tragy*, 51–52.
2. Leppmann gives 1898 as the date for the writing of the novella (Leppmann, 9). The table of contents in *Werke in drei Bänden*, vol. 3, says that the novella was "apparently written in the second half of 1898" (*WDB* 3:589).
3. Binion, 68, 81, 67.
4. Ibid., 97 and 107.
5. Leppmann, 73.
6. Livingstone, 46.
7. Binion, 353 and 374.
8. Binion; Livingstone; Ilonka Schmidt Mackey, *Lou Salomé: Inspiratrice et interprète de Nietzsche, Rilke et Freud* (Paris: Librairie A. G. Nizet, 1956); H. F. Peters, *My Sister, My Spouse* (New York, 1962).
9. Quoted by Livingston, 9, from Kurt Wolff, "Lou Andreas-Salomé. Ein Porträt aus Erinnerungen und Dokumenten," in *Gehört, gelesen* 10 (October 1963): 1191.

10. *The Letters of Rainer Maria Rilke and Princess Marie von Thurn und Taxis,* trans. and intro. Nora Wydenbruck (New York: New Directions, 1958), 241.

11. Letter dated May 18, 1897, quoted by Prater, 36, from a manuscript of a biography by Carl Sieber in the Rilke-Archiv at Gernsbach.

12. Quoted from *Lebensrückblick* by Leppmann, 81.

13. Quoted from *Lebensrückblick* by Prater, 39.

14. Leppmann, 80.

15. See Prater, 39, and Binion, 228–29 and 296.

16. Quoted from Rilke's diary by Leppmann, 79.

17. Quoted by Binion, 299, from *Rainer Maria Rilke—Lou Andreas-Salomé: Briefwechsel,* ed. Ernst Pfeiffer (Zürich: Max Niehans, Wiesbaden: Insel, 1952). Hereafter this volume of letters will be designated *Briefwechsel* in these notes. An expanded edition, published by Insel in 1975, will be cited hereafter.

18. *Briefwechsel,* 1975 ed., 55–56.

19. *Sämtliche Werke,* 3:171.

20. *Briefwechsel,* 60–61.

21. Letter of August 7, 1903; Ibid., 87.

22. Ibid., 76.

23. Ibid., 76–77.

24. Ibid., 125–26.

25. Ibid., 76–77.

26. Ibid., 90.

Chapter 5, Part II

1. Kohut, *The Analysis of the Self* (New York: International Universities Press, 1971), 116.

2. Kohut, *The Restoration of the Self,* 136.

3. Rilke, *Tagebücher aus der Frühzeit,* eds. Ruth Sieber-Rilke and Carl Sieber (1942; rpt. Frankfurt: Insel, 1973), 119.

4. Ibid., 115.

5. Rilke, *Letters to a Young Poet,* 49–50.

6. Rilke, *Tagebücher aus der Frühzeit,* 116 and 115.

7. Ibid., 118.

8. Ibid., 116.

9. Ibid., 117.

10. See Binion, 281.

11. *Briefwechsel,* 45; *Lebensrückblick,* 146.

12. Alice Balint, "Love for the Mother and Mother Love," chapter 6 of *Primary Love and Psychoanalytic Technique,* the rest of which was written by Michael Balint (New York: Liveright, 1953), 95–96.

13. Michael Balint, *Primary Love and Psychoanalytic Technique,* 83.

14. Alice Balint, 103.

15. Rilke, *Tagebücher aus der Frühzeit*, 115–16.

16. Ibid., 117–18.

17. Leppmann, 107–08.

18. *Briefwechsel*, 51.

19. See *Tagebücher aus der Frühzeit*, 346–49. The entry was written on the night of December 13, 1900.

20. *Briefwechsel*, 124–25.

Chapter 5, Part III

1. *Briefwechsel*, 60 and 61.

Chapter 6, Part I

1. Rilke, *Tagebücher aus der Frühzeit*, 237.

2. Ibid., 250.

3. Ibid., 250.

4. Hendry, 39–40.

5. Rilke, *Tagebücher aus der Frühzeit*, 250–53.

6. Ibid., 214.

7. Ibid., 237.

8. Ibid., 216.

9. Rilke, *Sämtliche Werke* 1:172–81.

10. Ibid., 374–75.

11. Ibid., 375.

12. Leppmann, 220–22.

13. *The Selected Poetry of Rainer Maria Rilke*, ed. and trans. Stephen Mitchell, intro. Robert Hass (New York: Random House, Vintage Books ed. 1984), 78–79. Hereafter page numbers will be cited in the text with the designation *SP*.

14. See Prater, 74.

15. Ibid., 76.

16. Ibid., 77.

17. Rilke, *Sämtliche Werke* 3:738–39.

18. Rilke, *Tagebücher aus der Frühzeit*, 115–16.

19. See Prater, 86, and *Paula Modersohn-Becker in Briefen und Tagebüchern*, ed. Günter Busch und Liselotte von Reinken (Frankfurt, 1979), 309.

20. Leppmann, 138.

21. Butler, 101.

22. Rilke, *Tagebücher aus der Frühzeit*, 250.

23. Ibid., 338–39.

24. *Sämtliche Werke*, 1:270–71.

25. Rilke, *Stories of God*, trans. M. D. Herter Norton (1932; rpt. New York: Norton, Norton Library 1963), 76–77.

26. Ibid., 77–79.

Chapter 6, Part II

1. Binion, 322.
2. Heinrich Wiegand Petzet, Foreword to Rilke, *Letters on Cézanne,* ed. Clara Rilke, trans. Joel Agee (New York: Fromm, 1985), xxv-xxvi.

Chapter 6, Part III

1. Sigmund Freud, "Mourning and Melancholia," in *Standard Edition* 14:239–258.

Chapter 6, Part IV

1. See Prater, 86, and *Paula Modersohn-Becker in Briefen und Tagebüchern,* 309.
2. Quoted by Leppmann, 140, from Rilke, *Briefe an Sidonie Nádherný von Borutin,* ed. Bernhard Blume (Frankfurt: Insel, 1973), 200–201.
3. Quoted from *Briefwechsel,* 259–61, by Prater, 209.
4. Leppmann, 263–64.
5. *Briefwechsel,* 88.
6. Ibid., 125–26.
7. Ibid., 126.

Chapter 7, Part I

1. Simenauer, 328.
2. Von Hattingberg, 8.
3. Searles, *Collected Papers on Schizophrenia,* chaps. 7 and 12.
4. Butler, 13.
5. Joyce Edward, Nathene Ruskin, Patsy Turrini, *Separation-Individuation: Theory and Application* (New York: Gardner Press, 1981), 63.
6. Ibid., 63.
7. Ibid., 25.
8. For the year in Rilke's life on which the story is based see Prater, 25.
9. Sieber, 101–02.
10. Rilke, *Ewald Tragy,* 21.

Chapter 7, Part II

1. Sieber, 73.
2. Letter to his mother from Linz, summer of 1892; Sieber, 103.
3. Leppmann, 28; Prater, 9.

4. Leppmann, 155.
5. Ibid., 4.
6. Ibid., 30.

Chapter 7, Part III

1. Sieber, 43.
2. Ibid., 42.
3. Ibid., 43.
4. Ibid., 101–2.
5. Prater, 3.
6. See Leppmann, 213.
7. Quoted from Hausenstein, 249–50, by Leppmann, 303.
8. Salomé, *The Freud Journal of Lou Andreas-Salomé*, 181.
9. Ibid., 184.
10. W. W. Meissner, *Internalization in Psychoanalysis* (New York: International Universities Press, 1981), 26. Meissner is influenced by but argues with Roy Schafer's definition of introjects in *Aspects of Internalization* (New York: International Universities Press, 1968).

Chapter 7, Part IV

1. Prater, 112.
2. Ibid., 118. Prater is quoting from a letter of March 2, 1905.
3. Ibid., 118; letter to Ellen Key, March 9, 1905.
4. Ibid., 118.
5. Ibid., 125.
6. See Simenauer, 320.
7. Quoted by Prater, 131, from Rilke, *Briefe 1904–1907*, eds. Ruth Sieber-Rilke and Carl Sieber (Leipzig: Insel-Verlag, 1939), 122.
8. Prater, 150.
9. Sigmund Freud, *The Ego and the Id*, trans. Joan Riviere, rev. and newly ed. by James Strachey (New York: Norton, Norton Library, 1962), 18–19; *Standard Edition*, vol. 19.
10. Freud, "Mourning and Melancholia," *Standard Edition*, vol. 14, 239–58.
11. See note 10 of part III, above.
12. Melanie Klein, "Mourning and Its Relation to Manic-Depressive States," in *Death: Interpretations*, ed. and intro. Hendrik M. Ruitenbeek (New York: Dell, Delta Book, 1969), 248–49. The essay is included in *Love, Guilt and Reparation, and Other Works 1921–1945*, vol. 1 of *The Writings of Melanie Klein*, ed. Roger Money-Kyrle et al., 4 vols. (New York: Free Press, 1975).

Chapter 8, Part I

1. Butler, 100.
2. See Rilke, *Tagebücher aus der Frühzeit,* 244 and 319–21.
3. See D. W. Winnicott, "The Relation of a Mother to Her Baby at the Beginning," in *The Family and Individual Development* (London: Tavistock, 1965), 17.
4. Prater, 7.
5. Schafer, 174.
6. Rilke, *Rodin,* part 2 (1907), in *Where Silence Reigns,* 143.
7. Letter dated March 17, 1926; Rilke, *Briefe,* 2 vols. (1897–1914 and 1914–1926) (Wiesbaden: Insel, 1950), 2:517.
8. Butler, 139.
9. See Sieber, 45–53.
10. See Edward, Ruskin, Turrini, 63.

Chapter 8, Part II

1. For a definition of transference in terms of recent psychoanalytic theory, see Meissner, 121.
2. Kohut, *The Restoration of the Self,* 137.
3. Kohut, *The Analysis of the Self,* xiv, 3, and 26–27.
4. Ibid., 37.
5. Ibid., 28.
6. Ibid., 46 and 48.
7. Kohut, *The Restoration of the Self,* 137.
8. Ibid., 155.
9. Arnold H. Modell, *Object Love and Reality: An Introduction to a Psychoanalytic Theory of Object Relations* (New York: International Universities Press, 1968), 147.
10. Ibid., 148.
11. Ibid., 56.
12. Freud, *Beyond the Pleasure Principle,* in *Standard Edition* 18:14.

Chapter 8, Part III

1. Norman Holland, *The Dynamics of Literary Response* (New York: Oxford University Press, 1968), 42. William Shakespeare, *Two Gentlemen of Verona,* act 3 sc. 1, lines 104–5.
2. Franz Kafka, *Letter to His Father,* trans. Ernst Kaiser and Eithne Wilkins (New York: Schocken, 1954), 19 and 21.
3. Ibid., 89 and 91.
4. Ibid., 17.

Chapter 8, Part IV

1. Winnicott, *Playing and Reality* (1971; rpt. New York: Tavistock, 1982), 1–25.
2. Rilke, "Some Reflections on Dolls," in *Where Silence Reigns*, 45–50. Von Hattingberg, 128–31.
3. Winnicott, *Playing and Reality*, 9–14.
4. See Rilke, *Tagebücher aus der Frühzeit*, 245.
5. Rilke, "An Experience (II)" (1913), in *Where Silence Reigns*, 37.
6. Modell, 38–39.

Chapter 8, Part V

1. Letter of Nov. 8, 1905. Quoted by Prater, 125, from *Lettres à Rodin* (Paris: Émile-Paul, 1931), 50–51.
2. Charles Brenner, *An Elementary Textbook of Psychoanalysis*, rev. ed. (1955; rpt. New York: Doubleday, Anchor Books, 1974), 89–90.
3. See Rilke, *Letters*, 1:210–16, and Prater, 132–33.
4. See Simenauer, 369–70.
5. Butler, 163.
6. Modell, 59.
7. Ibid., 58.

Chapter 8, Part VI

1. See note to this letter (no. 159) in *Letters*, 1:393.
2. Quoted from Rilke, *Letters à Rodin*, 76, by Prater, 152.

Chapter 8, Part VII

1. Prater, 156.
2. Ibid., 158.
3. Leppmann, 112.
4. Ibid., 112–13. See *Werke in drei Bänden* 1:17, 23, and 24–25.
5. Rilke, *Das Stunden-Buch*, Zweites Buch: "Das Buch von der Pilgerschaft" (1901), in *Werke in drei Bänden*, 1:68.

Chapter 8, Part VIII

1. Rilke, *New Poems*, trans. Edward Snow (San Francisco: North Point Press, 1984), 27–31. I have altered Snow's translation.
2. Ibid., 29.

Chapter 9, Part I

1. *The Letters of Rainer Maria Rilke and Marie von Thurn und Taxis,* 105.
2. Von Hattingberg, 87.
3. *Rilke and Benvenuta: An Intimate Correspondence,* 78 and 79. See also von Hattingberg, 91–92.

Chapter 9, Part II

1. Freud, *The Ego and the Id,* 18–25.

Chapter 9, Part III

1. Rilke, *The Sonnets to Orpheus,* trans. Stephen Mitchell (New York: Simon and Schuster, 1985), 159–60. Hereafter page numbers will be cited in the text with the designation *SO*.
2. Von Salis, 139.
3. Rilke, *Letters to Merline,* 47–48.
4. Rilke, *Sonnets to Orpheus,* trans. M. D. Herter Norton (1942; rpt. New York: Norton, Norton Library, 1962), 155.

Chapter 9, Part IV

1. Rilke, *Werke in drei Bänden* 1:106–7.
2. Quoted from J. Needham, *History of Scientific Thought,* vol. 2 of *Science and Civilization in China* (Cambridge: Cambridge University Press, 1956), 58, by Norman O. Brown, *Life against Death: The Psychoanalytic Meaning of History* (New York: Random House, Vintage Books, 1959), 134.
3. Freud, "Some Psychological Consequences of the Anatomical Distinction between the Sexes" (1925), trans. James Strachey, in *Sexuality and the Psychology of Love,* ed. and intro. Philip Rieff (New York: Crowell-Collier, Collier Books, 1963), 185; *Standard Edition,* vol. 19.
4. Freud, "Dostoevsky and Parricide," trans. D. F. Tait, rev. James Strachey, in *Character and Culture,* ed. and intro. Philip Rieff (New York: Crowell-Collier, Collier Books, 1963), 282 and 276; *Standard Edition* vol. 21.
5. Freud, "On Narcissism: An Introduction," trans. Cecil M. Baines, in *General Psychological Theory,* ed. and intro. Philip Rieff (New York: Collier Books, 1963), 74 and 80; *Standard Edition* vol. 14.
6. Freud, *The Ego and the Id,* 20.

Chapter 9, Part V

1. Paul Valéry in *Reconnaissance à Rilke: Les Cahiers du mois* 23/24 (Paris: Émile-Paul, 1926), 9f.

2. Winnicott, *The Maturational Processes,* 29.

3. Winnicott, *Playing and Reality,* 56, 64, and 65.

4. Winnicott, *The Maturational Processes,* 33.

5. Ibid., 32–34.

6. Ibid., 33–34.

7. Ibid., 34.

8. Ibid., 32.

9. Marthe Hennebert was seventeen when Rilke met her, according to Leppmann (261). She was eighteen at the time, according to Prater, (189).

10. *The Letters of Rainer Maria Rilke and Princess Marie von Thurn und Taxis,* 21n.

Chapter 9, Part VI

1. Winnicott, *Playing and Reality,* 73.

2. Ibid., 73–74.

3. Ibid., 77.

4. See Leppman, 300, 317, 382–83.

5. Winnicott, *Playing and Reality,* 78.

Selected Bibliography

Editions of Rilke's Works

Sämtliche Werke. Ed. Ernst Zinn. 6 vols. Wiesbaden and Frankfurt: Insel, 1955–66.

Werke in drei Bänden. Ed. Ernst Zinn. 3 vols. Frankfurt: Insel, 1966.

Rilke's Letters and Diaries

Sieber-Rilke, Ruth and Carl Sieber, eds. *Briefe und Tagebücher aus der Frühzeit 1899–1902.* Leipzig: Insel, 1933.

——. *Tagebücher aus der Frühzeit.* 1942; rpt. Frankfurt: Insel, 1973.

——. *Briefe aus den Jahren 1902 bis 1906.* Leipzig: Insel, 1930.

——. *Briefe aus den Jahren 1904 bis 1907.* Leipzig: Insel, 1939.

——. *Briefe aus den Jahren 1906 bis 1907.* Leipzig: Insel, 1930.

——. *Briefe aus den Jahren 1907 bis 1914.* Leipzig: Insel, 1933.

——. *Briefe aus den Jahren 1914 bis 1921.* Leipzig: Insel, 1937.

——. *Briefe aus Muzot 1921 bis 1926.* Leipzig: Insel, 1936.

Briefe. 2 vols. (1897–1914 and 1914–26) Wiesbaden: Insel, 1950.

Rainer Maria Rilke—Lou Andreas-Salomé: Briefwechsel. Ed. Ernst Pfeiffer. Expanded edition. Frankfurt: Insel, 1975.

Briefe an Auguste Rodin. Leipzig: Insel, 1928.

Letters of Rainer Maria Rilke. 2 vols. (1892–1910 and 1910–1926). Trans. Jane Bannard Greene and M. D. Herter Norton. 1945, 1947, and 1948; rpt. New York: Norton, Norton Library, 1969.

The Letters of Rainer Maria Rilke and Princess Marie von Thurn und Taxis. Trans. and intro. Nora Wydenbruck. New York: New Directions, 1958.

Letters on Cézanne. Trans. Joel Agee. Foreword by Heinrich Wiegand Petzet. New York: Fromm, 1985.

Letters to Merline, 1919–1922. Trans. Violet M. MacDonald. Intro. J. B. Leishman. London: Methuen, 1951.

Letters to a Young Poet. Trans. M. D. Herter Norton. Rev. ed. 1954; rpt. New York: Norton, Norton Library, 1963.

Rilke and Benvenuta: An Intimate Correspondence. Ed. Magda von Hattingberg. Trans. Joel Agee. New York: Fromm, 1987.

Translations of Rilke's Works

Gruenthal, Lola, trans. *Ewald Tragy.* New York: Twayne, 1958.

Houston, G. Craig, trans. *Where Silence Reigns: Selected Prose.* Foreword by Denise Levertov. 1960; rpt. New York: New Directions, 1978.

Leishman, J. B., trans. *Selected Works.* Vol 2: *Poetry.* New York: New Directions, 1960.

———. *Poems 1906 to 1926.* 2nd ed. London: Hogarth Press, 1968.

Leishman, J. B., and Stephen Spender, trans. *Duino Elegies.* 1939; rpt. New York: Norton, Norton Library, 1963.

Mitchell, Stephen, trans.. *The Notebooks of Malte Laurids Brigge.* New York: Random House, 1982.

———. *The Selected Poetry of Rainer Maria Rilke.* Foreword by Robert Hass. 1982; rpt. New York: Random House, Vintage Books, 1984.

———. *The Sonnets to Orpheus.* New York: Simon and Schuster, 1985.

Norton, M. D. Herter, trans. *The Notebooks of Malte Laurids Brigge.* 1949; rpt. New York: Norton, Norton Library, 1964.

———. *Sonnets to Orpheus.* 1942; rpt. New York: Norton, Norton Library, 1962.

———. *Stories of God.* 1932; rpt. New York, Norton, Norton Library 1963.

Snow, Edward, trans. *New Poems.* San Francisco: North Point Press, 1984.

Secondary Works

Alleman, Beda. *Zeit und Figur beim späten Rilke.* Pfullingen: Günther Neske, 1961.

Andreas-Salomé, Lou. *Rainer Maria Rilke.* Leipzig: Insel, 1929.

———. *Lebensrückblick: Grundriss einiger Lebenserinnerungen.* Rev. ed. Ed. E. Pfeiffer. Frankfurt: Insel, 1977.

———. *The Freud Journal of Lou Andreas-Salomé.* Trans. Stanley Leavy. New York: Basic Books, 1965.

Balint, Michael. *Primary Love and Psycho-Analytic Technique.* New York: Liveright, 1953.

Betz, Maurice. *Rilke vivant: Souvenirs, lettres, entretiens.* Paris: Émile-Paul Frères, 1937.

———. *Rilke in Paris.* Trans. Willi Reich. Zürich: Arche, 1948.

Binion, Rudolph. *Frau Lou: Nietzsche's Wayward Disciple.* Princeton: Princeton University Press, 1968.

Bollnow, Otto Friedrich. *Rilke.* 2nd ed., rev. Stuttgart: Kohlhammer, 1956.

Bradley, Brigitte L. *Zu Rilke's Malte Laurids Brigge.* Bern and München: Francee, 1980.

Brown, Norman O. *Life against Death, The Psychoanalytic Meaning of History.* New York: Random House, Vintage Books, 1959.

Butler, E. M. *Rainer Maria Rilke.* New York: Macmillan, 1941.

Chodorow, Nancy J. and Susan Contratto. "The Fantasy of the Perfect Mother." In Nancy J. Chodorow, *Feminism and Psychoanalytic Theory,* 79–96. New Haven: Yale University Press, 1989.

Delevoy, Robert L. *Dimensions of the 20th Century: 1900–1945.* Trans. Stuart Gilbert. Geneva: Skira, 1965.

de Man, Paul. *Allegories of Reading: Figural Language in Rousseau, Nietzsche, Rilke, and Proust.* New Haven: Yale University Press, 1979.

Demetz, Peter. *René Rilkes Prager Jahre.* Düsseldorf: Eugen Diederichs, 1953.

Edward, Joyce, et al. *Separation-Individuation: Theory and Application.* New York: Gardner Press, 1981.

Ehrenzweig, Anton. *The Hidden Order of Art.* London: Weidenfield and Nicolson, 1967.

Engelhardt, Harmut, ed. *Materialien zu Rainer Maria Rilke, "Die Aufzeichnungen des Malte Laurids Brigge."* Frankfurt: Suhrkamp, 1974.

Erikson, Erik, *Childhood and Society.* 2nd ed. New York: Norton, 1963.

———. *Identity, Youth and Crisis.* New York: Norton, 1968.

———. *Young Man Luther: A Study in Psychoanalysis and History.* New York: Norton, Norton Library, 1962.

Exner, Richard and Ingrid Stipa "Das Phänomen der Androgynie des Schaffenprozesses im späten Rilke: Das Beispiel. 'Solang du Selbstgeworfnes fängst...'" In *Rainer Maria Rilke,* ed. by Rüdiger Görner. Wege der Forschung, Vol. 638. Darmstadt: Wissenchaftliche Buchgesellschaft, 1987. 350–83.

Forrest, David V. "Poiesis and the Language of Schizophrenia." In *Language Behavior in Schizophrenia,* ed. Harold J. Vetter, 153–81. Springfield, Ill.: Charles J. Thomas, 1968.

Freed, Anne O. "Differentiating between Borderline and Narcissistic Personalities." *Social Casework: The Journal of Contemporary Social Work* 65, no. 7 (September 1984): 395–404.

Freud, Sigmund. *The Interpretation of Dreams.* Trans. and ed. James Strachey. New York: Avon Books, 1965.

———. *Introductory Lectures on Psychoanalysis.* Trans. and ed. James Strachey. New York: Norton, A Liveright Book, 1977.

———. "On the Universal Tendency to Debasement in the Sphere of Love," *Standard Edition,* vol. 11, 179–90.

———. "Mourning and Melancholia." In *Standard Edition,* vol. 14, 239–58.

————. *New Introductory Lectures on Psychoanalysis.* Trans. and ed. James Strachey. New York: Norton, 1964 and 1965.

————. *The Standard Edition of the Complete Psychological Works of Sigmund Freud.* Ed. James Strachey. 24 vols. London: Hogarth, 1953–74.

Hartman, Geoffrey H. *The Unmediated Vision, An Interpretation of Wordsworth, Hopkins, Rilke, and Valéry.* New York: Harcourt, Brace and World, Harbinger Books, 1966.

Hass, Robert. *Twentieth Century Pleasures: Prose on Poetry.* New York: Ecco Press, 1984.

Hattingberg, Magda von. *Rilke and Benvenuta.* Trans. Cyrus Brooks. New York: Norton, 1949.

Heidegger, Martin. *Poetry, Language, Thought.* Trans. Albert Hofstadter. New York: Harper and Row, 1971.

Heller, Erich. *The Artist's Journey into the Interior and Other Essays.* New York: Random House, Vintage Books, 1968.

————. *The Disinherited Mind: Essays in Modern German Literature and Thought.* Harcourt Brace Jovanovich, Harvest Books, 1975.

Hendry, J. F. *The Sacred Threshold: A Life of Rainer Maria Rilke.* Manchester, England: Carcanet New Press, 1983.

Holland, Norman N. *The Dynamics of Literary Response.* New York: Oxford University Press, 1968.

————. *Psychoanalysis and Shakespeare.* New York: McGraw-Hill, 1966.

Holthusen, Hans Egon. *Portrait of Rilke: An Illustrated Biography.* Trans. W. H. Hargreaves. New York: Herder and Herder, 1971.

Huyssen, Andreas, "Paris/Childhood: The Fragmented Body in Rilke's *Notebooks of Malte Laurids Brigge.*" In *Modernity and the Text: Revisions of German Modernism,* ed. Andreas Huyssen and David Bathrick, 113–41. New York: Columbia University Press, 1989.

Jacobson, Edith. *The Self and the Object World.* New York: International Universities Press, 1964.

Kafka, Franz. *The Penal Colony.* trans. Willa and Edwin Muir. New York: Schocken Books, 1961.

Kierkegaard, Søren. *Concluding Unscientific Postscript.* Trans. David F. Swenson and Walter Lowrie. Princeton: Princeton University Press, 1941.

Klein, Melanie. "Mourning and Its Relation to Manic-Depressive States." In *Love, Guilt, Reparation, and Other Works 1921–1945,* vol. 1 of *The Writings of Melanie Klein,* ed. Roger Money-Kyrle. New York: Free Press, 1975.

Kohut, Heinz. *The Analysis of the Self.* New York: International Universities Press, 1971.

————. *The Restoration of the Self.* New York: International Universities Press, 1977.

Komar, Kathleen L. *Transcending Angels: Rainer Maria Rilke's Duino Elegies.* Lincoln: University of Nebraska Press, 1987.

Lacan, Jacques. *Écrits: A Selection*. Trans. Alan Sheridan. London and New York: Tavistock and Norton, 1977.

Laing, R. D. *The Divided Self*. New York: Viking Penguin, Pelican Books, 1965.

Leppmann, Wolfgang. *Rilke: A Life*. Trans. Russell M. Stockman. New York: Fromm International Publishing, 1984.

Lesser, Simon. *Fiction and the Unconscious*. New York: Random House, Vintage Books, 1962.

Livingstone, Angela. *Salomé, Her Life and Work*. Mt. Kisko, N.Y.: Moyer Bell, 1984.

Martin, Biddy. "Women and Modernity: The [Life] Style of Lou Andreas-Salomé." In *Modernity and the Text: Revisions of German Modernism*, ed. Andreas Huyssen and David Bathrick, 183–99. New York: Columbia University Press, 1989.

Masterson, James F. *The Real Self: A Developmental, Self, and Object Relations Approach*. New York: Brunner/Mazel Publishers, 1985.

Meissner, W. W. *Internalization in Psychoanalysis*. New York: International Universities Press, 1981.

Modell, Arnold H. *Object Love and Reality: An Introduction to a Psychoanalytic Theory of Object Relations*. New York: International Universities Press, 1968.

Nietzsche, Friedrich. *Basic Writings of Nietzsche*. Trans. and ed. Walter Kaufmann. New York: Modern Library, 1968.

———. *The Portable Nietzsche*. Trans. and ed. Walter Kaufmann. New York: Viking, 1954.

Peters, H. F. *Rainer Maria Rilke: Masks and the Man*. New York: McGraw-Hill, 1963.

Prater, Donald. *A Ringing Glass: The Life of Rainer Maria Rilke*. Oxford: Clarendon Press, 1986.

Rolleston, James. *Rilke in Transition: An Exploration of His Earliest Poetry*. New Haven: Yale University Press, 1970.

Salis, J. R. von. *Rainer Maria Rilke: The Years in Switzerland*. Trans. N. K. Cruickshank. Berkeley and Los Angeles: University of California Press, 1964.

Schafer, Roy. *Aspects of Internalization*. New York: International Universities Press, 1968.

Searles, Harold F. *Collected Papers on Schizophrenia and Related Subjects*. New York: International Universities Press, 1965.

———. *The Nonhuman Environment in Normal Development and in Schizophrenia*. New York: International Universities Press, 1960.

Sewell, Elizabeth. *The Orphic Voice: Poetry and Natural History*. New York: Harper and Row, Harper Torch Books, 1971.

Shaw, Priscilla Washburn. *Rilke, Valéry and Yeats: The Domain of the Self*. New Brunswick, N. J.: Rutgers University Press, 1964.

Sieber, Carl. *René Rilke: Die Jugend Rainer Maria Rilkes*. Leipzig: Insel, 1932.

Simenauer, Erich. *Rainer Maria Rilke: Legende und Mythos*. Bern: Paul Haupt, 1953.

————. *Der Traum bei R. M. Rilke*. Bern: Paul Haupt, 1976.

Sokel, Walter H. "The Devolution of the Self in *The Notebooks of Malte Laurids Brigge*." In *Rilke, The Alchemy of Alienation*, ed. Frank Baron, Ernst S. Dick, and Warren R. Maurer. Lawrence: Regents Press of Kansas, 1980.

Steiner, Jacob. *Rilkes Duineser Elegien*. 2nd ed. Bern and Munich: Francke, 1969.

Stephens, Anthony, *Rainer Maria Rilke's "Gedichte an die Nacht."* Cambridge: Cambridge University Press, 1972.

Storr, Anthony. *The Dynamics of Creation*. New York: Atheneum, 1972.

Strauss, Walter A. *Descent and Return*. Cambridge: Harvard University Press, 1971.

Thurn und Taxis, Marie von. *Erinnerungen an Rainer Maria Rilke*. Frankfurt: Insel, 1966.

Webb, Karl Eugene. *Rainer Maria Rilke and Jugendstil: Affinities, Influences, Adaptations*. University of North Carolina Studies in the Germanic Languages and Literatures no. 90. Chapel Hill: University of North Carolina Press, 1978.

Winnicott, D. W. *The Maturational Processes and the Facilitating Environment*. London: Hogarth Press and the Institute of Psycho-Analysis, 1965.

————. *Playing and and Reality*. New York: Tavistock Publications, Social Science Paperbacks, 1982.

————. *Through Paediatrics to Psycho-Analysis*. New York: Basic Books, 1975.

Wood, Frank. *Rainer Maria Rilke: The Ring of Forms*. New York: Farrar, Straus and Giroux, Octagon Books, 1970.

Index

Aestheticism, 14–16
Albert-Lazard, Lulu, 243
Alcoforado, Marianna, 196
Angels: in First, Second, and Seventh Elegies, 139–40, 200, 232; as vital form of poet's genius, 224, 232–33
Andreas, Friedrich Carl, 88
Andreas-Salomé, Lou (Luise), 1, 7–9, 11–12, 16, 26, 40, 42, 45, 48, 52, 63, 66, 68, 71, 79, 81, 88–109, 110, 112–13, 116–18, 121–22, 124–28, 130, 132, 151–52, 154, 158, 163, 165, 176, 178, 182–83, 212–14, 218, 230, 237, 241; as a destroyer, 92, 107; empathetic responsiveness, 97–98; fantasy of unity with, 109; idealization of, 102, 107–8; as a maternal figure with the Creator's power, 90–92; maternal mirroring, 97–100, 102, 104; and Nietzsche, 88–89; oedipal dimension of Rilke's relationship with, 81–82; response to *Rodin,* 94–95; and Rilke's fear of a devouring mother, 92; on Rilke's growth as an artist, 94–96; Rilke's letters to, 174, 182; and Rilke's need of mothering, 88; Rilke's pain at separation from, 218–19; as second mother, 88, 91–92, 94, 100, 102, 105; as shelter, 109; as a source of Rilke's sense of his own reality, 94–95, 105–7; as a source of shame, 100; stature in German world of letters, 90; as informal therapist, 106
"Archaic love," 101

Aristocracy: friends and patrons, 55, 57, 59; fantasies of ancestral heroes, 143; myth of aristocratic Rilkes, 80, 81, 143, 173; Rilke's persona, 52, 58–59
Arnim, Bettina, von, 194, 225, 230, 231
Art: abstract form, 115, 146–47; "anonymous work," 19; autonomous art, 20–21; as an artist's defense against disturbance, 183; characterization, 146–47; childhood prototypes, 181; corrupted forms of writing in Rilke's view, 20; fragmentary form in *The Notebooks,* 2; fragmentary form in Picasso and Joyce, 2; indirection and concealment in, 53–54; irony, 53, 146–47, 149; metamorphosis in, 221, 224; modernists and post-modernists, 13, 46; "my art," 210; "objective expression," 20, 39; as an artist's means of objectifying and distancing, 159; portraits of Parisian figures in Rilke's letters, 95–96; "real, still things," 182; Rilke's conception of genius, 203, 216, 222–24; Rilke's contrast between sculpture and writing, 179–80; Rilke on unity of art object, 35; Rodin's disintegrative and reintegrating sculpture, 36; schizophrenic art, 46; writing as "self-treatment," 44. See also Andreas-Salomé, Lou; Creativity; Rilke's writings; Rodin, Auguste; Satiric irony in Rilke's writings; Transformation in Rilke's writings